Rejecting Rights

The language of rights is ubiquitous. It shapes the way we construct our debates over issues such as abortion, affirmative action, and sexual freedom. This provocative new study challenges the very concept of rights, arguing that they jeopardize our liberty and undermine democratic debate. By re-conceptualizing our ideas about limited government, it suggests that we can limit the reasons or rationales on which the polity may act. Whereas we once used the language of rights to thwart democratic majorities, Bedi argues that we should now turn our attention to the democratic state's *reason* for acting. This will permit greater democratic flexibility and discretion while ensuring genuine liberty. Deftly employing political theory and constitutional law to state its case, the study radically rethinks the relationship between liberty and democracy, and will be essential reading for scholars and students of political and legal philosophy.

Sonu Bedi is an Assistant Professor in the Department of Government, Dartmouth College.

Contemporary Political Theory

Series editor
Ian Shapiro

Editorial board
Russell Hardin
John Keane
Phillipe Van Parijs
Stephen Holmes
Elizabeth Kiss
Philip Pettit
Jeffrey Isaac

As the twenty-first century begins, major new political challenges have arisen at the same time as some of the most enduring dilemmas of political association remain unresolved. The collapse of communism and the end of the Cold War reflect a victory for democratic and liberal values, yet in many of the Western countries that nurtured those values there are severe problems of urban decay, class and racial conflict, and failing political legitimacy. Enduring global injustice and inequality seem compounded by environmental problems, disease, the oppression of women, racial, ethnic and religious minorities, and the relentless growth of the world's population. In such circumstances, the need for creative thinking about the fundamentals of human political association is manifest. This new series in contemporary political theory is needed to foster such systematic normative reflection.

The series proceeds in the belief that the time is ripe for a reassertion of the importance of problem-driven political theory. It is concerned, that is, with works that are motivated by the impulse to understand, think critically about, and address the problems in the world, rather than issues that are thrown up primarily in academic debate. Books in the series may be interdisciplinary in character, ranging over issues conventionally dealt with in philosophy, law, history and the human sciences. The range of materials and the methods of proceeding should be dictated by the problem at hand, not the conventional debates or disciplinary divisions of academia.

Other books in the series
Ian Shapiro and Casiano Hacker-Cordón (eds.) *Democracy's Value*
Ian Shapiro and Casiano Hacker-Cordón (eds.) *Democracy's Edges*
Brooke A. Ackerly *Political Theory and Feminist Social Criticism*
Clarissa Rile Hayward *De-Facing Power*
John Kane *The Politics of Moral Capital*
Ayelet Shachar *Multicultural Jurisdictions*

Rejecting Rights

Sonu Bedi

CAMBRIDGE
UNIVERSITY PRESS

CAMBRIDGE UNIVERSITY PRESS
Cambridge, New York, Melbourne, Madrid, Cape Town, Singapore,
São Paulo, Delhi

Cambridge University Press
The Edinburgh Building, Cambridge CB2 8RU, UK

Published in the United States of America by Cambridge University Press,
New York

www.cambridge.org
Information on this title: www.cambridge.org/9780521732154

First published 2009

Printed in the United Kingdom at the University Press, Cambridge

A catalogue record for this publication is available from the British Library

ISBN 978-0-521-51828-4 hardback
ISBN 978-0-521-73215-4 paperback

For my Parents

Table of contents

Acknowledgements

One of the greatest pleasures in writing this book was engaging its arguments with many friends, colleagues, and mentors. I owe them my gratitude. While any errors or missteps are my own, they have collectively made this book that much better. I take deep satisfaction in thanking them here. I did most of the writing while a student at Yale. Yale proved a fruitful, creative, and stimulating place to work. In particular, I thank Bruce Ackerman, Seyla Benhabib, and Ian Shapiro for their invaluable insights. Each in their own way has led me to craft a sharper, clearer argument. I could not have asked for better mentors. I especially thank Bruce Ackerman for his early enthusiasm and encouragement. His ability to home in on the weakness of an argument offering possible correctives still amazes me. This book would not have been possible without his support.

Dartmouth was an ideal place to finish the manuscript. I am privileged to have such collegial and supportive colleagues in the Department of Government. Additionally, I had the opportunity to participate in a manuscript review organized by the Dickey Center for International Understanding at Dartmouth. Participants included Amy Allen, Walter Sinnott-Armstrong, Michelle T. Clarke, Larry Crocker, Chandran Kukathas, Stephen Macedo, Lucas Swaine, James Murphy, and Christianne Wohlforth. This session proved crucial in clarifying and strengthening my arguments. I thank the Dickey Center, and in particular, Christianne Wohlforth, for organizing it. I owe thanks to Stephen Macedo and Chandran Kukathas who traveled to Hanover just to comment on my manuscript. My many conversations with them were extremely helpful. Walter Sinnott-Armstrong, Michelle T. Clarke, Larry Crocker, James Murphy, and Lucas Swaine provided additional comments and advice that I could not have done without.

I had the benefit of presenting portions of this book at various places including Dartmouth, Depaul Law School, MIT, Swarthmore College, University of Tulsa, and Yale. Receiving feedback as I tested my arguments in these venues proved quite useful. I also benefited from conversations with many dear friends including: Victoria Kennedy, Elvin Lim, and Tim Nguyen. Victoria Kennedy (thankfully) never stopped challenging me on my conclusions. Elvin Lim went above and beyond the call of duty, graciously editing portions of my manuscript while offering insightful criticisms. Tim Nguyen's sense of humor kept me in good spirits as I wrote the book. Through it all, my twin brother, Monu Bedi, was (and still is) my intellectual partner in crime. Without him, I would be lost.

At Cambridge University Press, I graciously thank my editor, John Haslam, for his early support of the project and for turning the manuscript into a book. I also thank Paul Stevens, Elizabeth Davey, and Mary Dalton for their invaluable editorial assistance. I thank the anonymous reviewers for their very constructive comments on an earlier version of the manuscript.

A portion of Chapter 7 appears in the following article: "Repudiating Morals Legislation: Rendering the Constitutional Right to Privacy Obsolete," 52 *Cleveland State Law Review* 447 (2006).

Finally, I thank my dear parents, Bhupinder and Anjali. They were the first to teach me the value of pursuing learning for its own sake. Their love and support know no limits. I am humbled and honored to call them my parents. This book is dedicated to them.

Table of cases

Introduction

I warn you from the outset that my argument may seem controversial, even highly counter-intuitive. After all, as my title suggests, I seek to reject rights. Yet, our intuitions here should only be thought of as knee-jerk. While they may rightly place the argumentative weight on me, they should not preempt an open mind. Like the prosecutor trying a case, I accept that the burden is mine. But just as a judge instructs jurors not to form any settled opinions of guilt or innocence until the trial is complete, I ask that you similarly withhold judgment until the end.

Imagine a polity passes the following law: blonds are forbidden from having sex with redheads. How would we respond to such a law? I'm confident that most (if not all) of us would immediately find it suspect. But why? Is it because the law violates a right to equality? That is, it discriminates on the basis of hair color. Or is it because the law violates a right to privacy? That is, it interferes with the intimate and personal decisions of redheads and blondes. I argue that the better argument stems from neither right. Rather, we need simply proclaim that the law is irrational, arbitrary even ridiculous. After all, there's no good reason for enacting it, for prohibiting blonds from sleeping with redheads. Reasons, not rights, ought to do the normative work. Once we realize this – once we turn our attention to the polity's reason for enacting the law – rights turn out to be unnecessary. This is the framework I deploy, a framework that asks us to reject conventional rights-talk and re-conceptualize the way we limit democratic government.

The conventional way of doing so specifies those areas, interests, spheres, or classifications that are off limits to state regulation. This is the typical view of limited government. Central to it is the private sphere. Whereas the state may legislate over public activities, it must refrain from interfering with private ones. Under the standard view, the state ought not to violate our rights to intimacy, religion, and property – rights that are seen as essential components of the private sphere.

Take as an example the argument for sexual freedom. The conventional account of limiting government suggests that I may sleep with the adult of my choice, because sexual activity occurs in private. I should be left alone in the personal and intimate areas of my life. The state ought not to regulate or interfere with behavior that occurs in it. Doing so violates one's right to intimacy. After all, as the argument goes, it is in this space that we articulate and ground our personal, idiosyncratic conception of the good, engage in basic human self-development, bond with others, and form our core identity. If there is anything that does not concern the state, it is this intimate sphere. Sexual activity is part of that sphere and thus off limits to state regulation, or so the conventional argument goes.

Similarly, the state ought not to violate rights to equality. Democratic majorities are forbidden from discriminating on the basis of various classifications such as race, sex, and sexual orientation. Considering the argument of sexual freedom, the conventional account also suggests that prohibiting sex improperly discriminates on the basis of sex or sexual orientation. A law mandating racial segregation is problematic precisely because it invokes race or discriminates against a particular identity group. It violates one's right to equal treatment. Such classifications are off limits to state regulation.

Rights, then, are seen as essential in limiting the scope of democratic decision-making. Any account of limited government must fulfill and balance two competing values: democracy as a matter of self-government and liberty as a matter of restraining government. First, it must provide space for democratic discretion, decision-making, and debate. It must permit the democratic polity to pass a wide range of laws. It must value democracy. Second, an account of limited government must ensure genuine liberty. It must appropriately thwart majority tyranny. Assuming that the values of liberty and democracy are important, rights represent the reigning method for best securing them. Rights are the traditional and widely accepted doctrines that thwart majority tyranny. They demarcate those interests, areas, spheres, or classifications off limits to state regulation. Conversely, under the conventional account, the state may regulate those interests and activities that do not violate such rights that are, for example, "public." The role for courts, then, is to strike down those democratically enacted laws that do encroach upon rights like our rights to intimacy and equality. This is the traditional methodology for balancing and realizing the values of liberty and democracy.

In fact, the essential purpose of constitutional law is to limit the reach of the state. Constitutions serve as basic constraints on the scope and reach of democratic government. In line with the conventional account of limited government, constitutions generally specify those rights the state may not violate. For instance, the First Amendment of the United States' Bill of Rights says in part that "Congress *shall make no law* respecting an establishment of religion; or abridging the free exercise thereof. ...."[1] The conventional argument secures religious liberty negatively by specifying religion as an area or interest the state may not interfere or legislate in.

The language of rights is ubiquitous. Most legal, political, and theoretical arguments concerning issues like abortion, affirmative action, and sexual freedom invariably appeal to such doctrines. Since *Roe v. Wade* (1973) (holding that the right to privacy protects a woman's decision to abort), the contemporary abortion debate has revolved around whether removing the fetus is about the right to life, a right to privacy, or about a right to women's equality. With the recent conservative appointments of Justices John Roberts and Samuel Alito framing the abortion debate seems even more salient. The Supreme Court's current jurisprudence on race-based affirmative action also trades in the language of rights, here the right to equality. The typical theoretical arguments juxtapose the rights of individuals – a notion of formal equality – with the rights of groups – a notion of anti-subordination. Moreover, defending sexual freedom including same-sex marriage is caught in the theoretical construct of the public and private divide. The alleged "private" nature of sex pushes for its protection requiring something else to permit the more "public" aspect of same-sex marriage.

Rights have set the terms of how we conceptualize and debate these and similar issues. It is difficult to pick up a book on contemporary theory, justice, or law or to watch a commentary on television that does not invoke these doctrines. Rights have a long pedigree stemming at least as far back as John Locke's classic depiction of them as natural or pre-political. Indeed, the rights to intimacy, property, and religion that make up the private sphere may have an even older history. Aristotle's distinction between the household and the polis stands as a testament to their enduring nature. Undoubtedly, these doctrines have great purchase.

Still, they have been criticized. Republican theorists have rightly charged rights with failing to offer a substantive role for democracy, with failing to honor the common good of a particular polity. According to this criticism, rights invite courts to frustrate our commitment to majoritarian decision-making. After all, they act as "trumps."[2] They fail to make room for genuine and robust collective, democratic discretion, treating individuals as atomistic, as un-connected to their fellow citizens. Others have accused the private sphere of serving as cover for the domination of workers, women, and minorities preventing the polity from doing anything about it. In particular, the right to property has stymied attempts by

---

[1] U.S. Constitution Amendment I (emphasis added).   [2] R. Dworkin 1984: 153.

the democratic majority to redistribute wealth making it difficult for the polity to pass legislation it deems desirable. Yet, rights seem firmly lodged as the only alleged way to secure equality and freedom.

As evidence of this prevailing attitude, much contemporary democratic theory recognizes some of the pathologies of rights but refuses to reject such doctrines. These democrats seek only to democratize rights, permitting the polity to reflect on and redefine their content. This is yet another instantiation of the conventional method of avoiding majority tyranny, of ensuring liberty while deferring to and permitting democratic decision-making. Again, in seeking to balance liberty and democracy, we are stuck within the conceptual framework of rights. These theorists merely "tinker" with this regime, offering a more reflexive, democratic-friendly conception of rights. But their failure to reject rights altogether permits rights to be interpreted so as to invite majority tyranny rather than thwart it. The conventional account of limited government is the reigning orthodoxy even for those who find it unsatisfactory. The language of rights seems entrenched.

I reject the conventional account. It fails as an account of limited government. I argue that we better ensure liberty simultaneously permitting robust democratic decision-making and debate by rejecting rights. We need simply re-conceptualize limited government as one where we limit the reasons or rationales on which the polity may act. I want us to look away from individuals and groups. We should turn our normative attention to the state itself. We should conceive of limited government *not* as carving out those areas, interests, or spheres off limits to state regulation. We should limit government by limiting the rationale or justification on which the democratic polity may act. In this way, we secure freedom and equality by contending that the state has no good reason for limiting whom we can sleep with, for segregating individuals on account of their race, or for curtailing religious liberty. Simultaneously, we value democracy. We permit the polity to pass a wide range of laws as long as it has a good reason to do so. The focus ought only to be on the polity's reason for acting not the area, interest, or sphere at issue. Our focus ought to be on reasons not rights.

Returning to the argument for sexual freedom, consider again a law outlawing consensual sex between redheads and blonds.[3] I contend that such a law is illegitimate *not* because it violates a right to equality or a right to intimacy. It is problematic *not* because it discriminates against a group and *not* because it interferes with behavior that is allegedly private or

---

[3] Throughout the book, I purposely use hair color rather than race, gender or sexuality. My concern is with the rationale behind the legislation, not the category of people affected. To highlight this crucial move in my argument, I often use the example of blonds and redheads.

intimate. All these invoke the conventional account of limited government. An account I argue is problematic. Such a law is illegitimate because there is no good reason for enacting it. Similarly, a contemporary sodomy law prohibiting me from sleeping with someone of the same sex is just as illegitimate – just as arbitrary – as one restricting sexual activity on the basis of hair color. We need not look to rights to deem it suspect. Once we turn our normative attention to reasons, realizing that the polity has no good reason to regulate activity in this way, rights turn out to be unnecessary. This is the theory I propose and defend in this book, one that contemporary liberal theory, albeit half-consciously, already endorses. We should reject rights, turning instead to this superior account of limiting government, to a particular theory of Justification.

This theory of Justification (I purposely capitalize the word), then, conceives of limited government as limiting the rationale on which the polity may act. What needs to be justified is the democratic polity's reason or purpose for acting. By adopting this theory of Justification we re-conceptualize limited government. No longer are certain areas, interests, or classifications off limits to state regulation. No longer must we speak in the language of rights to thwart democratic majorities. The democratic state may legislate in *any* area or sphere or invoke *any* classification as long as it has good reason to do so permitting greater democratic flexibility and discretion while ensuring liberty.

I hope to show that rights turn out to be *inadequate* to secure freedom and equality, also jeopardizing productive democratic debate. They have monopolized political and legal theory as well as political discourse for too long. Why do we insist on rights as *the* protector of our liberties, as if we were living in an age of monarchies and rights were "trumps" we could flail in their despotic direction? Gone are those days. Yet the same amulets that we deployed in those days have grafted onto our own democratic times. Why use rights against our democratically elected governments when we can demand that they *Justify* themselves instead? Surely, as I hope to show, this turn away from rights and towards Justification is at the heart of democratic government; one that is consistent with both the preservation of our liberties and the extension of democratic deliberation.

Though not directly aimed at the doctrine of rights, as a social theorist of possibility, Roberto Unger denounces "institutional fetishism," the nagging orthodoxy of the alleged necessity of certain concepts.[4] His charge against such orthodoxy is instructive here. The fetish for rights takes such doctrines as necessary to claims of justice. It proclaims that we

---

[4] Unger 1996: 7.

cannot do without talk of rights. Our unwillingness to think beyond them stymies, in Unger's lingo, our "transformative imagination," our ability to imagine alternatives.[5]

I seek to proffer such an alternative. Rather than asking whether a particular behavior falls under a right *to* something – a right to free speech, religion, or even equality – one need only ascertain the democratic polity's reason for acting – its reason for enacting a statute, passing a law, or enforcing a particular regulation. A court ought only to look at the legislative purpose behind a particular law rather than the alleged right it violates. This paradigmatic shift – from individuals to the democratic polity itself – constitutes the core of my argument.

I argue, in the spirit of John Stuart Mill, that we need simply specify the appropriate legislative rationale as one of only preventing harm. If the polity may only seek to prevent demonstrable, non-consensual harm, we have a philosophically sounder method of securing freedom and equality while informing democracy. The democratic polity must in good faith follow this justificatory constraint. By constraining democratic decision-making in this way, we avoid majority tyranny simultaneously making room for democratic flexibility. Doing so renders rights obsolete. This is the superior account of limited government I propose, one that finds life in American constitutional law and one that does all the work that the conventional locution of rights does, and more; while at the same time allowing our democratically elected legislatures to deliberate and decide on areas that a rights regime had previously declared off limits.

By Justification (again, I purposely capitalize the word) I mean a distinctive kind of legitimizing principle that stands as an *alternative* to rights. Conventional justifications are those that are used to arrive at something else: a schedule of rights, a mathematical proof, or a particular course of action. That is, such justifications are like ladders, discarded after they are used to climb up somewhere. They are single attempts to merely prove or establish something. This is not what I mean by Justification. I have a more specific and robust role for Justification. Justification is a constant, deliberative process, a mechanism that is perpetually appealed to in deciding whether the polity acts justly. Justification entails two necessary components: one, something needs to be justified (decided, talked about, agreed upon, etc.); and such justification takes place under some kind of justificatory constraints, limitations, or conditions. I argue that contemporary liberal political theory has already taken a turn to Justification.

---

[5] Ibid.: 6.

Ultimately, I proffer a *particular* theory of Justification that looks to legislative purpose contending that the state may only seek to minimize (mitigate, prevent, regulate, etc.[6]) demonstrable, non-consensual harm. What needs to be justified is the democratic polity's reason or rationale for acting (the first component) and this rationale may only be one of harm minimization (the second component).

A turn to this kind of Justification, to legislative purpose, is not merely semantic. It would be a mistake to interpret my theory of Justification as simply suggesting that as individuals we only have the right not to be harmed. Contending that the state may only act to prevent harm is not the same as suggesting that we have a right not to be harmed. Mine is a *justificatory* constraint on democratic decision-making. Rights attach to individuals and groups. They limit government by suggesting that certain areas, interests, or classifications are off limits to the democratic polity. Simply proposing that each of us has a right not to be harmed fails to balance and realize liberty and democracy. It represents an instantiation of the conventional account of limited government, one where rights are the regulatory principle that limits the scope or reach of the democratic polity – an account I reject.

On one hand, suppose this right not to be harmed applied against other individuals. That is, others could not go around harming you. Such a right would prove too much and too little. Imagine a polity that has a market economy. I'm an intrepid entrepreneur and open a new business near yours. Due to my shrewd business practices, your company is forced to shut down. My competitive actions have undoubtedly harmed you. Had I not started my company, you would not have lost yours. If we have a right not to be harmed by our fellow citizens, this would call into question all kinds of competitive behavior, behavior that we may not deem suspect. Moreover, what is to stop the *polity* from segregating us according to race or hair color or limiting whom we can sleep with? These tyrannical policies may not violate such a right, because the state is acting not our fellow citizens. It's problematic simply to say that we all have a right not to be harmed by others. Rights problematically distract us from considering the rationale on which the state acts.

On the other hand, if this right also applied against the polity – the state could not harm anyone – how can the state even imprison a murderer or, for that matter, impose any kind of behavioral constraint on its members? Here the state would be unable to do a wide variety of things we deem legitimate. In the end, invoking the language of rights simultaneously protects too much – it would force us to outlaw competitive behavior

---

[6] I use the locution of "minimizing harm" to cover all these possible meanings.

and prevent us from passing simple criminal legislation – and too little – it would give us no grounds on which to object to certain tyrannical policies.

Our normative attention ought to be on the polity's reason for acting, its rationale for imprisoning a murderer or segregating individuals on the basis of race or hair color. And once we reorient our attention in this way, we quickly realize that while there is good reason to imprison a murderer, there is no good reason to segregate individuals on the basis of race, hair color, or a wide variety of other characteristics. In fact, as I intimate throughout this book, we already think in these terms albeit half-consciously. I make explicit this focus on the polity's reason or purpose for acting. Once we realize this – once we endorse my theory of Justification – we no longer need to speak in the problematic language of rights. We can reject rights. I argue that once we constrain democratic government by contending that the polity may only seek to minimize demonstrable harm, we better balance and realize the values of liberty and democracy. We lose nothing in terms of liberty, while allowing democracy to pursue its own course. For too long we have had our cake but not been able to eat it. My account provides one way to do so.

Though equality and freedom are not identical, for much of this book I use them interchangeably, often utilizing the word "liberty" to stand in for both. Because securing one can be characterized as securing the other, my argument does not rest on neatly distinguishing between the two. Taken together, equality and freedom must be balanced against the value of democracy. It is adjudicating this balance – and ultimately the role of courts in reviewing democratically enacted statutes – that motivates my book.

My book is in three parts. Part I sets out the puzzle of rights, namely their inability to properly balance and realize the values of liberty and democracy. The conventional picture of limited government is flawed. Part II rejects such doctrines, offering my positive solution of Justification and its emphasis on the minimization of demonstrable, non-consensual harm as outlining the proper legislative purpose. I argue that this theory of Justification is a better account of limited government. In arguing for this particular justificatory constraint, I do not work up to it. Rather, I simultaneously present and apply it – demonstrating its superiority by its very application. Part III contends that American constitutional law has moved in the direction of Justification, rejecting the core rights of property, religion, and intimacy and should continue to do so.

Part I

Chapter 1 briefly outlines the "democratic deficit" in the classic depiction of rights. By articulating those interests, areas or kinds of behavior that the state ought not to interfere in, rights entail no genuine role for democracy.

By its very terms, the classic account of rights has no necessary relationship to a positively expressed democratic common good. John Locke articulates the paradigmatic classic account with his rights to life, liberty, health and property, rights that are purposely understood as natural or pre-political. They articulate normative obligations independent of the democratic decision-making process. Rights, as conventionally understood, fail to value democracy. The traditional account of rights does not strike the appropriate balance in limiting government. A more republican political alternative may cure such a deficit but at the cost of compromising equality and freedom. Appealing only to the democratic majority is problematic.

Chapter 2 critiques a dynamic, democratically informed characterization of rights. In an effort to balance liberty and democracy, avoiding the pitfalls of Chapter 1, reflexive theorists regrettably do not go far enough. In merely tinkering with a regime of rights rather than purging these doctrines altogether, these accounts needlessly invite majority tyranny, frustrating democratic debate. They still cling to rights in conceptualizing limited government.

Part II

Chapter 3 introduces my preferred mechanism of constraining democratic decision-making, Justification. I suggest that in the last fifty years or so contemporary liberal theory has, in fact, already taken a turn to reasons, a turn that has gone largely unappreciated. Specifically, I assay Bruce Ackerman's neutrality thesis, Jürgen Habermas' discourse theory, John Rawls' public reason, and Michael Oakeshott's civil association. These theories contend that something needs to be justified (decided, talked about, agreed upon, etc.) under some kind of justificatory constraints, limitations, or conditions. Though each is instructive in highlighting important aspects of an appropriate theory of Justification, I argue that these contemporary accounts fall short in doing the necessary work.

In drawing from them, Chapter 4 articulates my own theory of Justification. In doing so, I outline a superior account of limited government. I argue, in the spirit of Mill, that as long as the democratic polity may only seek to minimize demonstrable, non-consensual harm, we secure equality and freedom simultaneously valuing democracy. I elucidate the four central components of this justificatory constraint: state action, only demonstrable harm, consent, and democracy itself.

Chapter 5 contends we can reject the fetish for rights by accepting my theory of Justification, a theory that specifies the appropriate legislative purpose. By rejecting rights – rejecting the conventional account of limited government – we avoid the liberty-compromising features of such doctrines, permit needed democratic flexibility, and promote fruitful debate. We transcend (instead of merely "tinker" with) the distinction between an inquiry regarding the interests, spaces, and areas off limits to state intervention and an inquiry concerning self-mastery by the democratic polity.

Part III

Having made my argument in ideal theory, Chapters 6 and 7 contend that American constitutional law has moved in the direction of this theory of Justification turning away from the core rights of the private sphere: property, religion, and intimacy. In making a more modest argument in this part of my book, I argue in Chapter 6 that the Supreme Court has, as a general rule, repudiated the special status of property and religion. By subjecting economic regulations to mere rational review and treating religion like any other voluntary association, the Court effectively rejects such rights.

Chapter 7 makes the same argument for the right to privacy critically examining the Court's jurisprudence in this area. I interpret *Lawrence v. Texas* (2003) (declaring sodomy laws unconstitutional) as laying the foundation for the ultimate repudiation of the right to privacy. I argue that by repudiating morals legislation, *Lawrence* renders privacy constitutionally unnecessary. I suggest that, in line with my theory of Justification, the Court's abortion jurisprudence has also turned away from a focus on individuals to a focus on legislative purpose. In rejecting these core rights and turning entirely to the state's rationale for acting, constitutional law permits robust democratic flexibility. Properly understood, I argue that American constitutional law informs the re-conceptualized account of limited government proffered in Part II.

Chapter 8 seeks to replace the Court's current "equal protection" analysis with this theory of Justification. Though the doctrines of suspect class and classification are ingrained features of the constitutional landscape, I argue that the Court's use of them is internally problematic. By conflating classification with class, the Court fails to articulate a consistent equal protection doctrine, accomplishing neither formal equality nor anti-subordination. In accordance with my theory of Justification, we are better off asking the reason behind the legislation, instead of attempting to categorize legislation as affecting or invoking a suspect class or classification – as fulfilling a right to anti-subordination or a right to formal equality. Finally, I propose a more democratic role for judicial review given the turn away from rights towards the legislative purpose of only minimizing harm.

Part I

Rights

1 The classic conception of rights: the "democratic deficit"

How should we limit democratic government? Assuming we care about the competing values of liberty and democracy, what is the best regulatory principle for balancing them? Obviously, with no constraint on democratic government, there is nothing to thwart democratic tyranny. There is nothing to stop the polity from passing conventional sodomy laws or laws mandating racial segregation. We must limit democracy to some extent in order to ensure liberty. Alternatively, specifying all or even most of our normative obligations prior to any democratic decision-making may ensure liberty but leaves no place for democracy. We must be careful, then, not to go too far in limiting democracy. The puzzle is not whether or not to limit state power but *how* to do so. Consequently, I am *not* concerned with the following questions: Why should we limit democratic government? How do we arrive at such limits? How do we substantiate them? What are their foundations? Why do we even care about liberty and democracy? My book seeks only to answer "how": *How do we limit government so as to ensure liberty but simultaneously allow for and permit a good deal of democratic discretion?*

The conventional answer employs rights to balance and realize the values of liberty and democracy. I do not interrogate the philosophical foundation of rights.[1] Mine is an argument in political and legal theory not morality. It is an argument of application. I criticize the traditional method of limiting government by showing that it does not strike the appropriate balance between the values of liberty and democracy. As applied, it fails. We should reject it. I then propose an alternative way of limiting government, one that does a better job of realizing these values. I simply hope to reorient the way we think about and debate limited government. This is the nature and scope of my argument. In this way, it is both bold and modest: modest because I hope to propose a better way of

---

[1] For a foundational critique see, e.g., Bentham 1987 [1843], Burke 1973 [1790], MacDonald 1984; see generally Kramer *et al.* 1998.

conceptualizing how we limit democratic decision-making and bold because I do so by rejecting rights.

Rights undoubtedly have great staying power in both real world debates and academic scholarship. They are the fodder of much political and legal theory as well as political discourse. Issues like abortion, affirmative action, non-discrimination, welfare and same-sex marriage appear invariably to implicate talk of rights. In fact, the rights to property, religion, and intimacy that make up the conventional private sphere seem to have particular purchase in political theory and discourse. Rights carve out those areas, interests, and classifications off limits to state regulation. While the state may not legislate "private" matters, it may legislate "public" ones, or so the conventional argument goes. This chapter and the next argue that the conventional account is flawed. We should reject it. We should reject rights like the rights to free speech, due process, equality, property, religion, privacy and the like, turning instead to a particular theory of Justification.

For the purposes of my argument, rights have two salient features, features that are interrelated.[2] First, rights attach to individuals or groups of individuals. The traditional "subject" of rights is the individual.[3] We say that A has a right to x. Or that a group of Bs has a right to y. When the state violates a right, it has done a wrong to an individual or group. For example, a law prohibiting pornography may violate an individual's right to free speech. Or a law mandating racial segregation may violate a group's right to equality. Rights accrue to members of the polity. The state itself is not the beneficiary of rights. These doctrines are conceptually independent and distinct from the democratic state.

Second, a right is always a right to something: *to* free speech, *to* property, *to* privacy, or *to* equality. It protects a certain interest or area. If the activity implicates free speech, property, privacy, or equality, we deem it worthy of presumptive protection. For rights, the relevant inquiry is what specific category does the activity or behavior fall under? Rights carve out spaces or interests that the state ought not to interfere in or with. The methodology of rights functions negatively, articulating not what count as the relevant objects of state regulation but what are excluded from the purview of state power.

Rights represent the conventional account of limited government, an account that makes no necessary room for collective decisions by the democratic polity. This account does not explicitly value democracy, a particular polity's articulation of our normative obligations. After all, once

---

[2] Cf. Shapiro 1986: 14.   [3] Ibid.: 14.

we have specified those behaviors, activities, or interests of a person or group beyond the scope of state regulation, we leave little room for democracy.

Since the subjects of rights are members of the polity, and not the polity itself, there is no necessary connection to the democratic value of self-government. In his discussion of negative liberty, Isaiah Berlin says as much:

> But there is no necessary connection between individual liberty and democratic rule. The answer to the question "Who governs me?" is *logically distinct* from the question "How far does government interfere with me."[4]

If we focus simply on rights – this is the way we go about securing liberty, it does not matter whether our government is democratic or non-democratic. As long as our rights are not violated, why does it matter what government we find ourselves in:

> Just as a democracy may, in fact, deprive the individual citizen of a great many liberties which he might have in some other form of society, so it is perfectly conceivable that a liberal-minded despot would allow his subjects a large measure of personal freedom.[5]

In this way, the scope of liberty is "logically distinct" from democracy. As I argue, the classic conception of rights therefore entails a "democratic deficit." The puzzle is how to connect liberty to democracy – to limit government so as to ensure liberty while necessitating a robust role for democracy.

This very brief chapter lays out this motivating puzzle behind my argument leaving the ensuing chapters to answer it. It is in two parts. First, I explicate the "democratic deficit" in the classic characterization of rights, arguing that the conventional account of limited government fails to value democracy. Second, I argue that the republican alternative, an alternative that exemplifies and cures this deficit, fails to secure liberty.

The classic conception of rights

The following accounts of rights, though different in many respects, fail to value or allow for a robust role for democracy. These accounts (and this is not an exhaustive list) merely explicate what behaviors, activities, or interests of a person or group are beyond the scope of state regulation. In so doing, they do not contemplate a necessary role for democracy.

---

[4] Berlin 1970 [1958]: 130 (emphasis added).   [5] Ibid.: 129.

John Locke articulates the classic conception of rights. He argues that as *individuals* we have certain interests in securing our "Life, Health, Liberty, or Possessions."[6] Government is needed because our enjoyment of these rights is "uncertain" and "constantly exposed to the Invasion of others"[7] in the state of nature as it turns into a state of war. Because we cannot be judges in our own case – deciding when the "law of nature" has been broken – government is required.[8] If we are left to judge on our own, self-interest will lead us to do not what the law of nature requires but what is best for us. This precarious and dangerous state of affairs necessitates government.

Consequently, the social compact arises as a more satisfactory method of securing the rights to life, health, liberty, and property. Individuals do not give up their rights in civil society. They only relinquish their power to protect themselves and enforce such claims against each other.[9] The advent of government does not change, alter, or add to our rights. As individuals, we possess such rights in civil society as we did in the statute of nature. This renders them natural or pre-political.

Locke, then, separates the question of "who governs" us from the question of what interests we ought to be left alone in. Only after Locke has delineated our pre-political rights[10] does he move on to the question of government.[11] His answer does not connect with his earlier discussion of rights. As Locke explains, once individuals band together to form a society or "body politck,"[12] they must decide by majority rule on a particular form of government. Such possibilities include a democracy, oligarchy, monarchy (hereditary and elective) or a mixture of the three.[13] Moreover, this majority will also be the effective judge of when the government (that they have so entrusted the protection of their liberties to) has failed in protecting their rights, triggering dissolution of civil or political society.[14]

But majority rule serves no conceptual role in the Lockean argument. Though this kind of rule may be a practical, second-best solution, Locke offers no "necessary connection" between rights and the question of "who governs" us. For Locke, the rights a government must protect are conceptually specified prior to its creation. "The Obligations of the Law of Nature, cease not in Society. ... Thus, the Law of Nature stands as an Eternal Rule to all Men, *Legislators* as well as others."[15] Though any constraint on government – even the one I propose in Part II – is in a

---

[6] Locke 1988 [1690]: sec. 6.   [7] Ibid.: sec. 123.   [8] Ibid.: sec. 13.
[9] Ibid.: sec. 127–130.   [10] Ibid.: Ch. II.   [11] Ibid.: Ch. VIII.
[12] Ibid.: sec. 96–97, sec. 133.   [13] Ibid.: Chs. VIII, X.
[14] Ibid.: Ch. XIX; see also Shapiro 2003b: 325–332.   [15] Locke 1988 [1690]: sec. 135.

way pre-political, we should be careful not to impose too much of a constraint. We need to permit the polity to have a substantive (though not complete) role in defining our normative obligations. Locke provides no such role. It is no surprise, then, that Locke contemplates the existence of any number of governments. The kind of government – monarchic, oligarchic, or democratic – does not change the obligations it has to its members. His argument does not begin with the democratic state but rather with the individuals who will comprise it. This is the crucial difficulty with the classic conception of rights. The kind of government instituted is not a component in Locke's normative argument. If our primary political obligations are derived independently of the political process, what does it matter whether we live under a democracy or a monarchy? After all, the enlightened monarch could protect our rights as well.

Democracy is normatively unnecessary for Locke. Thus, the classic characterization of rights suffers from a "democratic deficit." If we care about affording democracy a substantive (but again not complete) role in defining our normative commitments (and I assume as much), Locke's account is inadequate. Locke is, at the conceptual level, no democratic theorist. If our key obligations are pre-political, as long as they are honored and enforced, the kind of government we happen to find ourselves in does not seem to matter. As long as our concern is with those behaviors, activities, or interests of a person or group off limits to state regulation, we need not worry or even care about "who governs" us.

This is clearest in considering the right to property, a staple in the conventional account of limited government. Such a right problematically ties the hands of the democratic majority. It leaves hardly any discretion for the state to redistribute wealth or pass welfare legislation. Rather, it requires a libertarian state, one where the polity may not regulate property. After all, this right carves out an area or sphere off limits to state regulation.

Robert Nozick is a defender of this conventional account of limited government.[16] He, more explicitly than Locke, argues for a libertarian state. He too leaves the value of democracy out of the normative equation. A democratic polity may not redistribute. It may not decide to be any more robust than a "minimal state." According to Nozick, to engage in redistribution is illegitimate. Why? As long as *individuals* are able to acquire holdings and transfer them, the state will need to constantly interfere to upset any pattern.[17] For Nozick, such interference violates

---

[16] Nozick: 1974.   [17] Ibid.: 150–164.

our rights. This is the classic depiction of the autonomous economic sphere. For instance, a series of consensual economic dealings that result in some having more property than others may not be un-done or regulated by the state. This precludes democratic flexibility, the ability of the democratic polity to redistribute or regulate. Even if we were to imagine our favorite initial distributive scheme (i.e. everyone gets an equal amount of stuff) the fact that individuals can consensually trade or give their stuff to someone else will invariably upset it. As Nozick suggests, it "is not clear how those holding alternative conceptions of distributive justice can reject the entitlement conception of justice."[18] Defining the substance of such a conception to include a justice in acquisition and a justice in transfer principle, Nozick argues that no pattern of distribution can long survive.

But it is this very assumption, namely that there even is an entitlement theory and that it includes certain principles, which sidelines democracy, excluding a role for democratic decision-making. Democracy or majority rule makes no appearance in Nozick's argument. After all, what if a democratic polity decided not to recognize the entitlement theory (rejecting the idea, for example, that we can even "own" something through our labor) or instituted, in Jeremy Waldron's language, a "collective property" regime instead of its more familiar private property counterpart?[19] In this way, Nozick articulates the economic claims of justice – I am entitled to this stuff and you are entitled to that – *without* appeal to democracy. There is no genuine room for it. The right to property prevents the polity from interfering in this area. Like Locke, Nozick takes democracy out of the normative equation. As a collective, the polity may decide to redistribute wealth, pass minimum wage legislation, or a host of other policies. The right to property and its attendant economic sphere preclude such democratic decisions. They do not make room for democratic decision-making in this area.

This is clearest in Nozick's characterization of rights as "side-constraints." Rights constrain the actions of the state.

There is no justified sacrifice of some of us for others. This root idea, namely, that there are different individuals with separate lives and so no one may be sacrificed for others, underlies the existence of moral side constraints.[20]

Redistribution violates the rights of individuals – once again exemplifying the concern not with the state (the state only comes in as the possible violator of rights) but with its members. In making his conceptual argument from dominant protective agencies to the minimal state, Nozick is careful to contend that no rights are violated. Whether or not his argument

[18] Ibid.: 160.   [19] Waldron 1985: 328–329.   [20] Nozick 1974: 33.

succeeds (whether "independents" can be forcibly included in the ambit of the dominant protection agency without violating rights) is not relevant here. What is significant is that Nozick makes sure to respect these "side-constraints" as he moves from the state of nature to the minimal state. Thus, such constraints, those behaviors, activities, or interests of a person beyond the scope of state regulation, are defined independently of the democratic process. The liberty inquiry is once again unconnected to its "who governs" counterpart.

Rather than posit a state of nature like Locke or Nozick, John Rawls articulates his famous "original position."[21] He asks what principles of justice would *individuals* behind a "veil of ignorance" agree upon. Individuals in this position are ignorant of such things as their "class position or social status," "fortune in the distribution of natural assets and abilities," "intelligence and strength," or their "conception of the good."[22] Rawls argues that these individuals would not only select an extensive compatible schedule of rights but also arrange social and economic inequalities so as to benefit the least advantaged while securing equality of opportunity.[23] As a contemporary Kantian, Rawls uses the veil of ignorance to achieve universalization. The principles arising from this device are those that all should agree to.

Because this Kantian argument abstracts from our contingent position, it must abstract from our membership in a democratic polity. Such membership is nothing other than our contingent, particular social preferences. The veil of ignorance by its very terms requires a "democratic deficit." The state is not the normative subject under the veil. Individuals are once again the only players. To have democracy play a role in the original position – informing Rawls' principles of justice – is to un-do the veil of ignorance. The abstracting quality of the veil entails that we leave behind our affiliation or membership in a democratic polity. After all, it is the a-contextual nature of the original position that supposedly generates the correctness of the two principles of justice. Since these principles are universal – they apply to all – a robust role for democracy is once more absent.

In putting forth his second principle of justice, Rawls effectively adds to the list of classic rights by including a certain right to social equality or what he calls democratic equality. This is his "difference principle." It postulates that obligations ought to be structured so as to benefit the "least advantaged."[24] Unlike Locke and Nozick, Rawls permits some kind of regulation in order to redress economic and social inequality at least for

---

[21] Rawls: 1971.   [22] Ibid.: 137.   [23] Ibid.: Ch. II.   [24] Ibid.: 76–83.

the worst off.[25] The upshot of such a principle is that it does seem to implicate a range of economic alternatives. Various kinds of economies could be said to benefit the worst off. Socialism and conventional market capitalism may very well meet the difference principle.[26] Rawls' second principle of justice goes some way in valuing the democratic context. It suggests that not every just polity need look the same.

Yet, Rawls shies away from explicitly embracing democracy as necessary to articulate such economic arrangements. He fails to realize that democratic polities may very well disagree over the meaning and scope of the "least advantaged."[27] And if they do, we must appeal to democracy to define our normative obligations. But Rawls' Kantian methodology that seeks to arrive at principles for all has no room for democratic context. My concern is not the feasibility or soundness of Rawls' two principles of justice. What is significant is that his methodology like Locke's and Nozick's does not go far enough in valuing democracy.

Just as Rawls is able to articulate a just state's obligations to its members on his own, so too can anyone else through the apparatus of the original position fulfilling the Kantian principle of universalization. Since all polities will, according to Rawls, accept these two principles of justice, we may secure equality and freedom but we do so at the cost of excluding a robust positive role for democratic decision-making. The later Rawls, as I outline in Chapter 3, does offer a more democratic-friendly account with his notion of public reason.

While these three rights based theories all suffer from an unacknowledged "democratic deficit," Ronald Dworkin is explicit about such a shortage.[28] He sees rights as "trumps," as superseding the welfare of the community.[29] Rights take precedence over decisions by the democratic majority. He holds that moral rights are normative obligations that the government may not un-do. Anyone who thinks that "men and women have only such moral rights as Government chooses to grant [...] means that they have no moral rights at all."[30] If rights are not understood in this privileged democracy-transcending way, we have none at all.

The democratic polity has little say in articulating our normative commitments or obligations. Dworkin, as a result, contemplates a strong and substantive role for a supreme court. A court must enforce these morals rights, even if such enforcement contravenes majoritarian decision-making.[31] To do otherwise is not to take "rights seriously."[32] Enforcing such rights must be done "even when the majority thinks it would be

---

[25] Ibid.: 75–83.   [26] Shapiro 2003c: 136–137.   [27] Benhabib 2004: 108.
[28] R. Dworkin 1978, 1984, 1985.   [29] R. Dworkin 1984: 153.
[30] R. Dworkin 1978: 185.   [31] R. Dworkin 1985.   [32] R. Dworkin 1978.

wrong to do it, and even when the majority would be worse off for having it done."[33] Dworkin, then, does not explicitly contemplate a democratically informed understanding of our rights or of our normative obligations to others. As individuals we hold "trumps" against the government. Since the normative subject in his argument is also the individual, there is no conceptual link to the question of "who governs" us. Dworkin's emphasis on the role of courts as opposed to the legislature points to a "democratic deficit." While any account of limited government must limit democratic decision-making, the classic conception of rights goes too far. It provides no genuine normative space for democratic discretion.

The republican alternative

Republican and some communitarian[34] theorists criticize the classic conception of rights in this very way. Drawing from the republican traditions of Jean-Jacques Rousseau and Aristotle and even Hegelian theory, these theorists contend that our normative obligations ought to be defined by the community.[35] Assuming that rights genuinely secure freedom and equality (I question this claim throughout the book), they do so by failing to offer a substantive role for democracy. If we care about affording democracy such a role (again, I assume we do), the classic accounts above are inadequate. We must reject them. My interpretation of the republican political alternative seems to do just that. Rather than look to the individuals of the democratic polity, republicanism turns to the democratic state, to the common good.

A commitment to the common good highlights the importance of the connectedness of individuals in a polity permitting democratic flexibility and discretion. What may be good for one community may not be good for another. Rights are universal. They apply regardless of the context leaving little if any room for democratic decision-making. In this way, rights based theories offer an unsatisfactory conception of the self. Michael Sandel argues that emphasis on the classic account of rights problematically treats the self as "unencumbered."[36] In specifically

---

[33] Ibid.: 194.

[34] In specifying our normative obligations, much communitarian thought looks not to democracy but to tradition, to practices or narratives passed down by the community (see, e.g., MacIntyre 1984, Taylor 1992 [1979]). Still, I believe this communitarian charge trades on a "democratic deficit." It trades on the fact that rights fail to take into account the preferences of the particular democratic majority. For instance, MacIntyre does not believe there are rights. For him, "belief in them is one with belief in witches and in unicorns" (MacIntyre 1984: 69).

[35] See, e.g., Pettit 1997, Sandel 1982, 1984, 1996, Walzer 1983.   [36] Sandel: 1982, 1984.

attacking the Rawlsian approach, Sandel finds the stripping away of our current characteristics, interests, social position, and aims as restricting and false:

> To imagine a person incapable of constitutive attachments such as these is not to conceive an ideally free and rational agent, but to imagine a person wholly without character, without moral depth. ... Denied the expansive self-understanding that could shape a common life, the liberal self is left to lurch between detachment on the one hand, and entanglement on the other. Such is the fate of the unencumbered self, and its liberating promise.[37]

Sandel's lament stems from the "democratic deficit" inherent in these classic rights based accounts. Since our individual normative obligations to others are pre-political, we do not need others to define them. There is no connection between liberty and the question of "who governs" us. Rights tie the hands of the democratic majority. By attaching to individuals regardless of their membership in a particular democratic polity, rights imply a conception of the self that is a-contextual and abstract. They preempt the polity from collectively defining a range of normative commitments.

Consequently, a republican alternative sees rights as anti-democratic. Such doctrines fail to look to the democratic majority in articulating our normative obligations. They fail to make genuine room for democracy. The republican charge is telling – demonstrating the "democratic deficit" of the classic characterization of rights.

However, having the democratic polity articulate our normative obligations fails to offer a workable political alternative. If freedom and equality are left at the mercy of the democratic common good, we have no way to avoid majority tyranny. With no limits on democratic government, we have no way to thwart it. As Amy Gutmann rightly contends:

> The common good of the Puritans of seventeenth-century Salem commanded them to hunt witches; the common good of the Moral Majority of the twentieth century commands them not to tolerate homosexuals. The *enforcement of liberal rights, not the absence of settled community*, stands between the Moral Majority and the contemporary equivalence of witch-hunting.[38]

Gutmann's concern is characteristic of much political theory, and I certainly share it. Leaving democracy – and nothing else – to articulate our normative and political obligations jeopardizes liberty. It invites oppression. The antebellum South valued slavery, Jim Crow saw "separate but equal" as legitimate, and currently many American states see marriage as the union of only a man and a woman.

---

[37] Sandel 1984: 91.   [38] Gutmann 1985: 319 (emphasis added).

These are no doubt instances of tyranny of the democratic majority. If we leave democracy to articulate our normative obligations, we open the way for oppression. Mill and Alexis de Tocqueville contend that we must guard ourselves against such tyranny.[39] After all, securing equality and freedom in the face of such majoritarianism stands as the motivation behind the classic account of rights explored above. I share the intuition that we risk liberty by leaving its protection entirely in the hands of the democratic majority. To ensure freedom and equality, we must limit democracy to some extent. Again, the question is *how* best to do so.

The political implications of the republican alternative, then, seem unpalatable. Tyranny of the majority cannot be overlooked or glossed over. It stands as a rightful worry. Though the republican alternative is correct in looking to the democratic state, turning its attention away from individuals or groups, it fails to secure liberty. While the classic conception of rights suffers from a lamentable "democratic deficit," the republican alternative that looks only to democracy seems equally objectionable. If democracy is a "nonnegotiable" value[40] and the prevention of tyranny of the majority is also non-negotiable, we must move beyond the options presented in this chapter. This is the puzzle of limited government, the puzzle of balancing and realizing the competing values of democracy and liberty. We must move beyond endorsing the simple options we have considered so far. In the next chapter, I evaluate such an alternative, namely a reflexive conception of rights.

---

[39] Mill 1989 [1859]: 8–9, Tocqueville 2000 [1835]: 239–242; see also Berlin 1970 [1958]: 171, 163.
[40] Shapiro 2003a: 1.

Reflexive rights: jeopardizing freedom,
       equality, and democratic debate

The classic characterization of rights fails to take seriously the value of
democracy. The republican alternative threatens liberty. How, then,
should we limit government? How do we balance the need for democratic
decision-making without falling prey to such tyranny? The reigning
answer seems to be a reflexive conception of rights.[1] It recognizes the
"democratic deficit" inherent in the classic characterization of rights.
It offers in its place a dynamic and active counterpart where rights are
(re)validated and (re)defined by the democratic majority.

Frank Michelman, for instance, recognizes that American constitutional
jurisprudence has commitments to both "self-rule" (to be governed by the
people) and "law-rule" (to be governed by the law).[2] Adapting Robert
Cover's term of "jurisgenerative,"[3] Michelman articulates a "jurisgenerative politics" where the aim of reconciling these two commitments stands at
the core of constitutionalism.[4] That is, we are both the "subject" and the
"author" of the laws.[5] Not only do we follow the law but also have a hand in
articulating and re-articulating it. Holding on to rights, the reflexive
account would have democracy inform and define those interests or areas
of the subject where the state ought not to interfere. The reflexive approach
aims to democratize rights, democratize the conventional account of
limited government. It aims to offer democracy a necessary role.

Seyla Benhabib describes her project as one of "democratic iteration."[6]
It emphasizes the reflexive and debatable character of rights. Rights claims
and principles must be "contested and contextualized, invoked and
revoked, posited and positioned."[7] Benhabib describes this approach in
the following way:

Whereas natural right doctrines assume that the principles that undergird democratic politics are impervious to transformative acts of will, and whereas legal

---

[1] See, e.g., Benhabib 1986, 1992, 2002, 2004, Cohen J. 2002, Cover 1983, Habermas 1990,
    1996, 2001, Michelman 1988, cf. Shapiro 1999.
[2] Michelman 1988: 1499.   [3] Cover 1983.   [4] Michelman 1988: 1502.
[5] Benhabib 2004: 181.   [6] Ibid.   [7] Ibid.: 179.

positivism identifies democratic legitimacy with the correctly posited norms of a sovereign legislature, jurisgenerative politics signals a space of interpretation and intervention between transcendent norms and the will of democratic majorities.[8]

She rightly seeks to avoid both a "democratic deficit" and majority tyranny. She like other reflexive theorists sees the democratic polity as interpreting rights, as defining their scope and meaning.

Jürgen Habermas, in fact, self-consciously sees his project as attempting to "strike a balance between popular sovereignty and human rights, or between the 'freedom of the ancients' and the 'freedom of the moderns'."[9] He sees himself as connecting liberty with democracy. I leave discussion of Habermas' discourse theory to Part II, suggesting that it articulates a theory of Justification. I am sympathetic to the turn away from static rights and towards a more dynamic, democratically informed counterpart. However, by clinging to rights, the reflexive approach fails to ensure genuine freedom and equality needlessly also frustrating democratic debate. By failing to reject the conventional way of limiting government, the reflexive approach problematically only "tinkers" with it.

In turn, this chapter is in three parts. First, I argue that the reflexive conception of rights is too prone to majority tyranny. It invites the very tyranny that rights are meant to thwart. Second, I specifically look at a reflexive right of privacy arguing that its regime of tolerance fails to achieve genuine liberty. Third, I suggest that such a dynamic account of rights frustrates democratic debate leaving opposing parties trapped between unnecessary, incommensurable positions.

The problem of scope and meaning

Integral to the reflexive or jurisgenerative approach is the democratic polity's ability to revise and reflect upon principles and rights, to define their scope. According to Benhabib, democratic majorities must be able to "*re-iterate* these principles and incorporate them into democratic will-formation processes through argument, contestation, revision, and rejection."[10]

Take the rights to property, religion, and intimacy that make up the conventional private sphere. These rights have permitted harm to vulnerable minorities in the name of protection within this sphere. History has shown that such rights have, for instance, condoned and shielded from state regulation harm to workers, women, and minorities.

---

[8] Ibid.: 181.   [9] Habermas 2001: 116.   [10] Benhabib 2004: 181.

The libertarian economic sphere and its accompanying right to property have made it difficult to permit regulation of the economy. If the right to property is pre-political representing just distributions that are independent of the democratic state, as Locke and Nozick would have us believe, altering such relations seems problematic. Adherence to this right allows courts to thwart majority decisions. For example, up until the New Deal, the Supreme Court struck down legislation that sought to do just that. The conventional account of limited government thwarted attempts by the democratic majority to increase welfare by interfering with market transactions.

Similarly, and perhaps even more egregiously, the right to privacy and specifically the realm of family and marriage have condoned violence against women. Again, the conventional account of limited government suggests that the realm of the intimate and familial is off limits to state regulation. But even Mill criticized the way the private sphere via the institution of marriage harmed women.[11] Until recently the common law saw husband and wife as one person. Spouses "could not be on opposite sides of any lawsuit for either personal injury or property damage."[12] Consequently, a husband could physically abuse his wife with no threat of legal sanction.[13] Linda McClain maintains that "the law's privacy is a sphere of sanctified isolation, impunity, and unaccountability."[14] The private sphere (as she goes on to state) "sanctions the violation of women by permitting those with power (men) to act with impunity ... toward the powerless (women)."[15] The private sphere has a historical legacy of allowing violence in the family, of serving as the cover for the domination of women.

Multicultural scholarship has also realized that in protecting religion (culture), the private sphere permits harm against minorities within minorities.[16] Okin, for example, chides practices such as "clitoridectomy, polygamy, the marriage of children or marriages that are otherwise coerced" done in the name of protecting culture – leaving them be in the private sphere – as they harm women and children.[17]

The claim that the private sphere with its rights to property, religion, and intimacy has compromised equality is certainly not novel. Karl Marx, in the *Critique of the Gotha Program*, recognized the problem of rights claiming that:

---

[11] Mill 1989 [1869].   [12] Epstein 1995: 944.   [13] Ibid.: 944.   [14] McClain 1995: 208.
[15] Ibid.; see also Allen 1999, West 1992.
[16] Benhabib 2002: 88–91, Kymlicka 1995: 39–42, Okin 1999, Parekh 2000.
[17] Okin 1999: 14.

Right by its very nature can exist only as the application of an equal standard; but unequal individuals (and they would not be different individuals if they were not unequal) are measurable by an equal standard only insofar as they are made subject to an equal criterion, are taken from a *certain* side only, for instance, in the present case, are regarded *only as workers* and nothing more is seen in them, everything else being ignored.[18]

In this way, rights and the ensuing account of limited government cover up underlying harm, harm that is allegedly beyond the scope of a state's ability to remedy, minimize or prevent.

As Benhabib contends:

All struggles against oppression in the modern world begin by redefining what had previously been considered "private", non-public and non-political issues as matters of public concern, as issues of justice, as sites of power which need discursive legitimation.[19]

In so far as the classic, static characterization of rights fails to permit such "re-definition" relegating harm beyond the scope of state regulation, we must reject it. However, Benhabib draws from this difficulty the conservative (or weak) conclusion that rights must be open to "democratic iteration." If the choice is between a static conception of rights and its reflexive, dynamic counterpart, perhaps the latter should be chosen. Yet, why keep such doctrines at all? If struggles in the modern world involve moving something from the "private" to the "public," is it not better to purge the distinction altogether? Why even cling to a distinction that has served as the cover for such domination? In criticizing the private sphere, Catharine MacKinnon claims that the "private is the public for those for whom the personal is the political. In this sense, there is no private, either normatively or empirically."[20] But she does not explicitly take the next step in rejecting the public/private divide, a divide that stands at the center of the conventional account of limited government.

I concede that perhaps the reflexive characterization of rights and its jurisgenerative counterpart are improvements on the classic account given in Chapter 1. By permitting the re-negotiation of the public/private divide – allowing the polity to (re)define the scope and meaning of the rights to property, religion, and intimacy – we can more easily allow the minimization of harm once thought beyond the scope of state regulation. However, having gone this far, why not reject such doctrines altogether? Why not reject the conventional way of limiting government? Why not simply reject rights? If reform takes place when a "private" matter is made public – the corresponding right is interpreted so as to permit

---

[18] Marx 1994 [1891]: 321.   [19] Benhabib 1992: 100.   [20] MacKinnon 1987: 100.

regulation – we are better off with no private sphere, with no rights to property, religion, or intimacy.

The reflexive theorists, borrowing Unger's terminology, only seek to "tinker" with an admittedly problematic doctrine.[21] They hope for gradual change in permitting the democratic polity to re-negotiate and re-define the scope of rights (and by implication the private sphere). They still look to the individual and the areas or interests she must be left alone in. According to the reflexive characterization of rights, the scope and meaning of such normative doctrines need to be (re)defined only because they have historically shielded harm from state regulation. The dynamic account, then, attempts to treat the symptoms – allowing the polity to engage in reform – neglecting the underlying disease.

We should scrap these doctrines altogether. The need for rights is an unnecessary pathology. We should seek transformative change by focusing not on the kind of activity at hand – is it "private" or "public," a matter of religion or property – but on the democratic polity's reason for acting, its rationale behind passing a particular law or regulation. As Unger quips more generally: "[W]hy should we stop so close to the surface?"[22] Once we have focused in on the private sphere as the culprit in perpetuating domination, why not reject rights altogether?

In fact, in its effort to overcome the "democratic deficit," the dynamic account of rights jeopardizes liberty. By merely tinkering with the system, by offering a middling approach that stops short of rejecting rights, the reflexive theorists invite the kind of majority tyranny rights are supposed to thwart. This is the most damning critique of the reflexive rights based alternative. Leaving the majority to define the scope and meaning of rights cannot be the solution. The majority can decide that pornography, controversial art, or even certain offensive books do not fall under the right to free speech or that the right to equality means "separate but equal" or that the right to intimacy does not include the freedom to engage in consensual sodomy.

For example, Jean Cohen specifically articulates a reflexive conception of the right to intimacy. "Indeed, privacy rights are (recursively) a condition of possibility of democratic contestation."[23] Recognizing as much, she concedes that *Bowers v. Hardwick* (1986) (held that sodomy is not protected under the right to privacy), though now overturned by the Court, interpreted the right narrowly so as to exclude gay sex. (I revisit this decision in more detail in Part III.) In Cohen's words, the debate over the constitutional right to privacy, "has been over whether [privacy is] to

---

[21] Unger 1996: 30–31.   [22] Ibid.: 31.   [23] J. Cohen 2002: 121.

be interpreted narrowly as protecting (privileging) only heterosexual marital relationships [...] or broadly as protecting the freedom of intimate association and all that it entails irrespective of marital status or gender." Of course, Cohen no doubt pines for a "broad construction."[24] But if she has so opened the right to privacy to such democratic (re)definition, she needlessly invites the majority to curtail equality and freedom. Having handed over to democratic majorities the power to define rights, she has no normative ground on which to now rein them in. If the limits placed on democratic government are themselves now open for revision, we jeopardize liberty. We effectively un-do limited government. While this may value democracy, we do so at the expense of liberty. Nothing stops the majority from defining the scope of such a right narrowly by, for example, prohibiting individuals from sleeping with someone of the same sex. The reflexive conception's attempt to connect democracy and liberty proves problematic.

A contemporary instance of this invitation to majority tyranny is the debate over same-sex marriage. Twenty-six American states have amended their constitutions to declare marriage between same-sex couples void or invalid. (And this does not include the nineteen states that have done so by statute.)[25] And these amendments took place as a response to the marriage litigation in the 1990s that sought equality for gays and lesbians. As amendments to a state constitution, these are paradigmatic instances of democratic decision-making. These twenty-six states did more than just pass a statute or a law through their legislative bodies. Rather, they engaged in the highest form of "democratic iteration" in their respective states by amending their constitutions. They interpreted the scope of the right to marry narrowly to *exclude* same-sex couples from its scope. During much of the twentieth century, American states had done the same for inter-racial marriage, restricting the right to marry to individuals of the same race.

Put another way, by simply tinkering with rights, the reflexive account cannot even tell us what rights we have. It cannot elucidate what limits, if any, to place on government. Do we have a right to marry someone of the same sex? Do we have the right not to be segregated according to certain characteristics like hair color? If not, what core rights, if any, do we have? And leaving this threshold decision to the democratic polity is unsatisfactory. The democratic majority may decide to recognize only a certain limited set of rights in order to tyrannize.

---

[24] J. Cohen 2002: 122.
[25] Human Rights Campaign. Statewide Marriage Laws (2007): www.hrc.org/documents/marriage_prohibit_20070919.pdf.

If we are authors as well as subjects of the law, criticism of such tyrannical "iterations" seems normatively impossible within the framework of rights. Taking the specific example of same-sex marriage, the reflexive theorist has two options. She can bite the bullet conceding that the democratic polity may exclude such a thing from the scope of the right to marry. Or she must maintain that the ability to marry someone of the same sex is an *integral* component of such a right thereby undercutting the allegedly dynamic (democratic) nature of the right. The former compromises liberty, the latter un-does the "jurisgenerative" enterprise collapsing into its static counterpart where rights are not open to revision or definition. The reflexive alternative either fails to overcome the "democratic deficit" or jeopardizes equality and freedom. It does not go far enough in scaling the pathology of rights and the fear of majority tyranny.

Leaving the definition and scope of rights at the mercy of the polity (not to mention what rights we have in the first place) cannot be the solution. Limiting government by permitting the polity to decide which areas, interests, or classifications are off limits to state regulation invites majority tyranny. Though we move one step forward – permitting "private" acts to be now made "public" – such a dynamic characterization of rights takes us two steps back – permitting the democratic majority to define away liberty. In fact, if a majority must validate rights, the reflexive account has the perverse advantage of giving such decisions an imprimatur of legitimacy. These rights (according to the reflexive theorist) derive their normative scope from the polity. At least the democratic polity in the republican alternative would be hard-pressed to hold out its decision as a conventional claim of justice having thrown out rights. But in the hands of the reflexive majority, such rights threaten justice but under the guise of ensuring equality and freedom. The reflexive account legitimizes these majority tyrannies.

The underlying problem with the reflexive account is its insistence on clinging to rights. Simply retooling the conventional account of limited government is not good enough. The fact that rights generally attach to individuals (specifying those interests or areas beyond the scope of state regulation) and the fact that democracy attaches to the community render any attempt to connect the two hopeless. It is like trying to stick a square peg in a round hole. It just cannot be done. Democratizing rights is not the solution.

The problem of tolerance

Tinkering with the classic characterization of rights is also insufficient in removing the problem of tolerance. Even if the democratic polity defined the right to intimacy broadly including gay sex within its ambit, the kind of protection this right offers is itself not genuinely equal. That is, the conventional way of limiting government actually fails to secure true liberty. Michael Sandel criticizes privacy – and here I mean a right to intimacy – in this very way, claiming it promotes tolerance rather than acceptance.[26] To understand why an acceptance regime is superior to a tolerance regime, it is crucial to realize that toleration, a widely touted liberal concept, is permission to *deviate* from a standard. The *Oxford English Dictionary* defines the technical use of "tolerance" as the "small margin within which coins, when minted, are allowed to deviate from the standard fineness and weight."[27] The *American Heritage Dictionary* defines tolerance as "leeway for variation from a standard."[28] In the religious context, Catholic theologian John Murray writes that toleration "implies a moral judgment on error and the consequent adoption of a moral attitude, based on charity, toward the good faith of those who err."[29] From all three definitional perspectives, tolerated behavior is erroneous, "deviant" behavior that is only reluctantly permitted. By forcing the act into the bedroom (this is the only way it can be protected), the act becomes unworthy of public consumption. It is a shameful practice that must stay behind closed, "private doors," or so this argument goes. Since the conventional account of limited government isolates interests, areas, or kinds of behavior deserving protection, the right to privacy must characterize gay sex as "private."

Sandel's lament here is one of disparity in respect or what Nancy Fraser calls the harm of "misrecognition."[30] While heterosexual sex, at least the monogamous, procreative kind, is no doubt valued in society – the goodness of this sexual activity is apparent – gay sex is short changed by being swept under the proverbial right to privacy rug. It is seen as a deviation that is reluctantly permitted. Effectively, while gay sex is simply tolerated, straight sex is accepted. "[B]y refusing to articulate the human goods that homosexual intimacy may share with heterosexual unions"[31] the right to privacy argument used to protect gay sex is woefully inadequate. It protects gay sex by invariably demeaning it, placing it in that sphere or space off limits to state interference. After all, I must characterize my sexual act as private to invoke the right to privacy argument.

Or, we can put the argument another way, not from the point of view of the "deviant" behavior, but from the point of view of the "normal" behavior. It is revealing that such a right is unnecessary for couples

---

[26] Sandel 1996: 106–108.   [27] www.oed.com.
[28] *American Heritage Dictionary* 2001: 858.   [29] Murray 1993: 150.
[30] Fraser 1997.   [31] Sandel 1996: 107.

engaging in procreative sex,[32] since such activity constitutes the standard. *Griswold v. Connecticut* (1965), the Supreme Court case that first articulated the due process right to privacy, involved a challenge to a law that prohibited the use of contraceptives for married individuals. The statute at issue effectively sought to outlaw *non-procreative*, heterosexual sex, sex that did not constitute the standard. Because the sex at issue was not "normal," privacy was necessary. Unsurprisingly, there is no worry that a democratic polity will pass a law outlawing conventional, procreative heterosexual sex within marriage. Even imagining the introduction of such a bill by a legislator seems outrageous. The "normal," gold standard of sexual activity need not be relegated to the private sphere in order to gain protection.

The right to privacy is simply unnecessary for protecting such activities, since most individuals have an interest in permitting them. As long as a majority of the polity cares about something equally, it can be left to the democratic process to ensure. For example, no one ever says to the straight married couple about to engage in procreative non-kinky sex, "what you do in your bedroom is your business!" Under a right to privacy, this often-used mantra is only for those acts we disapprove of but begrudgingly tolerate. Only deviations (leeway) from this standard *require* appeal to privacy.

Jed Rubenfeld argues that the right to privacy staves off normalization, ensuring that the government does not force or compel us to standardize ourselves, to live cookie-cutter lives.[33] For example, limiting sex only to heterosexual intercourse pushes us to lead a certain way of life. Privacy prevents this standardization, or so Rubenfeld contends. But by invoking the right to privacy or intimacy to protect certain behavior we have by this very fact deemed it abnormal. It is true that with a right to privacy, the state may not stop me from having sex with a man. Nevertheless, by the very fact that I must appeal to this right to protect my "life-style," the state has implicitly rendered it "deviant." As demonstrated above, this is Sandel's very critique of the right to privacy.

Since the protection of conventional heterosexual sex does not require the right to privacy, the state ends up compelling us to engage in certain sexual acts and not others. The fear of normalization that Rubenfeld so decries occurs not only by laws outlawing certain acts (it is illegal for me to have oral sex with a man) but also by the social stigma that attaches to

---

[32] Heterosexuals may also require the use of such a right. Non-procreative sex (oral sex, for example) may still be considered "abnormal" or "deviant." When I refer to heterosexual sex, I mean procreative, monogamous sex carried out within the bounds of marriage.

[33] Rubenfeld 1989.

sexual acts requiring the suspect appeal to privacy. By merely taking cover under a right to privacy, the state has stamped the sexual minority as unsuitable for the public. Rubenfeld is caught in a catch-22. Rubenfeld's reason for the right to privacy, his contention that the problem of normalization will disappear, pushes against privacy's very adoption. Rubenfeld's justification fails on its own terms. The problem of tolerance is inherent to a right to privacy.

Moreover, invoking this right with its regime of tolerance often suggests that such practices are crucial to the formation of identity. Since sexual acts may define who we are or play a large role in our self-definition, the state ought not curtail our ability to engage in them. Michelman makes just such an argument in his criticism of *Bowers*. "It seems very likely that among the effects of a law like Georgia's [the sodomy statute] on persons for whom homosexuality is an aspect of *identity* is denial or impairment of their citizenship, in the broad sense which I have suggested is appropriate to modern republican constitutionalism."[34] This republican conception of citizenship treats the regulation of gay sex as problematic, because such laws interfere with important identity-formation or self-definition.

But even assuming that we can figure out when such self-definition is at stake and thus when privacy should kick in, the problem is that sometimes we may engage in these acts for reasons unrelated to self-definition. Someone may partake in gay sex for purely physical pleasure having nothing at all to do with any gay-identity formation.[35] Michelman's focus on the "identity" forming nature of the sex act exemplifies the pathology of rights. The right to privacy seeks to categorize the relevant behavior or activity in order to determine whether it merits protection. This is the conventional way of limiting the scope of democratic government. If it is part of a sexual minority's identity formation, it falls within privacy's ambit or protection. But this overlooks the more important point. Who cares why the sex act is being done? Someone could engage in a night of gay sex to experiment, to honor a dare, to impress a friend, or to solidify identity. The motivation for the activity does not seem relevant. Rather, the sex act itself should be protected *regardless* of its intention or role in self-definition.

Now Sandel's panacea to the problem of tolerance is a move to a regime of acceptance. He argues that the solution is to create another, legitimate standard to stand alongside the traditional procreative one. By touting the obvious merits to gay intimacy, the state can set up another norm. As a republican, Sandel sees the positive act of democracy as necessary to validate such sexual behavior. Gay sex under an acceptance regime is no

---

[34] Michelman 1988: 1533 (emphasis added).   [35] Rubenfeld 1989.

longer just tolerated but actually *accepted* as another legitimate sexual activity. He writes that a "fuller respect would require, if not admiration, at least some appreciation of the lives homosexuals live."[36]

The problem is that this republican enterprise, if even possible, turns out to be too restrictive. Whom should we admit to this sexual Kingdom of Ends? Would Sandel have us publicly articulate the valuable qualities of sex that is anonymous or purely physical – the paradigmatic one-night stand or even the consensual bathhouse orgy? How many standards (or norms) do we create? Do we create one for experimentation? Or a standard for sex done to fulfill a dare?

And even if this is possible, how do we even go about extolling the virtues of these sexual practices? Suppose we decide upon certain criteria of worthiness – the values of love or monogamy. The problem is that in applying such values we invariably exclude those practices or behavior that fail to meet them. Paradoxically, Sandel's plea to accepting gay sex may very well turn out, in the lingo, hetero-normative – valuing such "deviant" sex by re-characterizing it as "acceptable" and "mainstream." This hetero-normativity may also exclude straight one-night stands, orgies, or consensual sadomasochistic sex. Though Sandel may very well be satisfied with such a result – he advocates a thick notion of respectable sexual behavior – his republican alternative is quite restrictive.

Put differently, the point is that while I may find no redeeming value in a one-night stand or a same-sex orgy, someone else may. The problem with a regime of acceptance is that it falls prey to a new kind of categorization with its new rules for defining the sheep from the wolves. Rather than categorizing behavior in a realm of the private and intimate (as in a regime of tolerance), acceptance seeks to characterize a list of activities as meaningful or valuable, and in so doing invariably excludes or demeans others. An acceptance regime, though preferable to a tolerance one, is unlikely to properly secure freedom and equality.

Add insult to injury, the conventional regime of limited government has the perverse consequence of making it that much easier for the state to tyrannize. By leaving "private" issues beyond the scope of state regulation, this regime invites the state to regulate those issues that are "public." A paradigmatic example is same-sex marriage. The privacy argument that gays should be allowed to sleep with the partner of their choice has no force with the issue of same-sex marriage. Marriage is a "public" benefit and does not implicate the same concerns. We can confidently champion the right to sleep with someone of your own choosing – given the regime of

---

[36] Sandel 1996: 107.

tolerance – but fail to extend this logic to same-sex marriage. Why? The pathology of classification permits one to categorize gay sex as a *different* issue than same-sex marriage, allowing the former and forbidding the latter. After all, according to the account of limited government I criticize, "public" activities are subject to regulation by the state. While what people do in their bedrooms is their business – the state may not pass a sodomy law – democratic majorities may regulate what they do outside of it – the state may prohibit same-sex marriage. The usual method of limiting government, then, is a double-edged sword. On one hand, as I suggest above, it shields harm from state regulation as it merely tolerates behavior. On the other hand, it permits the polity to jeopardize liberty.

Frustrating democratic debate

My final criticism focuses on that which the reflexive concept of rights holds in such high esteem, namely democratic debate. I argue that the language of rights renders debate unnecessarily frustrating. If various members in the democratic polity must discuss, validate, and define rights, the hope is that some common ground will be available. If the debate is incommensurable, if the opposing parties in the democratic polity talk past one another, "democratic iteration" seems at worst pointless and at best needlessly exasperating. I say "needlessly," because, as I will argue below, rejecting rights turning to Justification informs a more productive debate.

With rights, the debate is invariably about what relevant category should be invoked – is it, for example, an issue of privacy, or women's equality, or free speech or property. This leads to the problem of incommensurability. One group claims that the activity falls under a non-protected category and the other group claims the opposite. For example, affirmative action opponents contend that race-conscious programs are a kind of racial discrimination. These programs violate a person's right to formal equality. Proponents of such remedial legislation characterize the very same activity – treating individuals of one race differently than those from another – as an anti-subordinating measure, as truly promoting equality. According to this pro-affirmative action position, there is no violation of a right to equality. What category is relevant – formal equality or anti-subordination? How is it, then, we can even debate the issue? At best, we are stuck convincing each camp to re-characterize the activity as falling under the other.

Abortion is an even better example of the frustrating nature of debate carried out within the language of rights.[37] Since *Roe v. Wade* (1973), a

---

[37] MacIntyre 1984: 7; see also Glendon 1993: 47–75.

woman's decision to abort has revolved around whether removing the fetus is about the right to life, a right to privacy, or a right to women's equality. The political and legal debate is about which category abortion falls under. This is how the conventional view determines whether abortion is beyond the scope of state regulation. And the stated purpose of the reflexive account is to decide the meaning and scope of rights. According to the pro-lifer, abortion is about saving innocent lives. If this is the correct category abortion falls under, the woman may not remove the fetus. She must carry it to term. For the pro-choice counterpart, on the other hand, the very same activity is an issue of privacy (bodily integrity) or women's equality. Given this categorization, the woman has the option of removing it. One claims the right of the fetus or a right to life, the other the right to privacy or perhaps the right to woman's equality. Both sides look to the individual woman characterizing her behavior in mutually exclusive ways. Nothing can be said to the pro-lifer to convince her that the activity is not "murder" falling under the category of life. And the pro-choice advocate is firm on seeing abortion as a matter of privacy or women's equality.

In her scathing critique of "rights talk," Mary Ann Glendon argues that:

A tendency to frame nearly every social controversy in terms of a clash of rights ... impedes compromise, mutual understanding, and the discovery of common ground. ... A near-aphasia concerning responsibilities makes it seem legitimate to accept the benefits of living in a democratic social welfare republic without assuming the corresponding personal and civic obligations.[38]

Rights pose the wrong question. In asking what category the activity – removing the fetus, preferring the black candidate in lieu of the white one – falls under, we cannot help but run up against incommensurability. With no common ground, the debate over the correct characterization – privacy, life, formal equality, or anti-subordination – becomes quite frustrating. Short of what the relevant activity is, there is nothing that these opposing factions can agree upon. There is no way to decide or debate whether abortion is beyond the scope of state regulation. An appeal to spaces, interests, and classifications to limit democratic government is not fruitful in generating democratic debate.

Part of this problem is that rights are seen as the province of the law. They are legal constructs that require special training in constitutional law. All too often, we resign the issue to courts, placing our faith in their hands. Who else can adjudicate and decide upon the scope of these rights? Paradoxically, seeing the debate as one of rights problematically takes us out of it, relegating the decision to courts. In so doing, it is no surprise that

[38] Glendon 1993, xi.

the demos is likely to pass the buck – fail to take up their democratic role – simply because the debate is too often seen as one involving rights.[39]

In this way, deciding on what abortion is about – life or privacy – does not require a democratic decision. The inquiry simply concerns the correct characterization of abortion. It is as if the pro-lifers see the overturning of *Roe* as invariably deeming abortion illegal. At issue in *Roe* was a Texas statute outlawing abortion. A reversal of *Roe* would not mean that abortion is unconstitutional but only that the debate would be in the hands of the states, the relevant democratic polities. After all, even before *Roe*, four states – New York, Washington, Hawaii, and Alaska – freely permitted a woman to abort during the first trimester.[40] Even Justice Antonin Scalia, one of the most conservative members of the Court, does not contend that the Constitution *requires* that abortion be illegal, that the woman *not* be able to abort. Rather, Scalia argues that:

[B]y banishing the issue from the political forum that gives all participants, even the losers, the satisfaction of a fair hearing and honest fight, by continuing the imposition of a rigid national rule instead of allowing for regional differences, the Court merely prolongs and intensifies the anguish.[41]

Scalia desires to leave the issue in the hands of the states. But the pathology of rights – and its concern with individuals – has left the value of democracy in deciding the abortion question out of the debate. By failing to reject the reigning methodology of limiting government, the reflexive conception of rights threatens liberty while frustrating and even weakening democratic debate. I introduce my preferred solution in the next Part.

---

[39] Cf. Bickel 1986: 22.   [40] Burt 1992: 348.
[41] *Planned Parenthood v. Casey* (1992) at 1002, dissenting, J. Scalia.

Part II

Justification in theory

3 The turn to justification

Rights are deficient. Even tinkering with them by offering a more reflexive interpretation will not do. While rights are the most discussed doctrines in achieving the values of liberty and democracy, in this chapter I elucidate contemporary theory's turn to Justification, a turn that informs a distinctive way of limiting government.

Justification entails two necessary components: one, something needs to be justified (decided, talked about, agreed upon, etc.); and such Justification takes place under some kind of justificatory constraints, limitations, or conditions. How we justify this appeal to Justification or to my particular theory of Justification (the meta-justification of Justification) is not my primary concern.[1] Again, I put aside these foundational questions. My book seeks to convince those who already care about the values of liberty and democracy to endorse a theory of Justification. Establishing these values is not the aim of the book. The puzzle is to find the regulatory principle that best balances and realizes them.

Here I introduce my preferred solution – Justification. The following contemporary theories of Justification have not been categorized together in this way. In fact, they are usually seen as containing divergent accounts of justice. While they do differ in important ways, their common theme of Justification needs to be highlighted. Some of these authors do not even use the word "justification" in describing their accounts. Still, I group them under this banner even perhaps at the expense of passing over some of their important features for at least two reasons. First, I hope to establish Justification as a conceptual methodology to limit democratic

---

[1] Gaus (1996) devotes an entire book to what he calls "justificatory liberalism." He sees this project as one of articulating "publicly justified" principles. However, his conception of justification is not the Justification I put forth in this book. Rather, Gaus looks primarily at epistemology in articulating the necessary conditions for people to agree on certain principles. Of course, these principles could very well be a set of rights. In other words, Gaus is concerned with the meta-justification of a particular set of principles. This is not my project. Mine is putting forth a superior account of limited government.

government distinct and independent from the popular alternative of rights. Second, these theories set the stage for my positive account of Justification in the subsequent chapter. I outline the virtues and failings of these accounts in order to better craft my own theory of Justification. Each account below, albeit in different respects, then, proposes a theory of Justification.

Conceding that this is not an exhaustive list, I outline four contemporary theories of Justification: Bruce Ackerman's neutrality thesis, Jürgen Habermas' discourse theory, John Rawls' public reason, and Michael Oakeshott's civil association.

Ackerman's Neutrality Thesis

To a much greater extent than the others, Ackerman's account in *Social Justice in the Liberal State*[2] is self-consciously a theory of Justification. His stated goal is to outline the appropriate reasons that can justify power. The first component of any such theory is the "what" of Justification. That is, what needs justifying? Ackerman focuses on various kinds of power. He writes:

Even when our power is relatively secure, however, it is never beyond challenge in a world where total demand outstrips supply. And it is this challenge that concerns us here. Imagine someone stepping forward to claim control over resources you now take for granted. According to her, it is she, not you, who has the better right to claim them. Why, she insists on knowing, do you think otherwise? *How can you justify the powers you have so comfortably exercised in the past?* [3]

What are these "powers" that need justifying? They include economic wealth, genetic advantage, citizenship, a good education, and presumably exercises of state power. For example, a wealthy individual will have to justify her wealth to someone with less. If I am innately more intelligent – suppose I have a genetic predisposition to do well in math – I must justify this power as well. If the police officer comes into my bedroom mandating that I stop doing something, she must justify her actions too. By "power" Ackerman means to include a broad range of things: brute force by a state actor, anything of social or perhaps intrinsic value that someone can have over someone else.

How are these powers to be justified? The second component of Ackerman's theory of Justification is an appeal to neutrality. In justifying her power, the power holder *may not* assert:

---

[2] Ackerman: 1980.   [3] Ibid.: 3 (emphasis added).

(a) that [her] conception of the good is better than that asserted by any of [her] fellow citizens, or

(b) that, regardless of [her] conception of the good, [s]he is intrinsically superior to one or more of [her] fellow citizens.[4]

In justifying why I have more money or better genes than you, I may not simply say that I am a better person, or that my race, gender, hair color or sexuality warrants better treatment. Additionally, a police officer may not arrest me for engaging in gay sex simply because the state finds such practices immoral or disgusting. These kinds of reasons are ruled out by the conditions above.

These justificatory constraints seek to ensure freedom and equality. To ensure freedom, condition (a) prohibits the power holder from appealing to conceptions of the good. The power holders including state officials may not justify their power or their exercise of it by citing some religious or moral viewpoint. Ackerman is not the only theorist to advocate this doctrine of neutrality. Much liberal theory argues that the state is forbidden from legislating on comprehensive world-views.[5] Neutrality rules out reasons that invoke a certain conception of the good. This argument repudiates what is commonly referred to as morals legislation, legislation based simply on morality.[6] Furthermore, to ensure equality, condition (b) dictates that all citizens are on an equal footing. No one person is better or worse than another. I deserve as good an education as you do. I deserve the same opportunities, privileges, and benefits as you do regardless, for example, of my race, gender, hair color, or sexuality. No one is intrinsically better than anyone else.

In the ideal world where there exists a perfect technology of justice, Ackerman contends that there is no need for criminal legislation or punishment.[7] If everyone has a perfect ray gun that immobilizes anyone else taking action to violate the liberal conversational constraints, we rightly have no need for a police force or jails. No one will be able to violate the neutral constraints. However, this kind of argument holds little value in a world where punishment is an inescapable reality, where such a ray gun does not exist. We must be able to justify the enforcement of criminal legislation, legislation that reprimands anti-social behavior.

Ackerman seems to concede as much offering an explanation for punishment in the non-ideal world.[8] But his alleged neutral constraints end

---

[4] Ibid.: 11.
[5] See, e.g., B. Barry 1995, Brettschneider 2007, Larmore 1987, Rawls 1996b, cf. Scanlon 1998.
[6] For a good discussion of the legal history of morals legislation see Goldberg (2004b).
[7] Ackerman 1980: 31–83.   [8] Ibid.: 83–88.

up proving too much. Suppose I murder someone. As a result, a police officer attempts to restrain me. I ask the officer to justify her action. She must do so with an appropriate reason. Suppose her response passes condition (a) – she does not put forth an impermissible conception of the good. Condition (b) must also be met. As the officer seeks to take me to jail, I claim that I am as good as anyone else. Remember, the officer may not claim that she or anyone else is intrinsically superior to me. If others are not being detained (namely those who did not murder), why am I being singled out? Does this not violate (b)? According to Ackerman, the police officer responds by instructing me that "minimal prudence" is a requirement of citizenship in the polity given the features of a non-ideal world. If I go around killing others, I can no longer be considered a citizen. Hence, restricting me does not violate condition (b), since it presumably applies *only* to citizens.[9] But how is this "special restriction" (the perquisite of citizenship) justified? Now it seems we violate condition (a). Minimal prudence is, after all, a certain conception of good. It values the minimization of non-consensual harm. In moving to the non-ideal world, Ackerman's constraints have cut the ground from underneath him.

Taken together (a) and (b) leave us with no way out. In attempting to imprison or detain me, a murderer, the officer violates (b). She does not seem to treat me as well as others. Effectively, those not being detained are deemed superior. However, as we try to articulate why my detention (or punishment) is permissible, why the officer's varying treatment of me does not run afoul of (b), we violate (a). If (b)'s applicability is contingent on certain conditions – such as minimal prudence – we end up endorsing a particular conception of the good, namely the minimization of harm. This in turn contravenes (a). Ackerman's framework gives us no conceptual room to rightly detain the murderer. His argument proves too much seemingly *excluding* harm prevention as an appropriate reason.

As a result, the common threshold objection to neutrality is that the notion of a neutral state is a non-starter. If the state may not appeal to morality in legislating, then how can it for instance prohibit murder or other types of harm? This criticism of neutrality is not novel and has been proffered *ad nauseam*.[10] I find it convincing. Neutrality as such ought to be repudiated. I readily concede there is nothing impartial about neutrality.[11] If neutrality is meant to be a non-normative concept, Justification,

---

[9] Ackerman 1980: 3–35.   [10] See, e.g., Sandel 1982, MacIntyre 1988.
[11] Ackerman, in fact, recognizes that by neutrality, he does not mean a "value-free politics." Rather, neutrality "permits liberals to gain a deeper philosophical perspective on their own more obvious commitments and anxieties" (Ackerman 1983: 372).

understood as a neutral justificatory constraint, turns out an easily defeated straw man. This book assumes that we care about freedom, equality and democracy. It endorses these values to put forth a superior account of limited government.

While this pledge to neutrality is the target of most criticism of *Social Justice and the Liberal State*,[12] the more troubling aspect of Ackerman's theory of Justification is the limited role it gives democracy. This overlooked drawback threatens to leave us in the same predicament as the conventional way of limiting government: undercutting the value of democracy. Under the "what" component of Justification, Ackerman seeks to justify all kinds of power: economic, genetic, educational, physical, generational, etc. As a result, he eventually concludes that a "political community of diverse individuals" following his neutral constraints will make sure that:

(a) No citizen genetically dominates another.
(b) Each citizen receives a liberal education.
(c) Each citizen begins adult life under conditions of material equality.
(d) Each citizen can freely exchange his initial entitlements within a flexible transactional network.
(e) Each citizen, at the moment of his death, can assert that he has fulfilled his obligations of liberal trusteeship, passing on to the next generation a power structure no less liberal than the one he himself enjoyed.[13]

Consequently, (in a very similar way to Rawls' veil of ignorance) we have arrived at substantive results without the need for democracy. As argued in Chapter 1, the trouble with the classic accounts of rights is that once such doctrines are specified (we have a right to x, y, z ...) democracy serves *little* purpose. The Rawlsian veil of ignorance sets up a just regime without any interaction from fellow polity members. It necessarily entails a "democratic deficit." Every just polity will look the same. We know all our normative obligations without looking to our membership in a particular democratic polity.

Likewise, the results of applying Ackerman's neutral constraints can also be achieved without any such inquiry. Ackerman's book arrives at the five requirements above on its own. He imagines what a neutral conversation would be like and then tells us the results just as Rawls postulates an original position announcing his two principles of justice. Both are thought experiments. Of course, Ackerman does not generally talk of rights. His account only provides guidelines on how one goes about justifying power. However, because these guidelines aim at justifying *all* power in the social world, the

[12] See Barber 1983, Fishkin 1983, Flathman 1983, Williams 1983.
[13] Ackerman 1980: 28.

democratic polity has little flexibility or choice in articulating our normative obligations.[14] Ackerman has written out the value of democracy. What if, for example, a polity decided to use up all its resources before the next generation arrives? What if a polity, even in ideal theory, chooses to reject the very notion of private property, eschew the very idea that someone could be entitled to a thing – or in Ackerman's language "manna"? Or perhaps the polity decides not to remedy or compensate its members for genetic disadvantages? Suppose it decides to leave such inequalities where they stand. These options are not open to the polity under Ackerman's neutral constraints just as a kind of socialism is not permissible under Locke's or Nozick's schedule of rights.

Ackerman purports to offer a theory of Justification. Ackerman characterizes his account as dialogic, distinguishing it from the more rigid, un-democratic monologic ones explored in Chapter 1.[15] A conversation is presumptively necessary under his theory of Justification. He maintains that in persuading you to adopt "liberal principles" the "conversation I have with you can differ radically from the talk I have with somebody else."[16] The difficulty here is that while citizens of a polity may have different conversations, they ought to (under Ackerman's neutral constraints) arrive at the same set of substantive results: no genetic domination, a liberal education, initial equal entitlements to property, etc. Why do we need democracy? Since all polities must look the same, Ackerman ends up creating a *de facto* regime of rights. For instance, under Ackerman's account, every democratic polity must be one that redistributes wealth providing material resources for all. Whereas Nozick argues that every democratic polity must be libertarian, Ackerman argues that every polity must be a robust welfare state. Effectively, Ackerman has posited an affirmative right to welfare, forcing the polity to choose a particular economic regime.

I contend that a polity should have the democratic flexibility to create any number of economic systems: libertarianism, communism, and a robust welfare state, to name a few. My theory of Justification considers all these valid democratic decisions. After all, I reject both negative and affirmative rights. I suspect that Ackerman's argument is a response to those like Nozick who would prevent democratic majorities from passing welfare legislation. But there is no need to go so far as to *require* the democratic polity to pass such legislation. Doing so needlessly undercuts democratic flexibility and discretion. American legal history suggests taking a more modest approach to limiting government. After all, it has

---

[14] Shapiro 2003c: 113.   [15] Ackerman 1980: 355–359.   [16] Ibid.: 359.

been the maintenance of the autonomous economic sphere that has stymied actual attempts by the polity to redistribute wealth and ensure equality. Once we reject this sphere – as the New Deal Court ultimately did – we permit such legislation. As a historical matter, no affirmative right was needed. Turning away from rights and towards reasons permits the polity to structure the economy as it sees fit.

Admittedly, I find Ackerman's "liberal results" quite convincing. Barring problems with the misleading word "neutrality," they ensure equality and freedom. However, in making power the "what" of Justification, Ackerman has eviscerated the value of democracy. He has taken away the value of democratic flexibility. Total equality is achieved at the expense of democracy. Again, any account of limited government must balance these competing values. A theory of Justification that must justify *all* power relations is, as a result, deficient.

Habermas' discourse theory[17]

While Ackerman's theory of justification is not democratic enough, Habermas' discourse theory[18] goes too far in championing the role of the democratic community. Habermas (unlike Ackerman) does not focus on power. He does not seek to have the power holder justify her power whether it is genetic, economic, or social. What needs to be justified (the first component of a theory of Justification) is the opinion and will formation processes that take place among the members of a polity. Habermas writes that "[m]odern law is formed by a system of norms that are coercive, positive, and so it is claimed, freedom-guaranteeing."[19] It is the rule of law that Habermas seeks to justify, law that arises from decisions by the relevant political community. He looks to democracy to "bear […] the entire burden of legitimation."[20] He proposes a "two-track" model of democracy. Deliberation is carried out in formal governmental institutions (such as legislatures or parliamentary bodies) and informal – non-governmental – sites of civil society (such as voluntary associations, churches, coffee shops, and so on).[21] The relevant democratic body, identified by the "rule of recognition,"[22] decides on a particular course of action such as passing a law or enforcing a regulation. His discourse principle allows citizens to "judge whether the law they enact is legitimate."[23]

---

[17] Habermas' general argument also applies to issues of ethics and morality. I am not concerned here with the application of discourse theory to such issues. Rather, what is relevant here is how this theory bears on limiting democratic decision-making.
[18] Habermas 1990, 1996, 2001.   [19] Habermas 1996: 447.   [20] Ibid.: 450.
[21] Benhabib 2002: 115.   [22] See Hart 1994 [1961].   [23] Habermas 1996: 454–455.

These deliberative processes, then, need to be justified. By turning away from power and toward sites of discourse, Habermas opens the door for a greater substantive role for democracy. All power *need not* be remedied or minimized. It will be left to the individual polity to decide. For Habermas, then, most of our commitments are not articulated independently of the democratic process.

However, in valuing democracy Habermas fails to limit it. Much like the reflexive theorists above, he plainly invites majority tyranny. The troubling part of Habermas' account is the second component of a theory of Justification, namely under which conditions does such decision-making take place. In asking how the polity justifies such decisions (resulting from discussions taking place in the legislatures, local school boards, churches, coffee shops, and voluntary associations), Habermas (unlike Ackerman) fails to offer any meaningful constraints. He does not secure liberty. Whereas Ackerman goes too far in limiting democratic decision-making, Habermas does not go far enough. Habermas may cure the "democratic deficit," but he overshoots, threatening liberty.

I argue that Habermas' discourse theory articulates three distinct justificatory constraints: the ideal speech condition, the principle of universalization, and the right to equal liberty (effectively a reflexive notion of rights). Each is either too weak or vague to adequately ensure liberty. Each fails as an account of limited government. First, Habermas contends that opinion and will formation are legitimate as long as they take place under certain formal conditions or dialogic presuppositions.[24] These conditions require that everyone have an equal chance to speak, be heard and participate in the democratic, deliberative process. Benhabib summarizes these constraints as requiring the conditions of symmetry and reciprocity.[25] Such conditions are immanent to the very task of Justification. To argue against them is to be caught up in a performative contradiction. For instance, to argue that a regulation is legitimate and hence justified even though a certain group of persons affected by it are silenced and deemed unable to participate in the relevant decision-making process is to find oneself in a contradiction. By admitting that these individuals are affected by the regulation – they have interests, desires, and goals that are implicated – one has conceded that they have the capacity to participate and be heard.[26]

Though I agree with Habermas that such conditions are presumed by any theory of Justification – this is after all a vindication of the value of democracy – they turn out to be insufficient. What stops the polity from

---

[24] Habermas 1990: 86–94, 2001: 116–118.
[25] Benhabib 1986.   [26] Habermas 1990: 91.

passing sodomy and anti-miscegenation laws or instituting a regime of racial segregation? As long as the relevant racial or sexual minority had a chance to speak, debate, and be heard in the deliberations concerning such laws, the justificatory constraint is met. The conditions immanent to communication are still satisfied. Of course, if the majority sought to curtail a group's right to vote, prevent members of it from running for office, sponsoring a political association, or any number of laws aimed at restricting its democratic input in the opinion and will formation process, this would certainly run afoul of the communicative constraints. But regulations on inter-racial coupling or sodomy do not do this. A gay person can certainly be heard, vote, and run for office, even if she is unable to sleep with someone of the same sex. Consequently, if this is the "how" component of Justification, it does not go far enough in constraining democracy.

A second contender in Habermas' writings is the principle of universalization. Though more restrictive than the first, it also turns out to be too permissive.[27] This second constraint maintains that only those decisions, regulations, and laws are legitimate which "all who are possibly affected could assent as participants in rational discourse."[28] If this constraint is to have any plausibility, it must require putting ourselves in the position of those who are at the receiving end of the particular legislation.[29] It asks us to imagine the desires, preferences, and traits of those who would suffer as a result of the contemplated legislation.[30] Take a law against murder. The constraint requires that we imagine ourselves with the inclination or desire to murder and speculate how we would react to such a law. Presumably, most of us would have no problem with it. Even in imagining a situation where I feel like murdering, I would desire a law against it. I would want such behavior to be discouraged. A law prohibiting a particular minority from doing something (the infamous Black Codes of the South), for instance, also fails this universalization test. Requiring the majority to imagine themselves as victims of such nefarious legislation, and how they would vote as a result, seems to rule out its possibility. No victim of such *asymmetric* legislation would decide to vote for it. So far so good.

---

[27] McMahon (2000) distinguishes between the weak and strong dialogic versions of Habermas' discourse theory. The weak version corresponds to the formal presuppositions of the ideal speech condition and the strong with the principle of universalization.

[28] Habermas 1996: 458, 109 n. 38; see also Rehg 1991.

[29] T. M. Scanlon (1998) adopts a similar argument suggesting that: "The aim of finding and acting on principles that no one similarly motivated could reasonably reject leads us to take other people's interests into account in deciding what principles to follow" (Scanlon 1998: 202).

[30] Mackie 1977, McMahon 2000.

But under the test of universalization, there seems to be no difficulty in passing laws regulating certain kinds of behavior[31] like miscegenation or sodomy or even imposing a system of *symmetric* racial segregation. Such laws seem to pass universalization in the same way as laws against murder. The majority may very well believe that even if they had urges to engage in intercourse with someone of the same sex or opposite race or even opposite hair color, they would desire laws against it. Many could simply believe that such urges can (or at least ought to) be controlled. Just as a preference for murder is wrong (and must be outlawed) so too are certain sexual ones. Any allegedly "deviant" behavior could be outlawed under the constraint of universalization, because the majority could be quite comfortable with being victims of it. Furthermore, a white person could very well accept that if she were black, she would still desire to stay with those of her own race. As long as such segregation is empirically equal (and thus truly symmetric), the white segregationist would have no problem contending that all those affected could consent.

It will not suffice for Habermas to claim that in order to pass the universalization test, the legislation must be one for which the polity can proffer reasons that the relevant group will accept. Again, take as an example the prohibition on same-sex marriage. This interpretation of universalization contends that the polity must be able to offer reasons that gays could accept for the prohibition.

There are two problems with this test. First, why should we only ask gay people whether they find such reasons acceptable? After all, those against same-sex marriage will no doubt contend that heterosexuals are the primary group affected by the prohibition. It seems quite dubious to suggest that only a particular group such as gays is affected. Many would claim that the prohibition on same-sex marriage ensures the perpetuation of certain norms regarding sexuality. And this is a genuine concern for the majority of the polity. Hence, as long as the majority is satisfied with the reasons for the prohibition – as it no doubt is, because it voted for the law – the ban passes universalization.

Second, how do we even go about deciding who belongs to one group – gays – and who belongs to the other – straights? It requires we decide, for example, whether one is born gay or chooses such a "lifestyle." I argue in Chapter 8 that this focus on group differentiation turns out to be problematic. What does it matter if I'm gay or straight? Why must I be gay in order to object to the ban on same-sex marriage? This affirmation of group differentiation[32] needlessly pushes individuals into one group or another

---

[31] Lukes 1982.   [32] Fraser 1997.

even if they may not identify with it. Much contemporary multicultural and social theory already views such affiliations as partly socially constructed, suggesting that adherence to them problematically essentializes and reifies groups.[33]

Perhaps Habermas would respond that his test simply means that the polity needs a *good* reason for enacting a statute thereby avoiding the problem of group membership. While a polity has a good reason to outlaw murder, it does not have a good one for prohibiting gay or inter-racial sex. However, how do we define "good"? This is the crucial question that stands at the center of my book. And appeal to ideal speech conditions, the first of Habermas' justificatory constraints, will not aid us in defining it. Since anti-miscegenation laws and the like do not restrict the ability of individuals to participate in the democratic process, they do not violate any such speech conditions. Even in tandem, these justificatory constraints – ideal speech conditions and universalization – are insufficient. Obviously, those who support sodomy or anti-miscegenation laws no doubt believe there are good reasons to do so. Something more is needed to distinguish these cases, to fill in the content of our intuition that there is "good" reason to pass laws against murder but not gay sex.[34]

Unsurprisingly, Habermas has a third seemingly more robust justificatory constraint. Here he effectively retreats to a reflexive regime of rights by appealing to a principle of "private autonomy" that guarantees "the basic right to equal individual liberties."[35] As Habermas argues:

Rights, which make the exercise of popular sovereignty possible, cannot be imposed on this practice [discourse] like external constraints. To be sure, this claim is immediately plausible only for political rights, that is, the rights of communication and participation; it is not so obvious for the classical human rights that guarantee the citizen's private autonomy. The human rights that guarantee everyone a comprehensive legal protection and an equal opportunity to pursue her private life-plans clearly have an intrinsic value. They are not reducible to their instrumental value for democratic will-formation.[36]

Habermas concedes that his theory assumes certain "basic rights." The fetish for rights rears its ugly head. Like the reflexive theorists explored above, Habermas also sees citizens as serving as "addressees" and

---

[33] See, e.g., Appiah 1994, 1996, Benhabib 2002, Gilroy 1993, Hall 1992, Parekh 2000.

[34] Similarly, Philip Pettit's (1997) republican vision of government contends that freedom is "non-domination." He suggests that one "party dominates another just so far as they have the capacity to interfere on an arbitrary basis in some of the other's choices" (Pettit 1997: 272). But what does "arbitrary" mean? Certainly, those who favor laws against sodomy find such interference non-arbitrary. The claims to good or non-arbitrary reasons are on their own insufficient.

[35] Habermas 2001: 117–118; cf. Habermas 1996: 118–131.   [36] Habermas 2001: 117.

"authors" of such rights.[37] In having democracy affirm and inform these rights – this is how Habermas intends to connect democracy to the rule of law – we invariably revisit the difficulties explored in Chapter 2. Habermas falls into the trap of fiddling with rights. Habermas must either concede that sodomy and inter-racial marriage are integral to a right to privacy or "private autonomy" leaving the democratic polity unable to define their meaning and scope; or permit a narrow interpretation of such "basic rights" jeopardizing equality and freedom. Again, without collapsing into a static, conventional picture of rights à la Locke and Nozick, this dynamic characterization of rights invites majority tyranny.

Perhaps a more charitable reading of Habermas' characterization of such rights is his emphasis on the "right to equal individual liberties." Such a principle requires that participants in the democratic discourse see each other as equals, abide by a Kantian norm of equal respect.[38] Appealing to equal liberty as constituting the appropriate justificatory principle may, on its face, seem to cure the defects of the others. Presumably, such a constraint would not permit the polity to pass laws that regulate "deviant" behavior or discriminate against certain minorities. These would fail the requirement of equal liberty. Such laws do not seem to treat everyone with equal respect. Nevertheless, on a closer look such a principle turns out excessively vague, resulting in a constraint that is both too permissive and too strict.

On the one hand, the notion of equal liberty or equal respect turns out to be too accommodating. After all, racial segregation and anti-miscegenation laws can be seen as treating groups equally. They can be understood as equally affecting blacks and whites. Just as blacks may not marry whites, so whites may not marry blacks. This symmetric result may very well accord with equality.[39] The bare assertion of equal respect or equality is insufficient to rule such interpretations out. Sodomy laws, at least those that forbid oral and anal sex with someone of the same sex, are also equal in that they affect women and men equally. An appeal to equal liberty turns out too pliable to thwart these paradigmatic tyrannies of the majority.

On the other hand, this constraint proves too much. A law against murder no doubt discriminates between those who partake in this activity and those who do not. It does treat the former group differently than the latter. Hence, in response to such a law – one that every democratic polity

---

[37] Habermas 1996: 120.   [38] Larmore 1996: 205–223.
[39] See, e.g., *Pace v. State of Alabama*, 106 U.S. 583 (1883) (law that imposed higher penalty for inter-racial "fornication" or "adultery" passed equal protection because higher penalty applied to both blacks and whites engaging in such behavior).

will surely pass – why can't the murderer claim a violation of equal liberty? Why is proscribing sodomy a presumptive violation of equal respect but not a law against murder? We see the same problem with Ackerman's constraints. Something more is needed than the boilerplate language of equal respect or the right to equal liberty. These doctrines may seem attractive but are simply not specific enough to do the job. They either go too far in limiting government – threatening democracy – or don't go far enough – threatening liberty. Ultimately, if Habermas requires that we fill the content of such boilerplate with talk of "classical human rights" or "basic rights,"[40] his theory of Justification collapses into the reflexive account criticized above, or worse the classic ones of Chapter 1.

Habermas' goal to afford democracy a substantive role – to connect democracy to the rule of law – is important. His argument no doubt addresses the "democratic deficit" inherent in a regime of rights. Nevertheless, his various justificatory constraints are too permissive or vague to adequately protect our liberty. They fail as accounts of limited government.

Rawls' public reason

Unlike Ackerman and Habermas, Rawls may seem the least interested in proposing a theory of Justification. At first glance, *Political Liberalism*[41] seems like a normal, run of the mill (small 'j') account of justification for a certain schedule of rights. Whereas his *Theory of Justice*[42] sought to justify the two principles of justice (equal rights and liberties and the difference principle) by way of a philosophical, moral argument, here he proposes a merely political explanation of such principles. Specifically, Rawls suggests that the two principles of justice are arrived at by an overlapping consensus of the comprehensive religious and moral viewpoints held by the citizens of a polity. Just as the veil of ignorance is discarded after the two principles have been articulated, so too is the overlapping consensus. They are mere ladders, thrown away after their work is done. This, then, does not seem like a theory of Justification – where Justification is a constant process, a mechanism that is perpetually appealed to in determining justice in the polity. Political liberalism appears like any other account of rights rejected in the first part of this book.

---

[40] Habermas says as much: "Consequently, without the classical rights of liberty that secure the private autonomy of legal persons, there is no medium for legally institutionalizing those conditions under which citizens can first make use of their civic autonomy" (Habermas 1996: 455).
[41] Rawls 1996.   [42] Rawls 1971.

Nevertheless, I believe that alongside this political argument as an alternative grounding for *A Theory of Justice*, Rawls articulates a theory of Justification.[43] In fact, his account of public reason is best understood as a constraint on democratic deliberation. Specifically, in Lecture VI Rawls sees this conception of public reason as constraining and limiting public discourse. He writes:

> To begin: in a democratic society public reason is the reason of equal citizens who, as a collective body, exercise final political and coercive power over one another in enacting laws and in amending their constitution. The first point is that the *limits imposed* by public reason do not apply to all political questions but only those involving what we may call "constitutional essentials" and questions of basic justice. [...] This means that political values alone are to settle such fundamental questions as: who has the right to vote, or what religions are to be tolerated, or who is to be assured fair equality of opportunity, or to hold property.[44]

This is nothing other than a theory of Justification. It articulates the constitutional essentials as the "what" of Justification and appeals to public reason as constituting the "how." Moreover, these limits apply not only to "official forums" and "legislators" but also to the very act of voting where citizens exercise their coercive political power.[45] In the language of Ackerman, public reason is the Rawlsian conversational constraint.

Public reason appears to stand somewhere between Ackerman's rigid, undemocratic constraints and Habermas' permissive, liberty-compromising ones. In answering the "what" of Justification Rawls applies his constraint of public reason to only the constitutional essentials of a polity. Rather than have the particular power relation or disadvantage justified, Rawls (unlike Ackerman) looks to the fundamental decisions of the relevant democratic polity. He shies away from explicitly applying public reason to all decisions by the polity contending that its application only to constitutional essentials is the stronger argument. By limiting the "what" of Justification to higher lawmaking, Rawls leaves room for the substantive role of democracy. This account of limited government is friendlier to democracy than Ackerman's. Similar to Habermas, Rawls implicitly envisions that democratic polities could under the constraint of public reason draft different constitutions or at least reach different basic decisions.

In elucidating this account, Rawls argues that a supreme court stands as an exemplar of public reason.[46] Even after settling on the "how" of Justification some institutional mechanism must exist to enforce it. Ackerman's enforcement device is the Commander, a character with a perfect technology of

---

[43] Ackerman 1994, Wolgast 1994.   [44] Rawls 1996: 214 (emphasis added).
[45] Ibid.: 217.   [46] Ibid.: 231–240.

justice to make sure that the neutral conversational constraints are followed. Though instructive, such a device fails to highlight the reason component behind Justification. Courts, unlike other branches of government, issue decisions with justifications – with opinions. Such a practice is ideal for a theory of Justification where emphasis is on the rationale behind the polity's actions. This does not mean that other branches or officials cannot also oversee or apply such constraints. Emphasis on courts, though, highlights the fact that Justification is a wholly reason-driven enterprise.

However, in answering the "how" of Justification, Rawls effectively appeals to the problematic notion of neutrality that plagued Ackerman's account. According to Rawls, public reason does not aim to presuppose or endorse any particular comprehensive doctrine – any religious, political or moral viewpoint. Rawls hopes to articulate a constraint that is "political and not metaphysical."[47] The same trouble that accompanied Ackerman's conversational constraint that forbade appeal to any conception of the good applies here as well. Of course, Rawls hopes that his two principles of justice, equal liberties and the difference principle, meet this commitment of neutrality. But a true neutral (or merely political) position is impossible. Any political claim invariably appeals to and draws from a moral or metaphysical foundation.[48] This book, after all, seeks to realize the values of liberty and democracy. There is nothing neutral or non-moral about them.

In fact, after having endorsed neutrality Rawls unsurprisingly specifies the content of public reason as containing, among other things, certain "basic rights, liberties, and opportunities."[49] Rawls, then, falls back on the conventional method of limiting government. Much like Habermas' third formulation of the justificatory constraint, what began as a fruitful theory of Justification runs out of steam, retreating to a regime of rights or a vague, catchall claim to equal liberty and its attendant difficulties: being too permissive and too strict. Though equality is certainly important (one of the motivating principles underlying this book), we must realize it with a more specific and concrete justificatory constraint. Ackerman, Habermas, and now Rawls fail in doing just that.

Oakeshott's civil association

Ironically, Michael Oakeshott,[50] the alleged conservative of the group, ends up articulating the most persuasive general framework for a theory of

---

[47] Ibid.: 97.   [48] Steinberger 2000.   [49] Rawls 1996: 223.   [50] Oakeshott 1962, 1975.

Justification, for an account of limited government. Though the other three theorists are self-described liberals, Oakeshott has traditionally been viewed as a paragon of conservative thought[51] with some more recent liberal-democratic readings.[52] Even these more liberal interpretations fail to interpret Oakeshott as putting forth a theory of Justification.[53] In interpreting him as doing so, he turns out quite illuminating.

Oakeshott's purpose in Section II of *On Human Conduct*[54] is to theorize the civil condition. This is not an actual description of a polity or a present-day state. It is a Weberian ideal type that seeks to describe a particular "mode of association."[55] This mode has implications for the setup of a state or polity. But it is presented as a theoretical construct.[56] I submit that the civil condition is nothing other than a theory of Justification.

Again, any such theory must answer the "what" and "how" questions. Oakeshott describes a civil association as:

a practice or language of civil intercourse which they [members of the civil association] have not designed or chosen but within the jurisdiction of which they recognize themselves to fall and which, in subscribing to it, they continuously explore and reconstitute.[57]

The "what" of Justification is this "practice or language." The civil intercourse is the nature of politics. Like Habermas' discourse theory, Oakeshott also identifies political conversation (intercourse) as the lodestar of the democratic polity or state. He sees the importance of exploring and reconstituting such a practice. Moreover, these conversations take place in relation to the law, or *lex* as Oakeshott refers to it.[58] Such conversations or practices must take place in governmental bodies such as legislatures and city councils. Such is the political language of the civil association. Politics is this social exchange, this intercourse. It is a kind of technique that is acquired only by partaking in it, by engaging others in civil discussion.[59]

More importantly, this political conversation, this practice is undertaken under certain moral conditions. This represents the "how" of Justification.

---

[51] Plant 1972, Quinton 1978.   [52] Franco 1990a, 1990b, Grant 1990.

[53] Interestingly, in discussing Ackerman's conversational constraints, Flathman (1983) considers Oakeshott as putting forth a similar kind of argument.

[54] Oakeshott 1975.   [55] Ibid.: 108.

[56] I recognize that Oakeshott may not be comfortable with the blurring of this division between theory and practice (Franco 1990b: 161). But see Gerencser 1995.

[57] Oakeshott 1975: 183.   [58] Ibid.: 130–141.

[59] Oakeshott 1962: 15. R. Dworkin (1986) who has much in common with Oakeshott's legal theory views law as the internal, normative legal practice of what judges do. Only by doing it can one understand what law is.

Just as there are grammatical rules that constitute a language, so too are there moral conditions that constitute the practice immanent to civil association. These are, in the language of Justification, constraints. Such moral conditions, moreover, depend on the moral-historical context, "the jurisdiction" we happen to find ourselves in. By specifying the justificatory constraints as moral, Oakeshott flatly rejects neutrality, the "political and not metaphysical" nature of politics. Politics cannot be neutral. It invariably appeals to a certain conception of good, a certain moral nature.

However, these moral conditions are not goals or ends. The civil condition is not an enterprise association engaged in achieving a substantive aim or purpose. Rather, and here is the crucial point, such moral justificatory constraints are non-instrumental. The civil condition is "not concerned with the satisfaction of wants and with substantive outcomes but with the terms upon which the satisfaction of wants may be sought."[60] These "terms" do not have a desired purpose. They constrain only the political conversation but do not dictate its substantive outcome. This is his conception of the language of politics.

Oakeshott repudiates the conventional regime of rights. Realizing the frustrating presence of rights in civil discourse, he contends that the "language of rights is the language of pretend unconditionals and misdescribes the terms of civil association."[61] Rights entail certain end-states. They categorize behavior in order to decide its fate. Moral conditions, on the other hand, "do not enjoin, prohibit, or warrant substantive actions or utterances; they cannot tell agents what to do or say. They prescribe norms of conduct."[62] I suggest that the best interpretation of what Oakeshott means here is the difference between reasons and categorizations. In other words, "moral conditions" ("norms of conduct") outline the appropriate reason for acting. Such conditions are justificatory constraints such as the prevention of harm. "Substantive actions" on the other hand classify behavior. That is, if something is "private" or a matter of free speech, civil association must not interfere. If it is "public," the state has an interest in enjoining or prohibiting it. In this way, Oakeshott rightly realizes that rights and their accompanying methodology of classification leave the polity with fewer options. Justificatory constraints, on the other hand, do not dictate what the civil association must do – only under what "moral conditions" it may act. The emphasis in Justification is on reasons not categorizations or classifications.

---

[60] Oakeshott 1975: 174.   [61] Oakeshott 1962: 456.   [62] Oakeshott 1975: 126.

Consequently, Oakeshott's civil association leaves room for the democratic polity to decide a range of issues that a rights regime would declare off limits. It will be up to the democratic polity to decide what to enjoin or prohibit. For example, Oakeshott envisions a civil association choosing between a Nozickean minimal state and a more robust Ackerman-like one.[63] This contingent account of politics necessitates a significant role for democracy.[64] But in rejecting rights, Oakeshott does not automatically endorse its conventional republican alternative. After all, he repudiates any substantive purpose or goal of the civil condition.[65] He does not leave the democratic majority to do anything it pleases. If that were the case, he would have no need to describe the civil condition as containing such moral limitations. He seems implicitly to recognize that without such non-instrumental justificatory constraints, we invite majority tyranny.

Instead of separating the questions of "who governs me" and "how far ought government to interfere with me," Oakeshott constrains or limits the grounds on which the democratic state may act. He suggests that we ask the following question, one where reasons rather than rights do the normative work: "what is the appropriate rationale or reason on which the democratic polity may act?" In doing so, we simultaneously secure liberty – constraining the polity's reason for acting – while necessitating a role for democracy – after all, a *democratic* polity must proffer such reasons.

Rather than attempting to find a way to democratize rights by letting democracy define, validate, and inform them, we change the very question by looking solely to the legislative purpose of the statute, law, or regulation. Oakeshott's account of Justification affirms the importance of shifting our attention away from individuals or groups to the democratic polity itself. This transformative move turns out to be crucial in appropriately balancing and realizing the values of liberty and democracy.

Though Oakeshott lays out the framework for a workable theory of Justification, the elephant in the room is no doubt the *content* of these moral conditions. He articulates the correct question – seemingly rejecting rights – but fails to proffer an answer. Oakeshott does not give us this necessary key to reject rights. He does not tell what – at least in his historical-moral context – are the relevant moral constraints. He does not articulate what reason or rationale the polity ought to act upon. Why? I suspect that he sought only to give us the ideal parameters of a theory of Justification, leaving it to practitioners to specify their content. He warns us at the start that a civil condition does not represent an actual or even realized state. I interpret him as laying down the gauntlet in

---

[63] Oakeshott 1962: 456.   [64] Mapel 1990.   [65] Franco 1990a.

re-conceptualizing limited government. He rightly limits government by limiting the reason or rationale on which the polity may act. But to make this re-conceptualization persuasive and thereby reject rights, we must go farther. Since so much turns on these non-instrumental moral conditions, their content is essential. The next chapter provides what Oakeshott's theory fails to, namely an answer to the question of what are the legitimate grounds on which the state may act.

4   A theory of justification: specifying the appropriate legislative purpose

Having outlined contemporary political theory's turn to Justification, I draw from these other accounts to propose my own, a theory that aims to better ensure and balance the values of liberty and democracy. My method of argumentation is to make my particular theory of Justification – my account of limited government – attractive through its application. Rather than arguing to my justificatory constraint – mine is not a foundational argument – I first present it constantly proving its superiority to the more conventional regime of rights.

My account of limited government turns our attention to the state's reason or rationale for acting. It reorients the way we think about limiting democratic majorities. Again, the two central questions in any theory of Justification are: what needs justifying and how is it justified? I submit that the "what" component is state action and the "how" is the minimization of demonstrable, non-consensual harm. In other words:

The democratic state may only seek to minimize (mitigate, prevent, regulate, etc.) demonstrable, non-consensual harm.

This is the only reason that the state may appeal to justify its actions. This is what it means for a democratic state to act with good reason or to act non-arbitrarily. Rather than specify activities that the state may not infringe upon (or must respect), this theory of Justification identifies the rationales that the polity must proffer to support a particular decision. I do not consider variations on this justificatory principle. I concede that it could be the case that a different reason or rationale may proffer a more persuasive theory of Justification. After all, this chapter proposes *a* theory of Justification.

Yet, this misses the force of my argument. I seek to introduce a new framework for limiting democratic decision-making reorienting the way we conceive of the relationship between liberty and democracy. Once we agree that the best way to limit democratic government is to limit the reason or rationale on which the polity may act, the next step is to hammer out and debate the appropriate theory of Justification. But again, abandoning the standard account of rights is quite counter-intuitive. Thus, in ultimately persuading you to do so, I spend the rest of my book working out the implications of a particular justificatory constraint in part despite (and perhaps because of) its elegance; it parsimoniously does the laborious work of rights. It does quite well in balancing and realizing the values of liberty and democracy.

Instead of having democracy inform and validate rights – in line with the reflexive theorists explored previously – the democratic polity should reflect on what demonstrable harm(s) it desires to minimize and how it plans on minimizing them. This is the concrete alternative I offer. As I hope to suggest, we more satisfactorily connect democracy to the rule of law – suitably limiting government – by articulating the appropriate *grounds* upon which the polity must act. The role for the courts, then, is to invalidate those laws, regulations, or statutes that rest on something else. This is the account of limited government I defend.

There are four components to it: state action, only demonstrable harm, consent, and, less apparent but just as important, democracy.

State action

Somewhat like Habermas and the later Rawls, but unlike Ackerman, my theory of Justification applies only to state actors or actions by the state. In asking what needs to be justified, a wide range of answers is possible: any exercise of power (Ackerman), all sites of discourse or deliberation (Habermas), or constitutional essentials (Rawls). My account applies only to state action. That is, it constrains the grounds upon which the democratic polity may act – passing laws, enacting statutes, enforcing regulations, and the like.

Ackerman's focus on justifying the power itself – such as all social inequalities – leaves little substantive room for democracy. It leaves an actual polity with few (if any) substantive choices. Though Habermas rightly focuses on the decisions by the democratic polity – the relevant representative body – he needlessly extends the justificatory constraints to other sites of discourse. After all, only the state has the presumptive monopoly on legitimate force. Moreover, it is practically difficult to enforce these constraints against such Habermassian sites, unlike decisions by the state legislature, for example, which bear a more direct line of responsibility. Most importantly, by rejecting rights, there is nothing beyond the scope of state regulation; accordingly, there is no need to apply justificatory constraints to non-state actors.

Rawls' emphasis is seemingly too narrow. He answers the "what" question of Justification by looking only to the constitutional essentials of the democratic policy. However, in elucidating a better account of limited government, such justificatory constraints must be constantly enforced against *all* decisions by the polity. If we see constitutional essentials as applying to all lower law-making decisions, Rawls' answer to the "what" of Justification turns out similar to mine.

What does state action consist in? In its purest form it applies to laws, statutes, regulations, and ordinances passed by national, state, or local legislatures or any other political body specified by the "rule of recognition." Such laws and statutes must be appropriately justified. Even if a particular regulation passes muster, those that enforce it may run afoul of the relevant justificatory constraint. Thus, my theory of Justification applies to all kinds of state actors: legislators, executive officials, and judges. How the law is administered must also meet the justificatory test.[1] Questions no doubt arise at the margins. Do actions by a shopping mall[2] or a company town[3] count as state actors? Just as American constitutional law has been able to adjudicate the line, or at least draw it somewhere, these borderline cases need not deter us here. As a general principle state actors are those that are backed by the state's monopoly of legitimate force. Police officers, for example, stand as the paradigmatic example of state actors. Their actions when carried out as protectors of the state no doubt come with the coercive backing of the state. They enforce legislative decisions, decisions that by definition constitute state action. Judges and executive officials, of course, also count as state actors. After all, judicial decisions generally carry the backing of police power. My justificatory constraint then applies to all such decisions. In carrying out their civic duties, they must not run afoul of it: they must only seek to minimize demonstrable, non-consensual harm.

Moreover, as Rawls points out courts stand in an ideal position to determine whether such a constraint has been met. A court does not just render decisions – saying this party wins and the other loses – but offers reasons to support them. What then should we (or the court) look to in evaluating whether such a constraint has been met? Charles Larmore, who offers a very instructive theory of legitimacy, unfortunately obscuring it with the label of "neutrality," claims that the neutral state "is not meant to be one of outcome, but rather one of procedure."[4] My justificatory test is

---

[1] See, e.g., *Yick Wo v. Hopkins*, 118 U.S. 356 (1886) (court found discrimination in the administration of a facially neutral statute).

[2] See *Lloyd Corp., Ltd. v. Tanner*, 407 U.S. 551 (1972) (property does not lose its private character merely because the public is invited to use it for designated purposes), *Pruneyard Shopping Center v. Robins*, 447 U.S. 74 (1980) (left states to decide the question of access to privately owned shopping centers).

[3] *Marsh v. Alabama*, 326 U.S. 501 (1946) (company town was taken as being a "state").

[4] Larmore 1987: 44.

evaluated by appeal to the *aim or intent* of the statute, law, regulation, or its administration by officials, not its effects. We best limit government by evaluating the polity's reason or rationale for acting.

For instance, it could turn out that a particular policy fails to minimize harm. Suppose that in order to stop the spread of a disease believed to be spread by mosquitoes, lawmakers in good faith develop and release an airborne chemical toxin allegedly fatal only to these flying insects. While such a program meets the justificatory test, it could turn out that the chemical kills certain other insects leaving the disease unregulated. Such legislators may be voted out of office but they have not violated my justificatory constraint. Rather, laws and their administration must merely *aim* in good faith to minimize demonstrable, non-consensual harm.[5] These laws must be plausibly justified. This does not mean that effects are irrelevant. Naturally, the disparate impact of certain laws (though not sufficient on its own) may be evidence for an improper rationale.[6] Deciphering the legislative purpose may very well involve looking at the impact of the particular law or statute.

In passing a statute, individual legislators may have various, even diverging motivations in mind. Most problems with deciphering legislative intent occur when a statute's purpose is unclear or ambiguous.[7] Here the debates over originalism, history, and principle become relevant, informing various theories on how courts should ascertain legislative purpose. But these debates are not about whether the statute seeks to minimize harm. They entail other institutional or jurisprudential concerns such as whether the statute intends to exceed legislative authority, whether it aims to apply only to certain transactions or cases, or whether it seeks to have retroactive effect. My book avoids these thorny issues, because my argument does not require determining what the legislative purpose is. Rather, my argument simply requires that courts determine whether the legislative purpose *is* one of only minimizing harm *or* not. Smoking out a plainly illegitimate purpose is conceptually prior and more straightforward. This task does not involve deciphering the motivations of legislators, though an inquiry into purpose may very well reveal them. Mine is a workable account of limited government. I show that an improper purpose, one other than harm minimization, is apparent on a statute's face. It is discoverable by the language of the statute and whether the polity has or has not passed other relevant laws. This will become clearer as I outline cases

---

[5] Cf. Rawls 1996: 193.

[6] See, e.g., *Washington v. Davis*, 426 U.S. 229 (1976) (in upholding an employment test that disproportionately affected blacks, the Court held that disparate impact is one factor among many).

[7] See, e.g., Breyer 2005: 85–102, Scalia 1997, R. Dworkin 1986: 313–354.

where judges have deployed these very techniques to smoke out an illicit purpose, a purpose other than harm minimization.

Only demonstrable harm

The intent or reason behind the law or its enforcement must only be the minimization or mitigation of demonstrable, non-consensual harm. Minimization is a catchall word that includes prevention, regulation, mitigation, and the like. There are three distinct but related components to this condition: a concern with harm, a requirement that it be demonstrable, and a requirement that the polity exclusively minimize it. My argument, of course, takes off from John Stuart Mill, who famously contended, "the *only* purpose of which power can be rightfully exercised over any member of a civilized community, against his will, is to prevent harm to others."[8] In appealing to harm, I no doubt invoke a word with a much-belabored pedigree. Admittedly, since Mill's famous *On Liberty*, the "harm principle" (as it has come to be known) has been pretty much discussed to death. Still, as I will argue, this principle, properly understood, constitutes the cornerstone of my theory of Justification.

Now let me concede from the outset that Mill may not have understood his principle as merely articulating the rationale or grounds upon which the state may act. My argument is not about "getting Mill right," though I do believe this is a fruitful interpretation of his "harm principle."[9] It suggests an illuminating method of limiting government. Much of the trouble with interpreting Mill rests on his seemingly contradictory commitments to utilitarianism and liberalism. Reading *Utilitarianism*[10] would have one believe that justice requires maximizing utility or minimizing disutility. Reading *On Liberty*[11] one may believe that justice requires that we be left alone in certain areas or interests. Pursuing the former strategy seems to run up against the latter. If we are to be left alone in certain areas – that is, as individuals we have certain rights – how can we simultaneously adopt a principle of utility, a principle that seems indifferent even hostile to rights? In his introduction to three of Mill's essays, Richard Wollheim chides scholars for setting aside this commitment to utility by grounding *On Liberty* in values that are seemingly inconsistent with it.[12]

---

[8] Mill 1989 [1859]: 13 (emphasis added).
[9] Ten (1980) briefly suggests this as an interpretation of Mill's principle of liberty. "What is crucial to Mill's defence of liberty is therefore his belief that certain reasons for intervention – paternalistic, moralistic, and gut reactions – are irrelevant, whereas the prevention of harm to others is always relevant" (Ten 1980: 41). See also Waldron 2007.
[10] Mill 1979 [1861].   [11] Mill 1989 [1859].   [12] Wollheim 1975: xiii.

I suspect much of the conventional framing of this tension in Mill's corpus – between liberalism and utilitarianism – arises from an adherence to rights. As long as we interpret Mill's harm principle as implying or entailing a schedule of rights, his utilitarianism will be hard to reconcile with his commitment to liberty. And many scholars of Mill do just that. They interpret the harm principle either as a right not to be harmed or as entailing a private sphere of self-regarding action beyond the scope of state regulation.[13] Doing so invariably collides with Mill's commitment to utilitarianism.

But by latching onto the rationale of preventing harm there is a way to reconcile these arguments. If we turn our focus away from rights – the commitment that individuals ought to be secure in certain interests, areas, or spheres – and toward the democratic polity itself, we simultaneously value utility and liberty.

This does not mean the democratic state must minimize harm. If that were the case, we would have to ascertain the effects of a particular law rather than its aim or intent. Rather, in passing legislation, the polity's *reason or rationale* must be one of harm prevention. It must undertake this cost/benefit analysis in good faith. This means that various polities may arrive at different or even contradictory legislation. I see this as a virtue of my account, one that reinforces our commitment to democracy while appropriately limiting it.

We should interpret Mill's harm principle as entailing neither some kind of self-regarding private sphere off limits to state regulation nor a list of rights. Instead, we should understand harm prevention as a constraint on democratic decision-making, as a constraint on the appropriate reason(s) on which the polity may act. Reasons not rights ought to be our focus. This blending of utility and liberty goes some way to re-characterizing Millian liberalism as more of a democratic enterprise.[14] It lodges the utilitarian calculus – harm mitigation – in the hands of the democratic polity. I concede that much more needs to be said to work out this interpretive argument. I use Mill simply to introduce and elucidate my theory of Justification.

My theory of Justification (and by implication my interpretation of Mill) necessitates a wide understanding of harm. In this way, I hopefully overcome a threshold objection that this justificatory principle is too narrow, permitting the polity merely to prevent the intentional, punch-someone-in-the-face kind of harm. I reject such an interpretation. I understand harm broadly, precisely because this affords the polity substantive

---

[13] See, e.g., Gray 1983, Rees 1966.   [14] Cf. Devigne 2006, Urbinati 2002.

discretion in passing various laws. The polity, then, need not remedy, mitigate, or prevent all such harms or even a majority of them. With this broad interpretation of harm, we rightly allow the demos to decide how much the state should be involved in our lives.

Some scholars of Mill proffer such an expansive reading of harm.[15] According to Nadia Urbinati, a

comprehensive interpretation explains Mill's composite notion of harm. Harm refers both to individual actions that directly injure others ("wrongful aggressions") and to forms of human relations that inhibit people's chances to make independent decisions and plans ("wrongful exercise of power over some one").[16]

This broad conception of harm accords with much contemporary political theory. Even though the literature may shy away from using the word,[17] most theories of justice in one way or another invariably invoke it. For example, theorists talk about power over another,[18] disadvantage,[19] and domination.[20] These are all just ways of characterizing or describing harm. A genetic disadvantage, an innate inability to do mathematics, for instance, is a harm, as is any kind of domination over another. Having fewer resources than others – material, genetic, social, etc. – demonstrably hinders and limits one's chances and opportunities in life. Unequal social and economic structures invariably harm individuals in this way. Removing, remedying, and curbing such structures are all attempts to prevent harm. In the same way, the polity could (but need not) decide to prevent environmental damage, halt the loss of an animal species, or even stymie market breakdowns. By interpreting harm expansively, we inform our commitment to democracy, leaving the democratic polity to pass (if it so desires) a wide array of legislation.

But if the polity may only seek to prevent harm, what of the polity that desires to establish parks, museums, or other kinds of public goods? Here too my justificatory principle is capacious enough to permit such legislation. After all, harms could include economic inefficiencies, the externalities associated with the failure of the state to provide such goods. In asking how a liberal state can justify the provision of such goods, Ronald Dworkin characterizes them in just this way: "Public goods are those whose production cannot efficiently be left to the market because it is impossible (or very difficult or expensive) to exclude those who do not pay from receiving the benefit and so riding free."[21] To remedy such

---

[15] Lyons 1994: 89–109, Dyzenhaus 1997: 31–53, Urbinati 2002: 161–172.
[16] Urbinati 2002: 165.   [17] *Pace* Feinberg 1988.
[18] Ackerman 1980.   [19] G. Cohen 1989.
[20] Gaventa 1980, Shapiro 1999, Pettit 1997, Hayward 2000.   [21] R. Dworkin 1985: 223.

inefficiencies – to thwart the "tragedy of the commons" – the polity may decide to pass laws establishing parks and the like.

But would this economic analysis apply to museums? On first glance, it seems a bit tortured to suggest that the justification for publicly funded museums is to remedy inefficiency. In fact, for these kinds of public goods, Dworkin ultimately appeals to justifications that center on sustaining or informing the "structural aspects of our general culture."[22] But by appealing to such rationales, Dworkin invariably invites rationales that are not about preventing harm.

I suggest a different take on public goods, one that accords with my theory of Justification. We can all agree that without museums, artwork would be primarily in the hands of the wealthy. That being the case, publicly funded museums provide opportunities – here the ability to look at artwork – to those who otherwise would not have them. The harm is simply a lack of access, a lack of opportunity. In this way, it is not that museums seek to promote some kind of good – e.g., make individuals worldly or provide them with better taste. Rather, museums are best seen as remedying or mitigating access. And this is nothing other than preventing harm.

It is no coincidence that such "high art" unlike its more popular counterpart correlates with high socioeconomic status. Remedying access is not an issue with wrestling or racecar driving. It so happens that our contemporary society does not consider these cultural activities as "high art." Consequently, there is no worry that without state funding such activities would be seen only by the wealthy. In such cases, there is no "cultural" monopoly. We justify state funding, then, not because the polity deems that museums are good for the citizenry in ways that wrestling or racecar driving are not. Rather, it is the fact that without state intervention, certain activities – and these could change from one period or generation to the next – would be primarily in the hands of the wealthy. And, as long as the polity only seeks to do so, it may pass laws in order to remedy or break up this "cultural" monopoly, to prevent this kind of harm. Our focus ought to be on the monopoly part not the cultural part. While more may need to be said to fill in this argument, such an analysis suggests that harm prevention has the potential to justify such legislation.

Still, the nature of my justificatory constraint (it dictates what the state may only do, *not what it must do*) leaves the polity to decide which kinds of harm to minimize and how to do so. For example, the polity need not

---

[22] Ibid.: 229.

provide public goods. It need not do anything. It is just that when the polity acts, it must do so only to prevent harm.

But the polity may not seek to prevent all harms, only those which are demonstrable. By demonstrability, I mean two distinct, but related notions. First, the democratic polity may choose only those harms for which we can in good faith proffer some kind of publicly ascertainable evidence or proof. For example, harm in a possible afterlife cannot be publicly ascertained. Because there is no genuine evidence for such harm, we as a democratic polity cannot discuss or debate it. As a collective, we do not have access to such harm. Thus, legislation seeking to minimize or prevent it is unacceptable. Second, assuming that there is demonstrable harm, the means the polity selects to minimize it must also be made in good faith. Claiming that outlawing gay sex will reduce the murder rate would violate this condition. There is no plausible evidence for it. The role for a court is to strike down wayward laws that fail demonstrability.

Turning to reasons invites and requires democratic decision-making. Such democratic deliberation would be nearly impossible without publicly ascertainable harms. Imagine democratic citizens discussing the harm in a possible afterlife. With no tangible harm in play, what is there to discuss? If I believe that it's just wrong or offensive for blonds to have sex with redheads, how is this something the polity can genuinely debate? Knee-jerk reactions and mere proclamations that something is wrong, offensive, or disgusting do not make for fruitful democratic debate.[23] I specify that the polity's attention must be on *demonstrable* harms, precisely because I place this justificatory constraint on democratic decision-making. After all, it will be up to the polity to make the normative judgment about which of these demonstrably harmful activities, if any, to minimize and how to do so.

This criterion of demonstrability is not novel. As intimated above, much scholarship already advocates it under the misleading and unfortunate label of neutrality. When contemporary theorists speak of neutrality, I suggest that they have in mind this notion of demonstrability. I want, then, to make explicit my two-fold criticism of contemporary theory's commitment to neutrality. After all, my account of limited government shares many of the intuitions behind it. First, the very term incorrectly connotes a theory that is valueless that does not endorse any principle or position. Yet since this is a function of using the wrong word, much of the criticism of neutrality is simply about terminology. As a result, my positive account drops the word "neutrality" focusing on the minimization of demonstrable, non-consensual harm as the relevant justificatory principle.

---

[23] Cf. Gutmann and Thompson 1996.

Second, and more importantly, neutrality is a commitment to excluding certain reasons from the relevant decision-making discourse. Generally, as Ackerman and Rawls contend, this exclusion applies to conceptions of the good.[24] By proceeding negatively – specifying what we are *forbidden* from appealing to – neutrality turns out vague and infeasible. It is difficult to see what reasons would pass neutral dialogue or even the veil of ignorance. For example, does harm minimization pass neutrality? And if so, does the harm of a troubled afterlife count? By failing to stipulate the positive form an appropriate argument must take, these conventional neutral arguments prove un-instructive, seemingly excluding everything. It seems odd that contemporary neutral theorists have not articulated demonstrable harm minimization as the appropriate justification.

I suspect that their reluctance to declare as much is a symptom of an adherence to the methodology of rights. Just as rights prevent the state from acting in certain ways by classifying an activity as being of a certain kind, so too do these conventional neutral arguments – excluding reasons rather than specifying their appropriate form.

Neutrality's turn to reasons is a step in the right direction. But by specifying rationales the state may not use, it fails to offer genuine guidance. The list of unacceptable reasons seems *infinite*. Who knows what kind of crazy, arbitrary rationales a polity may proffer for its legislation. Trying to capture all of them seems impossible and pointless. Similarly, trying to lay out the scope and meaning of rights seems a hopeless task. Do we have a right to marry someone of the same sex? Do we have a right to equality and, if so, does it include treating murderers the same as non-murderers? The perverse need to carve out that which the state may not intrude upon or those reasons the state may not appeal to is unnecessary and problematic. Moreover, as a practical matter, this strategy invites problems of statutory interpretation. It requires that we ascertain what the purpose of the statute is in order to determine if it passes neutrality. Again, my justificatory constraint requires that we ascertain not what the purpose is but whether this purpose is one of harm prevention.

Neutrality theorists should not shy away from *positively* articulating the mark of all good arguments for state action. The conventional claim that the state ought to be neutral to various conceptions of the good is better

---

[24] Ackerman 1980, Rawls 1996. In line with neutrality, Corey Brettschneider also argues for a conception of public reason. He deems arguments "based on a particular conception of the good life that is not acceptable to all reasonable citizens" as outside the boundaries of state coercion (Brettschneider 2007: 81). But he, like other theorists of neutrality, neglects to spell out what counts as "acceptable to all reasonable citizens."

understood as a simple criterion of demonstrability. Very much like Oakeshott and implicitly like Ackerman and Rawls, I see Justification as, at least, thinly moral in nature. The values of freedom, equality, and democracy underlie my enterprise here. My theory of Justification undoubtedly endorses a conception of the good,[25] a certain "fighting creed."[26] While Oakeshott failed to articulate exactly what this "moral practice" amounted to, I submit that it values the minimization of demonstrable harm. Simply put, there has to be publicly ascertainable evidence that a particular activity, externality, loss, damage, etc. is harmful.

Richard Posner, for example, properly understands this notion of demonstrability arguing that sexuality ought to be approached functionally. Rather than speaking in the confusing talk of neutrality or of rights, he advocates an understanding of sexual activity that is "resolutely secular, scientific in either a broad or narrow sense."[27] Consequently, demonstrability ensures that alleged moral harms may not be minimized. Simply claiming that certain kinds of sexual conduct are wrong or not valuable, as much natural law theory does,[28] fails this criterion of demonstrability. For instance, the following rationales for state legislation (all of which do appeal to some non-demonstrable harm) are immediately inadmissible: the virtuous path of monogamy; God deems gay sex (even certain kinds of heterosexual sex for that matter) a sin; marriage is a sacred institution between only a man and a woman; inter-racial sex is disgusting. These rationales are just as illegitimate, just as arbitrary as ones that suggest that marriage is a sacred institution between those of the same hair color, or that oral sex between a redhead and a blond is disgusting. They are arbitrary, because they do not seek to prevent some *demonstrable* harm. How can a democratic polity properly discuss and debate such rationales? By picking out some kind of non-publicly ascertainable harm, these reasons are not democratic ones. We should immediately deem them inadmissible.

As Posner rightly points out, Lord Patrick Devlin[29] does not and could not support his famous claim that allowing gay sex would lead to "national disintegration."[30] Devlin makes gestures to the conclusion that "a recognized morality is as necessary to society as, say, a recognized government" but simply fails to offer the necessary evidence.[31] If anything, the fact that same-sex marriages are and have been taking place in Massachusetts, and the state government there has not (yet) crumbled or disintegrated, goes a way to refuting Devlin's claim. I do not object to Devlin's standard – after

---

[25] Galston 1991, Larmore 1996.   [26] Rockefeller 1994: 90.   [27] Posner 1992: 220.
[28] See, e.g., George 1993, Finnis 1994.   [29] Devlin 1971 [1965].
[30] Posner 1992: 234.   [31] Ibid.: 234.

all, disintegration of government counts as a demonstrable harm. We could, for example, point to riots, widespread disregard for the law, and the like. But Devlin offers no evidence to suggest that permitting gay sex or even same-sex marriage leads to such harm.

Of course, I assume that the alleged disintegration would occur in a democratic polity. A non-democratic society could not avail itself of the Devlin standard. That is, it could not claim that it must prohibit a certain practice in order to protect its non-democratic institutions. For example, during apartheid, certain white South Africans would have undoubtedly contended that permitting inter-racial marriages would erode or threaten the current political system.[32] However, since the political system itself was not democratic – black South Africans did not have the right to vote – we do not even meet the threshold requirement of my theory of Justification, namely the presence of a democracy. Again, I seek to limit democratic government, balancing and realizing the values of democracy and liberty. Both are necessary. After all, as I argue below, democracy ensures some freedom. While Devlin may not have considered democracy crucial to his argument, it is vital to mine. My justificatory constraint constrains decisions by a *democratic* polity. Given the existence of a democracy, such a constraint rules out mere moral condemnation.

Conversely, again with a focus on the relevant rationale, I may worship as I choose simply because the state has no good reason to tell me to do otherwise. Suppose I, as a Satanist, want to start my own church. In order to shut my church down, the state may only seek to minimize demonstrable, non-consensual harm. The state is prohibited from saying that Satanism is merely a bad thing or it is not a real religion (these are all concerns that are not demonstrably harmful). Effectively, my freedom is secure. Imagine instead that as part of my Satanist ritual I seek to kill a victim; and, the state prevents me from doing so. Here the state may seek to stop my religious ritual, because it is seeking to avert demonstrable harm.

Neutrality does not explain the difference between laws against murder and laws against sodomy or laws mandating racial segregation – leaving us with all or none at all. What this characterization really amounts to is that murder, unlike the others, is a harm that can be supported by evidence. But the democratic polity will be hard pressed to justify sodomy laws. Such laws seek to prohibit "victimless" crimes. The characterization of them as "victimless" suggests that there is no genuine harm at stake, only an inchoate, nebulous, and hard to pin down notion of disgust or offense.

---

[32] Apartheid South Africa passed the Prohibition of Mixed Marriages Act in 1949.

We will see in Part III that even those Justices who find sodomy laws *acceptable* concede that there is no plausible harm in play, invariably characterizing such laws as "morals legislation." Laws against murder or assault are entirely inapposite. Here there are victims. There is publicly ascertainable harm. How the polity goes about mitigating or minimizing such harm – for example, what harms to assign to the tort law as opposed to the criminal law, when to use a strict liability or a negligence standard and the like – is up to it. This way of limiting democratic government ensures such democratic discretion.

Now in many other cases there will be good faith disagreement over demonstrability, whether a particular activity leads to harm. We could disagree about what is the best kind of economic system, whether illegal immigration helps the economy, whether certain kinds of evidence are reliable for criminal investigations,[33] or whether affirmative action remedies harm. This kind of disagreement entails the need and appeal for democratic decision-making. There are no right answers here, only good faith decisions by the majority. In these cases, courts should defer to the democratic process. The fact that people can sometimes genuinely disagree over demonstrability suggests the need for democratic flexibility and discretion. It suggests we should accept rather than reject such a condition. More importantly, it stands as a reason not to constrain such democratic decision-making by invoking rights. This informs our commitment to democracy. The courts should step in when the polity fails to engage the issue of demonstrability in good faith.

But how do we know when this happens? One sure indication is when the polity fails to *exclusively* prevent harm, when it violates the "only" requirement. Mill argues that "preventing harm" is the *only* principle on which the state may act. Mill could have contended that *a* purpose or one of the purposes on which the state may act is harm prevention, leaving open the admissibility of other rationales. But he explicitly writes that this is the "only purpose." I take his words literally in putting forth my own theory of Justification, one where harm minimization is the sole or exclusive rationale on which the state may act.

The recent controversy over partial birth abortions is an illustrative example. In *Gonzales v. Carhart* (2007) the Court upheld the Congressional Partial Birth Abortion Act of 2003.[34] The federal law prohibits a certain kind of abortion procedure referred to as a partial birth abortion. In such a procedure – called an intact abortion – the

---

[33] There is disagreement over the reliability of scientific testimony concerning fingerprints and handwriting identification. See, e.g., Saks 1998, Stoney 2005: 189–207.

[34] 18 U.S.C. § 1531.

fetus is partially delivered before it's destroyed. The Court upheld the law reasoning that Congress had a legitimate and substantial interest in "preserving and promoting fetal life."[35]

In connecting theory to actual constitutional practice, I criticize this case for failing to properly endorse Justification. Specifically, the case neglects to apply the "only" constraint. If the concern is truly with preserving fetal life – preventing harm to the fetus – it is illuminating that the federal law will not save one fetus. After all, the law merely prohibits one kind of abortion procedure. It leaves open other procedures such as medical induction, hysterotomy, and even removing the fetus piecemeal, a non-intact abortion,[36] procedures that straightforwardly also destroy the fetus. Thus, and this is where the "only" constraint becomes relevant, what reason does Congress have for drawing a line between one procedure and another? Such a line seems arbitrary. It is unconnected to the goal of preventing harm to the fetus. It suggests that Congress' purpose is not exclusively to minimize harm.

As a practitioner of Justification, Justice Ruth Bader Ginsburg implicitly endorses the "only" constraint. She dissents from the decision citing the arbitrary nature of the ban. That is, she argues that there is no *rational* reason to explain why the ban is under-inclusive. And here I quote from her dissent at length:

The Court offers flimsy and transparent justifications for upholding a nationwide ban on intact D&E *sans* any exception to safeguard a women's health. Today's ruling, the Court declares, advances ... the Government's "legitimate and substantial interest in preserving and promoting fetal life."... But the Act scarcely furthers that interest: The law saves not a single fetus from destruction, for it targets only a *method* of performing abortion... As another reason for upholding the ban, the Court emphasizes that the Act does not proscribe the nonintact D&E procedure. But why not, one might ask. Nonintact D&E could equally be characterized as "brutal," involving as it does "tear[ing] [a fetus] apart" and "rip[ping] off" its limbs. "[T]he notion that either of these two equally gruesome procedures ... is more akin to infanticide than the other, or that the State furthers any legitimate interest by banning one but not the other, is simply irrational." ... Ultimately, the Court admits that "moral concerns" are at work, concerns that could yield prohibitions on any abortion ... Notably, the concerns expressed are untethered to any ground genuinely serving the Government's interest in preserving life. ... "Our obligation is to define the liberty of all, not to mandate our own moral code." *Lawrence* v. *Texas* (2003)... Revealing in this regard, the Court invokes an antiabortion shibboleth for which it concededly has no reliable evidence.[37]

---

[35] *Gonzales* at 15.   [36] Ibid.: at 9–10.   [37] Ibid.: at 13–15, dissenting (citations omitted).

Ginsburg contends that the federal ban seeks to do more than simply prevent harm to the fetus. It seeks to impose some kind of moral code or, as Ginsburg writes later in her dissent, to oppress women, rationales that render the law unconstitutional. She cites *Lawrence v. Texas* for the proposition that the state may not justify laws on the basis of enforcing morality. I analyze *Lawrence* in more detail in Chapter 7. She sees the law as a kind of morals legislation, legislation whose purpose fails my theory of Justification. She, but not the majority, rightly deploys the task of Justification – and in particular the "only" constraint – to smoke out such "flimsy and transparent" rationales. Rather than looking to the rights to privacy or equality to invalidate the law, Ginsburg, in line with Justification, turns to reasons. She proclaims that the partial birth abortion ban is "simply irrational," precisely because it does not serve the "interest in preserving life." This is a practical instantiation of re-conceptualizing limited government in this way. Reasons not rights can do the constitutional work.

But in turning to reasons do we not invite the polity to trump up claims of harm in order to satisfy Justification? After all, the mid twentieth century saw the advent of scientific racism, or Social Darwinism. Claims of demonstrability were used to justify the unequal treatment of blacks and racial minorities.[38] Blacks and racial minorities were considered genetically inferior to whites mandating differential treatment especially in the context of miscegenation. My response here is two-fold. First, scientific racism has undoubtedly been repudiated. It is not considered genuine science.[39] In fact, even at that time many scientists objected to the tenets of scientific racism.[40] We should deem such claims just as irrational as those that contend that hair color tracks biological inferiority. Do we believe that tomorrow or at some later date, we'll find some kind of evidence justifying racism? We'll find that piece of paper that says – aha! – one race is inferior to another. Rather than holding out for this possibility, we should simply say that it could *never* be the case that such evidence is one day uncovered. We should categorically rule it out.

Thus, a polity that acts on such a rationale does so in bad faith – the science bit being just a pretext. Put simply, claims that laws banning sodomy or mandating racial segregation aim to prevent harm, then, are baseless. They are just as silly as ones that seek to segregate or regulate

---

[38] See Pascoe (1996) for an excellent survey and analysis of miscegenation laws in twentieth-century America.

[39] Boas 1940, Dobzhansky 1955, Gould 1981, Montagu 1997.

[40] See, e.g., *Statement on the Nature of Race and Race Differences* by Physical Anthropologists and Geneticists – June 1951, flatly rejecting that "race mixture produces disadvantageous results from a biological point of view" (UNESCO).

sexual activity on the basis of hair color. We ought not to take them seriously, deeming them inadmissible.

Second, even conceding that Justification is prone to corruption (as is any principle), history shows that we are *not* better off with a regime of rights. After all, segregation and anti-miscegenation laws were, until *Brown v. Board of Education of Topeka* (1954) and *Loving v. Virginia* (1967), respectively, seen as passing the Fourteenth Amendment's requirement of "equal protection."[41] As argued above, symmetric legislation – legislation that seemingly burdens both groups – could be said to treat persons equally.[42] Just as blacks may not associate with whites, so whites may not associate with blacks. Even a right to privacy (until *Lawrence v. Texas* (2003)) was unable to secure the freedom to sleep with the adult of one's choosing. No doubt those who advocated laws against miscegenation could have similarly argued that a right to marry only means the right to marry someone of the same race. As argued in Chapter 2, this approach trades on the scope and meaning of rights. It problematically leaves the content of rights open to equally coherent positions.

Rights turn out to be more susceptible to such tyrannies of the majority than my justificatory constraint. Even conceding the bogus claims of scientific racism, the alleged harm in miscegenation – dilution of racial purity – would be consensual. Under the consent requirement explored below, the state may not minimize consensual harm – only its nonconsensual counterpart. Thus, even armed with the claims of pseudo-scientific racism, if a white person in 1966 chooses to "dilute" her/his racial purity, there is nothing the state may do. Even though such laws may very well pass a regime of rights, they fail the condition of consent in addition to being irrational. Moreover, segregation in non-educational contexts seems entirely un-connected to the allegations of scientific racism.[43] The relevant harm here (as the scientific racists would contend) is the *genetic mixing* of the races. Segregation on buses, though, seeks to do something other than minimize such harm, perhaps oppress or punish one group by privileging another. Unlike a regime of rights, these rationales could not possibly pass my justificatory constraint. Rights can more easily mask tyranny by categorizing it in a certain way. Since my theory of Justification focuses on the reason behind the law, as a mechanism of legitimation, it is less prone to such corruptions. Even in the darkest

---

[41] U.S. Constitution Amendment XIV § 1 ("No State shall ... deny to any person within its jurisdiction the equal protection of the laws").

[42] See fn. 39, Ch. 3.

[43] The assertion that certain groups are genetically less intelligent than others would only seemingly permit segregation so as to further perverse educational goals.

moments, demonstrability and consent as justificatory constraints are more vigilant in securing liberty than rights.

But if I entertain a broad, wide-ranging definition of demonstrable harm, what about the troublesome case of emotional harm? What if a society bent on passing sodomy laws does so by articulating the following rationale: sodomy is to be outlawed not because it is sinful or disgusting (recognizing that this fails demonstrability) but rather because it causes net emotional trauma? A majority of the polity suffers emotional harm knowing that gay sex is legally taking place. Suppose the majority's emotional suffering is in total greater than that experienced by the gay minority balking at the enactment of a sodomy law (assume that such interpersonal intensity comparisons can be made). Why can't the polity simply decide to minimize net emotional harm? In seeking to do so, why can't it pass such a law? Why won't this reason pass my justificatory constraint?

Rejecting the constitutional right to privacy, Robert Bork, an extreme judicial conservative who failed to win confirmation to the Court in 1987[44] makes this very argument. He claims that permitting gay sex "may surely be *felt* to be as harmful as the possibility of physical violence ... The Court has never explained, nor has anyone else, why what the community feels to be harm may not be counted as one."[45] Simply put, why may the state not legislate to minimize such a feeling – to mitigate emotional harm? In implicitly accepting the condition of demonstrability, Bork does not point to any vague, inchoate idea of "moral harm" but rather to straightforward, demonstrable emotional harm. The religious zealot can certainly explain how angry or offended she feels knowing that anal sex is occurring right down her street. Certain physiological and chemical imbalances that arise in her can point to the plausibility of such harm. According to one political theorist, this objection of emotional harm stands as the central barrier in endorsing the principle of harm minimization.[46] I suspect that this nagging objection, and it is no doubt a serious one, has led theorists to stick with and retreat to a regime of rights – including the allegedly necessary right to privacy.

However, by the very terms of my argument the polity may not seek to minimize this kind of emotional harm. It may not seek to minimize the offense individuals feel or experience. If our preferences – we desire gays not to have sex or blacks to be treated as second-class citizens or redheads to sit at the back of the bus – can cause us to suffer emotional harm when the state does not accede to them, we have moved away from caring about just harm minimization to caring about mere majority preference. The

[44] McGuigan and Weyrich 1990.   [45] Bork 1990: 249 (emphasis added).
[46] J. Cohen 2002: 106.

brute fact that a majority of individuals want, desire, or prefer a particular kind of legislation is not sufficient to pass it. According to my theory of Justification this is not a permissible rationale on which the state may act. Just because most individuals want x does not constitute a good reason for the polity to do x.[47] Appeal to such emotional harm is nothing other than a pretext for simply going along with the preferences of a majority. By its very nature, emotional harm cannot be separated from the preferences that engender it, preferences that can be for anything. If emotional harm can be used to justify any legislation, we have effectively removed any constraint on democratic decision-making. We no longer have a theory of Justification. If in the name of preventing emotional harm the polity may do *anything*, this is no longer an account of *limited* government.

In fact, though they do not convincingly explain why, scholars of Mill reject this kind of distress, because it rests on a belief that a particular action – gay sex, redheads sitting at the front of the bus, etc. – is wrong.[48] Consider the act of murder. Most, if not all of us, would consider it wrong to murder. We would feel emotional harm knowing such an activity was going on. But under my justificatory constraint, the polity prohibits murder *not* to reduce such emotional distress. Rather it prohibits murder, because the very act of murdering is harmful, harm that is independent of the pain we may feel knowing it is taking place.

This points to the fatal flaw with Bork's proposal. The problem with this kind of emotional harm or distress is its elastic nature. Unlike all other demonstrable harms, there is a strategic quality to it. Those who find gay sex disgusting or any kind of activity wrong have every incentive to become even more emotionally charged and thus harmed by the lack of a law prohibiting it. They can genuinely rouse themselves up so as to claim that such a law needs to be passed. And there is no way for the polity to deem such harm disingenuous. After all, as long as one feels it, it's genuine. It exists. This kind of harm is not independent of the law seeking to minimize it. At least with physical or genetic harm, the polity's decision to minimize it is independent of its existence. There's no way someone can strategically "up the amount" of physical or genetic harm. You cannot be any more physically hurt than you are or any more genetically disadvantaged than you are.

Suppose a polity does not currently minimize genetic harm. An interest group forms with the explicit task of persuading the majority to pass legislation compensating those who are genetically disadvantaged. It may hand out certain kinds of literature, have its members deliver speeches, or take out television ads. Whatever the interest group does in

[47] Cf. R. Dworkin 1978: 234–239.   [48] See, e.g., Waldron 1987, Wollheim 1973.

making its case, the genetic harm that it seeks to minimize will remain the same. Nothing the group does will increase the amount of genetic disadvantage. Said differently, efforts to persuade the majority to minimize genetic harm will have no effect on the existence or level of this harm.

Emotional harm based on the belief that something is wrong, on the other hand, *is* dependent on a group's efforts to minimize it. Suppose that individuals desire sodomy laws in order to minimize overall emotional distress. In convincing people to vote for such legislation – by using ads or sending out literature outlining the deep and felt pain of knowing that such "sinful" behavior is taking place – the interest group can increase the overall amount of emotional harm. By rousing people up, emotional harm invariably intensifies. But this intensification did not exist until the push to minimize it. Yet, if a polity may minimize such harm, we have no way of deeming it illegitimate. Emotional harm serves as a perfect cover for all kinds of liberty-compromising laws, laws that aim to privilege a certain sexual practice or oppress a certain group. The self-fulfilling nature of this kind of emotional harm renders it particularly ripe for such manipulation. Our only option is to reject it as a possible harm that the state may minimize.

Bork wonders why "what the community feels to be harm" cannot be counted as one just as "physical violence" is counted as one. Quite simply, unlike physical harm (or any non-emotional demonstrable harm), emotional distress serves as a foolproof *pretext* for pure majoritarianism, a pretext for simply acceding to majority preference that something is wrong. Because its self-fulfilling nature renders it both very difficult to contest and prone to manipulation, it may not be a legitimate object of state regulation. If the polity in the name of minimizing this kind of distress may do anything – individuals can be sufficiently riled up about anything – Bork's proposal must be about something *more* than mere harm minimization. And this fails my justificatory constraint. The strategy of minimizing this kind of emotional harm is impossible to distinguish from a strategy to simply oppress or subjugate. We should properly reject it in elucidating an account of limited government.

Consent

Whereas demonstrability ruled out morals legislation, the condition of consent repudiates paternalism.[49] The state may only minimize harm that is demonstrable and non-consensual. Consent is only possible by

---

[49] Joel Feinberg, for instance, distinguishes among four kinds of harm: harm to others; offense to others; harm to oneself (paternalism); and moral harm (morals legislation) (Feinberg 1988). He rightly argues that the law should not criminalize the third and fourth

competent adults. Though the lines between competence and incompetence or adult and child are no doubt important, they are not my primary concern. Such line drawing is certainly do-able – all countries set standards for competency and adulthood. In line with my commitment to democracy, these boundaries may very well be drawn in different ways. And even if there is genuine disagreement, the adult, competent individual is easy to spot. Thus, in so far as paternalistic legislation regulates consensual harm, my justificatory constraint generally rules out laws against suicide, drug abuse, gambling, and the like.

Mill quite rightly articulated the importance of consent. Those things that affect others but "with their free, voluntary, and undeceived consent and participation" are immune from state regulation.[50] Ackerman also finds refuge in the doctrine of consent. Though Ackerman characterizes his neutral constraints in negative terms (what reasons the power holder may not give), the flip side of his argument is what reasons are, in fact, permitted. Under his theory of Justification, if you question why I have more money than you, I can properly respond that you consensually squandered your initial amount of resources, manna, or money. For Ackerman consent would be the most common legitimate response in justifying power. The state ought to be in the business of minimizing non-consensual harm leaving its consensual counterpart un-regulated. Again, non-consensual harms may include unwanted physical attacks as well as, in Rawls' language, the panoply of morally irrelevant factors such as "the accidents of natural endowment and the contingencies of social circumstance."[51]

But if I am able to consent to anything, may I consent to being killed? May I consent to being a sacrificial victim in a religious ritual? May I consent to becoming a slave? With a thorough rejection of paternalism these scenarios are no doubt possible. In the case of consensual killing[52] we must only make sure that the adult victim did, in fact, consent. Since the victim is no longer able to express her consent – she is dead – the state may very well take precautions to ensure that consent did occur.

---

categories. That is, the state should not pass paternalistic or morals legislation. He implicitly seems to appeal to demonstrability and consent to reject paternalism and morals legislation. But he problematically accepts entirely the "offense to others" category, perhaps failing to realize the aforementioned problem of this kind of emotional harm or disgust.

[50] Mill 1989 [1859]: 15.   [51] Rawls 1971: 14.

[52] This is like the case of Armin Meiwes who killed and ate a consenting victim. In fact, he had a videotape proving that the victim had so consented. Since the harm here is consensual, there is no good reason to punish Meiwes. news.bbc.co.uk/2/hi/europe/3286721.stm.

More interesting is the example of voluntary slavery. Ever since Mill argued that his theory of liberty excludes contracts to slavery, theorists have been plagued with this apparent counter-example to a regime that repudiates paternalism by valuing consent.[53] However, we avoid this difficulty as long as the state treats this contract like it does any other. Discussion of the slavery contract begins with a false premise, namely that a legitimate contract is one where the state forces the parties to carry out its terms where breach is impermissible. For example, in trying to clarify Mill's argument, David Archard poses the issue in the following way: "The problem for Mill's critics lies in the reasons he can offer for refusing to recognize and enforce what is, after all, a freely entered-upon agreement."[54] Archard rightly contends that a "contract without sanctions to enforce it is, in effect, an empty pseudo-contract."[55] But he mistakenly assumes that enforcement means that the parties *must* fulfill the terms of the contract.

If I contract to sell you my lamp and then later decide to keep it, I have breached our contract. Generally within most jurisdictions in the United States[56] you can recover monetary damages to put you in the position you would have been in had the contract been fulfilled. The victim of a breach of contract is entitled only to *damages*.[57] Neither does the law "impose criminal penalties on one who refuses to perform one's promise, nor does it generally require one to pay punitive damages."[58] In no contract is breach illegal or unlawful. But if I assault you, I may not simply compensate you by paying damages. I will probably be prosecuted by the state. Contractual duties are unlike criminal ones. Conflating the two has, I suspect, needlessly posed problems for the philosophical debate over the slavery contract.

The apparent trouble with the slavery contract arises only if one assumes that the party consents to give up or alienate her autonomy or freedom.[59] Rather, given the remedy available to victims of a breach of contract, we should view the slavery contract as one where the party alienates the *value* of her autonomy – not her actual autonomy. Imagine that you contract to become my slave. After a month of fulfilling my commands, you decide to end our agreement. Of course, if you have

---

[53] Mill 1989 [1859]: 102–104, Arneson 1980, Ten 1980: 117–119.
[54] Archard 1990: 455.   [55] Ibid.: 455.
[56] Contract law allows for specific performance only in those unusual cases where damages are not an adequate remedy. Restatement of Contracts (Second) (1981: §. 359–69).
[57] Restatement of Contracts (Second) (1981: Sec. 346).   [58] Farnsworth 1999.
[59] By assuming that the contracting party alienates her autonomy or freedom, Radin (1987) needlessly runs into problems. He fails, like Mill, to characterize the contractual relationship as an alienation of value.

alienated the value of your freedom to me for your entire life, I will no doubt be entitled to a good deal of monetary damages. But that is all I will be entitled to. We therefore accept the voluntary slave contract in line with our commitment to anti-paternalism by treating it like any other personal service or employment contract.

Still, the appeal to consent has been criticized by feminists. These criticisms seem to fall into two camps. Though the first camp claims to be taking aim at the doctrine of consent (or contractualism) it really has its sights set on something else – sexist laws or the private sphere. For example, Catharine MacKinnon argues:

The law of rape divides women into spheres of consent according to indices of relationship to men. Which category of presumed consent a woman is in depends upon who she is relative to a man who wants her, not what she says or does.[60]

According to this objection, the problem is not with consent *per se*, but rather that in certain contexts such consent is erroneously (or hastily) presumed. In fact, the maintenance of the private sphere (as outlined in Chapter 2) has made harm in marriage, family, and our alleged "private" lives difficult to prevent. But where the harm occurs or to whom should not automatically render it consensual. After all, husbands can rape their wives just as a john can rape a prostitute. Feminist theory is correct in pointing out that harm can befall any woman – or anyone for that matter – regardless of her context. Once we purge political and legal theory of the private sphere, all forms of sexual relations are on an equal footing permitting the legitimate use of consent. We need not throw out the baby with the bath water. The two need not fall together. I suspect that most criticism against consent is really an indictment against the private sphere.

The second camp seems to have its sights set more directly on the doctrine of consent. Here the charge is one of false consciousness: even though I think I have consented (I may even expressly have done so), such consent is not real and hence false. For example, and this is commonly appealed to as the paradigmatic instance of false consciousness, though a prostitute may expressly consent to sex for money – the "sexual contract" – such consent is not real.[61] That is, even if conditions are equal – laws are not sexist, the private sphere is abolished, etc. – "sound prostitution"[62] cannot work. The consent is bogus. For Carole Pateman in particular, this

---

[60] MacKinnon 1989: 175.
[61] K. Barry 1995, Jeffreys 1997, Pateman 1988. As Davidson (1998) rightly points out if consent in prostitution is impossible, then there is no legal or normative difference between it and rape.
[62] Ericcson 1980.

is evident because not only are most clients in the sexual contract men (this is not merely a "contingent" fact) but also the services desired are sexual in nature.[63]

Yet, the prostitute's consent would seemingly suffice in *other* contracts or contexts. Her consent would be "authentic" in a situation where she contracted to sell an old piece of furniture for instance. To argue otherwise would render the woman incapable of consenting to any set of obligations – an untenable position that I doubt Pateman or any feminist would be willing to make. That being the case, Pateman's objection is not that the woman who happens to prostitute now and then may not consent *tout court* but only that she is unable to do so in the sexual contract. In other words, she has the capacity to consent in most situations just not in this one. But why? Why is her consent acceptable in other contracts but not the sexual one?

Assuming that such problems are not largely corrected by repeal of the private sphere, those in the false consciousness camp routinely appeal to the presence of male-dominated social relations to un-do consent. They see the "sexual contract" as imbued with such patriarchy. As Pateman writes:

> The patriarchal construction of sexuality, what it means to be a sexual being, is to possess and to have access to sexual property. How access is gained and how the property is used is made clear in the story of the demand of the brothers for equal access to women's bodies.[64]

Given the presence of such male domination in the "sexual contract," consent is not real.

But, and here's the trouble, such male hierarchical structures should prevent consent in a wide variety of other contracts as well. Patriarchy occurs in voluntary associations too not just the "sexual contract." Take as a prime example the Catholic Church. Undoubtedly, the practice of ordaining only men, repudiating homosexuality, and extolling traditional conceptions of marriage, to name just a few, create and reify patriarchy. Would Pateman find problems, then, with the "Catholic contract"? Should we prevent Catholic women from attending church services officiated by priests on the grounds that their consent is not real or false? I doubt Pateman would go that far. Since the false consciousness camp takes aim at only the "sexual contract," its concern cannot be with just the harm of male domination. A worry about male domination and patriarchy would invariably un-do consent in a variety of other contexts.

---

[63] Pateman 1988: 190–193.   [64] Ibid.: 185.

Rather, there is something peculiar about the sexual contract and prostitution having nothing to do with patriarchy that seemingly prevents consent by the woman. But then what is this concern but blatant paternalism? Paternalism admits that the party has consented to drug use or suicide, but contends that it is in their best interests to refrain from engaging in it. Similarly, the prostitute does not know what is in her best interest. If this paternalistic rationale underlies a prohibition on prostitution, it is plainly illegitimate. Paternalistic legislation fails the requirement of non-consent.

Interestingly, Sandra Schneiders, a feminist theologian who outlines the debilitating patriarchy in the Catholic Church, holds out for a "feminist spirituality" to overcome such male-dominated structures.[65] Rather than question the consent of Catholic women – prohibit the "Catholic contract" outright – she hopes such women will reform and transform the church. In this way, by honoring an adult woman's consent in such voluntary associations – associations that may very well be patriarchal – we allow women to internally reshape such sexist practices.[66]

In fact, in advocating for equality, prostitutes have also sought to characterize themselves as just like other legitimate workers.[67] The alleged presence of patriarchy and male domination should not be sufficient to un-do it. By acknowledging the presence of consent, these women are in a position, if they so desire, to change or alter the practice. Adherence to false consciousness undercuts the adult woman's ability to critique and reform the patriarchal practice from the inside. If her consent is false, she is *not* a legitimate member of the group or the practice, her effective voice is silenced.

I do not deny that perhaps prostitution and maybe even the Catholic Church harms or dominates women. Such patriarchal structures may have harmful consequences for all women. But the polity may not act on behalf of the *contracting* party – the prostitute or the Catholic. If the woman chooses to join the Church or chooses to prostitute herself, under my theory of Justification, the state may not interfere on grounds that such activity is not in the best interests of the participating women. It may not un-do her consent. Yet, as we will see in the next chapter, if the polity genuinely regulates or prohibits prostitution to minimize the non-consensual harm to *others* (not focusing on the best interests of the prostitute but perhaps women in general), it may do so.

---

[65] Schneiders 2004.   [66] Cf. Y. al-Hibri 1999.   [67] Jeffreys 1997: 162–168.

Democracy

While demonstrability and consent are the most explicit justificatory constraints, democracy itself works as an important mechanism in this theory. Unlike the conventional account of limited government, my theory of Justification explicitly requires the need for democracy. After all, together with the limitation on *only* minimizing harm, democratic considerations ensure much of our freedom and equality. Much like Habermas, I see democracy as integral to a regime of limited government. There are many kinds of democracy: minimal, deliberative, participatory, etc. This book is not directly about democratic theory – nor need it be. My argument works with various kinds of democracies. It assumes that, at the very least, a democratic polity is one where institutions properly ensure, *inter alia*, the ability to vote and participate in elections.[68] My purpose is to uphold the need for majority rule balancing it with liberty. I use a somewhat stripped-down version of democracy to emphasize the problem of majority tyranny. Obviously, if one, for example, assumes a thicker notion of democracy or assumes that under proper deliberating conditions or circumstances, people will on the whole act better, rendering tyranny less likely, the problem of balancing liberty and democracy is assumed away. Moreover, if a stripped-down version of democracy is sufficient in establishing my positive argument, any more robust conception of democracy will *a fortiori* work.

Those who reject democracy wholesale, who refuse to believe that value exists in a democratic arrangement, will no doubt find my general argument unconvincing. Again, I assume we care about democracy. I take it as rightly non-negotiable. We care about the minimal republican insight that the will of the majority has some independent value. Democratic flexibility permits various polities to decide what is in their best interest. The real task is how to limit democracy just enough to ensure liberty.

That said Habermas erred by going too far in relying on it. Mere democratic procedures and nothing more are *unable* to ensure equality and freedom. Without the constraints of demonstrability and consent, the democratic majority may pass sodomy or anti-miscegenation laws, restrict a group's freedom by imposing a system of segregation on the basis of race or hair color, or limit the institution of marriage to opposite sex couples.

---

[68] Perhaps Robert Dahl's eight requirements for a basic democracy would serve as a non-controversial definition of it: "1. Freedom to form and join organizations," "2. Freedom of expression," "3. Right to vote," "4. Eligibility for public office," "5. Right of political leaders to compete for support," "6. Alternative sources of information," "7. Free and fair elections," and "8. Institutions for making government policies depend on votes and other expressions of preference" (Dahl 1971: 3).

For these freedoms, faith in the democratic majority is ill placed. I suspect that Mill, Tocqueville, and Berlin had these kinds of scenarios in mind when worrying about democratic oppression. This is why we must limit democratic decision-making.

But this is not to say that democracy does not guarantee *some* freedom. My theory of Justification appeals to the overlooked constraint of democracy in doing just that. My account of limited government, unlike the conventional one, specifically entertains and requires a role for democracy. Robert Dahl, for instance, claims that democracies are better at protecting certain rights and liberties than non-democracies.[69] He contends that a democracy will ensure certain freedoms.[70] Since democracy already assumes that individuals will have the same basic freedom to vote, run for office, speak and associate, these are guaranteed by democracy's very existence. More significantly, taking Dahl's argument farther, bodily integrity and some kind of due process are also assured because as human beings we all have interests in providing ourselves with such freedoms. As long as we all value an interest equally – all of us would desire to be free from physical harm or be afforded criminal due process – the majority will provide it.

After all, my theory simply outlines the appropriate rationale for state action. *How* and *if* the democratic majority minimizes the relevant harm is entirely up to it. Leaving the democratic polity to do so permits and entails the need for "democratic iteration" while simultaneously securing equality and freedom. My constraint does not require the polity to prevent or minimize demonstrable, non-consensual harm. Theoretically a democratic majority could decide *not* to prevent any harm at all. Again, it need not institute a robust welfare state. Following Habermas, mine is a maxim-testing device: "Practical discourse is a procedure for testing the validity of hypothetical norms, not for producing justified norms."[71] It dictates what the polity may do, not what it must do. In the language of Oakeshott, it is non-instrumental. This means that the polity need not do anything. Limiting government in this way places the burden to act on the democratic majority.

Even Mill interprets his simple principle of harm prevention in a maxim-testing way. Once harm has been identified, "society has jurisdiction over it, and the question whether the general welfare will or will not be promoted by interfering with it, becomes open to discussion."[72] Mill does not *require* that the state prevent or remedy harm. Mill says that the "only purpose for which power *can* be rightfully exercised over any member of a

---

[69] Dahl 2001.   [70] Ibid.: 132–139.   [71] Habermas 1990: 122.   [72] Mill 1989 [1859]: 76.

civilised community, against his will, is to prevent harm to others."[73] Mill could have said that power *must* be exercised to prevent harm. But he specifically uses the word "can" instead of "must." This implies that the polity need not seek to prevent harm. It need not, for example, pass laws against murder. Rather, *when* it acts, it must seek to prevent such harm. This rightly leaves decisions about how and whether to prevent harm "open to discussion," open to "democratic iteration."

The necessity of democracy should now be apparent. Although possible, who would refuse to vote for legislation outlawing murder or rape? What legislator or relevant democratic representative would refuse to propose such a bill? If exit costs are the same for everyone, democracy will provide the benefit. Admittedly, this pure appeal to democracy will only *ensure* a few minimum guarantees such as physical security. But that is sufficient to make my argument. We are free from acts of physical harm in the democratic polity not because of some right that transcends the democratic process. Instead, since actual members of a democratic polity will undoubtedly provide for such protection, its presence is guaranteed by the democratic community not some a-contextual, normative right or commitment to bodily integrity.

In the same way, we have every reason to believe that a democratic polity will provide for some kind of due process. Since everyone has a chance of being wrongly caught up in the criminal justice system, the majority will pass laws affording such process. In fact, no democracy – present or past – has refused to protect its members from acts threatening their physical security or honor some kind of due process for its citizens. It is this insight that under-girds the constraint of democracy. As long as the franchise is extended to all members of the polity, we can rest assured that the majority will pass laws against murder and the like as well as securing some kind of criminal due process.

Guido Calabresi makes a similar point cashing out this argument in terms of costs.[74] He argues that as long as costs are borne equally by all members of the polity and not just by a particular group, we should not fear a commitment to majoritarian rule.[75] This is not a thought experiment where we imagine that most individuals would pass laws against murder and the like. The constraint is not one in theory – like Rawls' veil of ignorance – but one grounded in real world democratic communities. Actual embodied individuals in democracies have as an empirical matter passed such legislation.[76] By doing so, we leave the community to define our normative obligations.

---

[73] Ibid.: 13 (emphasis added).   [74] Calabresi 1990.   [75] Ibid.: 91–103.

[76] Empirical research bears out the argument that the existence of a democracy reduces repressive behavior. See, e.g., Davenport 2007, Poe and Tate 1994.

For instance, the polity may create any number of economic systems – libertarianism, communism, and a robust welfare state, to name just a few. There is no need to go so far as to *require* the democratic polity to pass certain kinds of legislation. Doing so needlessly undercuts democratic flexibility and discretion by positing affirmative rights.

But could the polity pass a law to limit how much sex someone may have? Could it decide that on a certain day, it is illegal to engage in it? Imagine that the polity can demonstrate in good faith that refraining from sex can increase efficiency in terms of economic productivity. Given my commitment to the minimization of demonstrable harm, these are no doubt possible scenarios. The polity may pass any kind of legislation as long as it has a good reason to do so. Again, I entertain a broad notion of harm, one that includes inefficiency. But the democratic polity will have to decide to curtail sex in this way. If everyone must bear the cost of such proposed legislation, we should be less concerned (if at all) about these hypotheticals becoming reality.

Suppose though these same legislators desired to pass a law that minimized physical harm only if it was inflicted on a certain group or prohibited only a certain group from having sex to increase productivity. For instance, imagine a law that minimizes such harm only if it is visited on redheads but not on others. Or a law that says only those with long hair are prohibited from having sex. Or, suppose the legislation fails to mitigate harm in the family or in certain religious or cultural groups but minimizes it in other areas. These kinds of legislation would undoubtedly fail my theory of Justification. Here the problem is the "only" provision of the justificatory constraint.

In limiting the law's application to only those of a particular race or those with a certain hair color, the polity obviously seeks to do *something else* in addition to minimizing harm – perhaps it hopes to oppress a certain group or to privilege another. These limitations in the law are irrational or arbitrary. These are barred by my justificatory constraint. This is Justice Ginsburg's very objection to the partial birth abortion ban. As Ginsburg correctly points out, the ban does not save one single fetus. The majority must *exclusively* seek to minimize harm. To limit the law to certain individuals and not others or to certain activities and not others suggests that an improper motive is afoot. This was the intrinsic problem with an appeal to emotional distress.

In asking the legislators why they have limited the law's application to certain individuals and not others, they would have to appeal to something other than the overall goal of minimizing harm – unless, of course, some are harmed less. Put more perspicuously, the polity would need to offer plausible evidence to show that limiting the law's protection of individuals with a certain color or length of hair aids in the minimization of harm. This does not necessarily rule out "one step at a time" measures, measures that inform a commitment to democratic flexibility. A polity may very well decide to minimize only some portion of the relevant demonstrable harm. It may decide to leave the rest for another day. It is up to the polity to carry out the relevant cost/benefit analysis. But this is possible as long as there is a rational reason for the partial harm minimization. Again, as Ginsburg points out in *Gonzales*, Congress did not have a rational reason to prohibit one kind of abortion procedure but not others. After all, there has to be a good faith basis why the polity has chosen to minimize harm in a particular way.

Suppose the polity decides to remedy the economic harm of high prices by subsidizing farm products. In order to test the policy, it chooses wheat farmers because the price of wheat is particularly high or because the law's effect on that industry would be particularly instructive in determining the feasibility of a more comprehensive measure. Here the decision to minimize economic harm is no doubt rational. The polity's choice to minimize harm in this way makes sense. Of course, if the democratic polity subsidizes only farmers with blond hair, this does not seem to relate to the overall rationale of reducing economic harm. This democratic choice is irrational – un-connected to harm minimization – and thus barred by my justificatory constraint. Such a policy does not only seek to minimize harm. It fails my account of limited government.

The Supreme Court faced this exact issue in *Railway Express v. New York* (1949). In seeking to minimize traffic nuisances – a demonstrable harm to be sure – New York prohibited all vehicles from affixing advertising signs to their vehicles that were unrelated to the drivers' businesses. The Court held that the distinction between an advertising sign that is related to one's business and a sign that is not so related does not run afoul of the equal protection clause. In other words, the distinction is permissible. The Court reasoned that as long as such a distinction is related to mitigating the harm, it is acceptable. For example, the Court noted that those signs unrelated to the driver's business might be more obnoxious or distracting than those signs that are so related.[77] Though not mentioned by the Court, it could also turn out that given the city's resources and personnel, it is easier to crack down on those whose signs are unrelated to their business. Put in my lingo, there must be some publicly ascertainable reason related to the minimization of harm to justify the distinction, the decision to focus on certain signs and not others.[78] Contrastingly, if the

[77] *Railway Express* at 110.
[78] Justice Jackson's concurrence (111, Jackson concurring) in the case, however, seems too permissive. He contends that even if the two signs were equally obnoxious, the city could

city only prohibited signs on trucks driven by redheads, this distinction – redheads versus non-redheads – seems unrelated to mitigating traffic nuisances. Such a distinction would be irrational.

We must ascertain whether the polity *exclusively* seeks to prevent such harm. As I've intimated, this is not merely whether the law is over or under inclusive. Such considerations may be indicia that the polity seeks to do something more than prevent harm but they are not dispositive. Rather, we must ascertain if the polity has a good reason – one related to harm prevention – that explains why the law is over or under inclusive. Here we may have to look beyond the particular law itself examining other policies or laws the polity has promulgated or failed to promulgate.

Consider the following example. Suppose a polity contends that preventing gay sex prevents the spread of various kinds of sexually transmitted diseases (STDs) such as HIV/AIDS.[79] This is no doubt a proper reason on which the polity may act. It appeals to some demonstrable harm. The distinction between those that engage in gay sex and those that do not may very well be rational to remedying this harm. Again, this does not end the inquiry. We must ascertain whether the polity *exclusively* seeks to prevent such harm. For example, does the law prohibit promiscuous risky heterosexual sex – also a cause of STDs? There may be a good reason why the law is under inclusive – only prohibiting gay sex but not its straight counterpart. Maybe gay sex is riskier than straight sex. But then we must ask whether the law prohibits *protected* homosexual sex. Here there must be a good reason why the polity is being over inclusive – prohibiting protected and unprotected sex. If the polity truly cares about only preventing demonstrable harm – the spread of STDs – why is it needlessly casting such a wide net? These are the kinds of questions we can ask to smoke out illicit rationales.

Even more telling is whether the polity prohibits same-sex marriages, marriages that may very well encourage less promiscuity and thus less risky sexual behavior among the gay population. If the polity prohibits same-sex marriage how can it consistently also contend that it prohibits sodomy to prevent the spread of STDs? If the concern is truly with the spread of sexually transmitted diseases, why not encourage monogamy by permitting same-sex marriage? The reason I suspect is one of bad faith. We should be quite skeptical of the claim that such a polity *only* seeks to prevent harm. After all, it is no surprise that those who are for sodomy laws are against same-sex marriage. This is because these individuals cannot

---

still operate under this distinction. As a result, my position tracks the majority opinion. There has to be something about the distinction that somehow aids in the minimization of the harm.

[79] Cf. Harcourt 1999.

care about simply preventing the spread of STDs. If they did, they'd be far more likely to *champion* same-sex marriage in the hope of reducing risky sexual practices. Instead, they actively repudiate same-sex marriage, indicating that their genuine rationale is patently homophobic. They really seek to root out some kind of non-demonstrable harm. Harm prevention turns out to be nothing more than a pretext. A simple holistic look at the relevant laws and policies suggests that something more than mere demonstrable harm prevention is afoot, thereby failing my justificatory constraint.[80]

The language of rights distracts us from this kind of inquiry. By scrutinizing the polity's reason or rationale for acting in this way, we fetter out "flimsy and transparent" justifications. And in doing so, a court need simply invalidate laws that rest on such disingenuous claims of harm prevention. We need not deploy the right to privacy or the right to equality to thwart such tyrannies of the majority. Simply interrogating the polity's genuine rationale for passing a law is sufficient.

My account of limited government hinges on making sure that the polity acts in good faith. The "only" requirement ensures this. It is no surprise that actual sodomy laws prohibit oral and anal sex whether committed by men or women. It is telling that there has been no confirmed case of female-to-female sexual transmission of HIV in the United States.[81] This suggests, then, that a polity that passes such a sodomy law does so on the pretext of preventing demonstrable harm. Such a polity may seek to oppress a group or prevent some kind of non-demonstrable harm, rationales that fail my justificatory constraint. Consequently, the "only" requirement – ensuring the polity only prevents harm – smokes out disingenuous claims of demonstrable harm prevention. But again, Justification does not dictate substantive outcomes – e.g., gay sex or any kind of sex may never be regulated – but only the reasons the polity may proffer in passing legislation.

---

[80] In his work on profiles and probabilities, Frederick Schauer (2003) also implicitly endorses the "only" constraint. He argues that race, sex and the like may very well be non-spurious indicators or proxies for legitimate traits such as upper body strength or likelihood of carrying drugs. However, if the relevant actor uses only this proxy, it suggests that something other than mere efficiency is afoot. "To pick out only one from a large array of nonspurious proxies for material qualifications strongly suggests that the employer has a goal other than that of using efficient proxies in making employment decisions, for if that were the case then some of the other proxies would have been employed as well" (Schauer 2003: 148). Thus, we can determine whether the polity exclusively seeks to prevent harm by examining what other policies it employs or fails to employ. Cf. Macedo 1995.

[81] Center for Disease Control Fact Sheet Regarding *HIV/AIDS among Women Who Have Sex With Women*, 2006, www.cdc.gov/hiv/topics/women/resources/factsheets/wsw.htm.

Laws fail my account of limited government when they inappropriately aim to elevate one group over another or to minimize some non-demonstrable injury. For example, it is the existence of the private sphere that permitted husbands to physically abuse their wives with impunity. Such distinctions (single woman, prostitute, wife) are effectively ruled out by my theory of Justification, a theory that rejects the private sphere. Similarly, limiting the law's reach to only the public sphere, as the conventional account of limited government suggests, is just as irrational as Devlin's claim that society will crumble if gay sex is officially allowed.

Similarly, armed with this democratic constraint, we can dispense with the troubling conventional examples of utilitarianism without appeal to rights. For instance, take the familiar example of the surgeon who can save five people by forcibly harvesting the organs of one healthy one.[82] Suppose a polity decides to implement legislation to that effect: a person in the polity will be chosen at random and her organs forcibly harvested to five sick individuals suffering from the non-consensual harm of organ failure. The polity decides to minimize net harm in this way. Most conventional responses to such a scenario appeal to non-democratic solutions.[83] For example, such a law would violate some deontological theory – here the right to be free from unwanted intrusion of bodily integrity. The conventional method of limiting government rules such scenarios out, because they violate our rights. This is why framing Mill as the paradigmatic rights-based liberal is at odds with his commitment to utilitarianism.

But, in accord with my account of limited government, democracy is our best response against the forced organ donor legislation. The democratic regime may theoretically institute it. As long as everyone is allowed to vote and participate in the decision to carry out such a proposal, there is no ground on which to overturn it. In removing organs to save more lives, the polity is certainly minimizing demonstrable, non-consensual harm and nothing more. This possibility exemplifies Mill's commitment to utilitarianism, placing the utilitarian calculus of harm minimization in the hands of the democratic polity.

Nevertheless, and here's the rub, who would vote for such legislation? What actual democratic community would do so? If anyone can be the victim of such harvesting, there is every reason to believe that the polity will vote down such legislation. In fact, a legislator would be foolish to even introduce it. Though a possibility open to the polity, it is hard to

---

[82] Thompson 1976.

[83] See, e.g., Rawls (1971) and Nozick (1974). Both appeal to some version of rights to reject utilitarianism. In Samuel Scheffler's (1998) volume, various authors criticize utilitarianism by appeal to some kind of agent-relative moralities or constraints.

imagine such legislation being contemplated in a legislature. We would not need a court to strike down such a statute – it would almost certainly never pass. I know of no extant or past democracy that has instituted anything like a forced organ transplant system. As we will see in the abortion debate, the common law does not even recognize a minimal duty to help.

This exemplifies the appropriate relationship between democracy and the rule of law. We need a democratic decision – a law – to protect our bodily integrity. When a contemplated policy must affect everyone (that is, it may not be un-equally imposed on a singled-out group) and everyone values its non-implementation equally, democracy functions as the appropriate constraint. By its very terms, my justificatory constraint does not compel action by the state. By adopting it, we can and should reject rights. This is the explicit task of the next chapter.

5   Rejecting rights

By simply holding that the democratic polity may only seek to minimize demonstrable, non-consensual harm, rights turn out to be obsolete. We should confidently reject them. Accepting my theory of Justification, we bypass the need to connect liberty with the question of "who governs" us. We need not struggle over getting the square peg in the round hole. Our normative attention is rightly just on the democratic state.

In this chapter I further explore and outline this argument by considering the ramifications of rejecting rights. Admittedly, I do not explore in detail every application of this justificatory constraint. Doing so would lose sight of the proverbial forest. Rather, I highlight its salient features, examining the general way in which this re-conceptualized rubric of limited government works. To that end, this chapter is in three parts. First, I show that a turn to Justification not only avoids a "democratic deficit" but also permits a more rewarding and productive democratic debate. My account of limited government better values democracy. Second, I examine the rights to intimacy, property, and religion, rights that have particular purchase as components of the conventional private sphere. I argue that we are better off repudiating them, turning to legislative purpose. Third, I argue that theorists have unfortunately failed to realize that an appreciation of Justification renders rights obsolete.

Promoting democratic debate

By appropriately constraining democratic decision-making, rejecting rights may (hopefully) not seem so alarming. The constraints of demonstrability and consent repudiate morals legislation and paternalism – without the need for the rights to privacy or equality. And democracy itself ensures that the polity will pass laws securing bodily integrity and due process. Appeal to the relevant right is unnecessary. A turn to legislative purpose, to the democratic polity's reason for acting, is sufficient.

Even the right to free speech – a staple in the regime of rights – is obsolete under my account of limited government. Some principle of free speech stands at the core of democracy.[1] Freedom to speak, publish, and associate is "critical to the functioning of an open and effective democratic process."[2] In order to realize a genuine democratic form of government, individuals must be able to speak and associate freely. How else can we choose democratic representatives who will sufficiently represent our interests? We preserve free speech by way of a commitment to democracy. After all, my theory of Justification assumes the existence of democratic institutions. According to Habermas, democracy requires that everyone have an equal chance to speak, be heard and participate in the democratic, deliberative process.[3] Such conditions are immanent to the very task of Justification.

Additionally, what reason could the polity proffer for severely limiting what we say or even whom we associate with? Such legislation would violate the requirement of demonstrability. The democratic majority will be hard pressed to limit what people say or do or engage in on grounds of decency or offensiveness. Such rationales seek to minimize some non-demonstrable harm or problematically regulate emotional distress. For example, mere exhortations that pornography or controversial art is displeasing are insufficient to pass my justificatory constraint.

But the polity may decide to censor material in order to minimize physical harm, exemplifying the value of democratic flexibility. Polities may very well disagree in good faith about how much free speech to restrict. For example, the fault standard for establishing libel depends on the notoriety or fame of the plaintiff in the United States – making it harder for a famous person to recover damages – but is generally uniform under English law – making it easier.[4]

Even American case law permits the regulation of speech that is "directed to inciting or producing imminent lawless action and is likely to incite or produce such action."[5] In this important respect, the debate over heterosexual pornography can only rest on whether such material harms women.[6] As long as the polity acts in good faith, the majority may decide to regulate or prohibit it for this reason. However, simply proclaiming that pornography is too shocking, depraved, or offensive will not suffice as appropriate justifications. These rationales are plainly inadmissible under my justificatory constraint.

---

[1] The democratic defense of free speech is most closely associated with Meiklejohn (1948).
[2] John Ely 1980: 105.   [3] Habermas 1990: 86–94, 2001: 116–118.
[4] Glasser 2006: 51, 208.   [5] *Brandenburg v. Ohio*, 395 U.S. 444 (1969).
[6] For example, there are some who maintain such material invariably causes sexual crime (A. Dworkin 1981, MacKinnon 1987, Jeffreys 1990) and others who find the claim unsupportable (R. Dworkin 1985). For an interesting debate on how Mill would respond to the harm of pornography, see Dyzenhaus (1997) and Skipper (1997).

Unfortunately, much of the pornography debate trades in the language of rights or classifications. Some see it as a women's issue. Others view it as a private matter – holding fast to the right to privacy. Constitutional scholars even debate whether pornography is speech at all.[7] As a deliberative democrat, Benhabib validates the substantive role of democracy but problematically links it to rights. She writes:

> Whether pornography is to be defined as a question of the reasonable limitations to be imposed upon the First Amendment right of free speech; whether pornography is to be thought of as a private, moral issue concerning matters of sexual taste and style; whether pornography is to be thought of as a matter of aesthetic-cultural sensibility and as a question of artistic fantasy – we simply cannot know before the process of unconstrained public dialogue has run its course.[8]

Benhabib rightly looks to a decision by the democratic majority but needlessly obscures it. Who cares what box pornography belongs in – art, taste, fantasy? If such material does not lead to harm, there is no good reason to prohibit it. If it does, then there is a good reason to do so. By focusing on the rationale behind the polity's decision to act, leaving behind any concern with individuals or groups, we keep the debate relevant and focused.

Issues like abortion and affirmative action are also beset by the frustrating talk of rights. Here I analyze abortion leaving the debate over affirmative action for Part III. The abortion debate is too often marked by stark, mutually exclusive choices. I argue that my justificatory constraint opens up the range of democratic options simultaneously securing liberty. Take the two most extreme opposing positions in the abortion controversy: the pro-lifer who says no abortion even in the case of rape or incest and the pro-choicer who says abortion for any reason. My hope in simply thinking through these extreme cases is to generate a clearer, more convincing argument. If the turn to legislative purpose can provide even these positions with democratic room to talk *to* one another instead of past one another, its superiority to a rights regime should be easier to see.

Turning to legislative purpose to limit government immediately places the burden on the pro-lifer to justify the abortion statute. With no such statute, a woman would be able to abort. The pro-lifer must profess a reason for a law against abortion. And, given my justificatory constraint, this rationale must be one of minimizing harm.[9] The pro-lifer would

---

[7] In *Roth v. United States*, 354 U.S. 476 (1957) the Court held that obscenity is not protected under the First Amendment. Frederick Schauer (1979) makes a similar argument about pornography. But Kalven (1960) criticizes these cases, arguing that this non-speech approach fails to home in on the issue of whether such material (here obscenity) causes harm.

[8] Benhabib 1992: 99.

[9] In fact, there is also the harm the woman suffers from the fetus itself. Regan and Thompson also argue that abortion is justifiable as a kind of self-defense (Regan 1979: 1611–1618,

contend that an abortion law seeks to prevent harm to the fetus. Pro-life advocates see the fetus as a person.[10] Suppose that the majority decides that *failing* to carry the fetus to term – deciding to terminate the pregnancy by removing the fetus – is a harm. No matter how the woman got pregnant (be it by rape, incest, or consensual sex), the innocent life in her must be saved from harm, or so the pro-lifer contends. As a result, the majority passes a law outlawing abortion. Even though the pregnant woman has no desire to carry the fetus to term (presume she can do so without herself dying), the polity has decided that she must do so.

Under my theory of Justification, the polity may make this decision. Passing an abortion statute does not seem to run afoul of the constraint. It seeks straightforwardly to minimize harm to the fetus. However, this may very well commit the polity to passing more than just laws against abortion. Judith Thompson in her famous defense of abortion argues that even if the fetus is a person, this does not preclude abortion.[11] She imagines that we wake up one day attached by a tube to a famous violinist. Suppose the violinist will most certainly die if the tube is removed just as the fetus will die if it is removed from its mother. Thompson, in appealing to rights, argues that we have a right to remove the tube even though as a result the violinist will die.

Unfortunately, her famous example has been used to claim that there is such a right, that women must have the right to abort. The more illuminating point of Thompson's example is not that we have a right to remove the tube – such a position brings us back to the problematic options explored above – but that if we prohibit abortion, we *may also have to* pass a law requiring that the tube not be removed. Doing anything else is irrational. Why? If the polity has decided to compel the mother to minimize harm, it has no rational reason not to compel others in similar situations to help as well. Said differently, if the polity considers cutting the umbilical cord an act of "killing" the fetus, it must consider removing the tube an act of "killing" the violinist.

After all, if the pro-lifer imposes the burden of carrying the fetus on the pregnant women who was raped, she should compel me to stay attached to the violinist. Specifically, and this is the crucial point, the "one step at a

---

Thompson 1971: 50–53). Since the law already allows self-defense against an "innocent attacker" there is no good reason why the fetus cannot count as one (Regan 1979: 1617, Thompson 1971: 52). A turn to harm minimization leaves this kind of argument very much alive and relevant. The polity would have to offer a reason – one related to minimizing harm – that does not consider terminating the pregnancy a kind of self-defense. It would have to justify this "one step at a time" measure. The connection between self-defense and abortion goes unnoticed given the presence of rights.

[10] Similarly, the polity may decide that killing animals constitutes a harm as well. Of course, doing so may pose problems for eating meat; but again, this is for the polity to decide and work out.

[11] Thompson 1971.

time" measure of forcing women to minimize harm by carrying the fetus to term but no one else seems unrelated to the goal of harm minimization. Like the federal partial birth abortion ban, such a distinction seems arbitrary.

As Donald Regan, a legal academic, rightly makes clear, American law does not generally require such compelled Samaritanism.[12] If the rationale behind passing a law against abortion is to ensure that someone sustains a life even against her will, why is this obligation only visited upon women? Why does the woman "kill" the fetus when she fails to sustain it, but I don't "kill" the violinist (or any such individual) by failing to help? Only by rejecting the distracting doctrine of rights can we appreciate the force of this charge. If the polity decides to minimize the net harm of failing to aid by forcing women to do so for nine months, it seems irrational not to require anyone else to do the same.

Even the objection that the pro-lifer cares about harm to innocent life, not just any life, is unpersuasive. Suppose I happen to come across a drowning child in a lake who through no fault of her own finds herself in this predicament. Imagine someone else threw her in. Imagine further that to save her, I need only get my pants wet. If the pro-lifer cares about minimizing harm to the fetus by forcing the mother to carry it to term, she must *a fortiori* care about the harm to the child, a child who can only be saved by forcing the bystander to help. (We can imagine a scenario where the violinist is innocent as well.) Since a law against abortion effectively conscripts a woman's body to save life, the polity must so conscript others. Otherwise, the rationale cannot be one of only harm minimization.

But the current state of American law repudiates such forced Good Samaritan duties. It flatly rejects such conscription. The Restatement of Torts says as much: "The fact that the actor realizes that action on his part is necessary for another's aid or protection does not itself impose upon him a duty to take such action."[13] Moreover, the majority of states in the United States fail to legally compel this kind of aid.[14] In other words, failing to help the drowning child – "killing" her – is not a crime in most

---

[12] Whereas Regan (1979) primarily looks to the common law in arguing against abortion laws, Andrew Koppelman suggests that the Thirteenth Amendment's prohibition on involuntary servitude stands as the best constitutional basis to invalidate them (Koppelman 1990). See also Tribe (1988: 1354). Though I am sympathetic to this argument, Koppelman fails to realize that this conscription argument has been drowned out by the needless talk of rights.

[13] Restatement 1965.

[14] Only Minnesota (M.S.A. § 604A.01 (2001)) and Vermont (12 V.S.A. § 519 (1968)) have such required Good Samaritan laws. Six other states (Hawaii, Massachusetts, Ohio, Rhode Island, Washington, and Wisconsin) have adopted more limited Samaritan statutes requiring that the bystander know that a crime is being committed that would expose the victim to bodily harm (Eisenberg 2002: 654, fn. 25).

places. Said differently, the law does not generally *require* that I help others in critical need.

Yet, the current abortion debate in the United States entirely ignores the issue of compelled aid or forced Samaritanism. I suspect if it did, perhaps the pro-life position would seem unpalatable, even to those who currently advocate it. Instead, pro-life supporters only seem to care about visiting this burden of nine months of Samaritanism on pregnant women. They do not challenge the current status of the law that explicitly neglects to compel aid. Their concern is only about pregnant women, about the health of fetuses not the health of others. There is no reason why we cannot have laws compelling aid or help. Turning to legislative purpose permits this democratic flexibility. But with nothing to explain this "one step at a time" measure, simply requiring women to do so suggests that something else in addition to harm minimization is going on.

Perhaps the pro-lifer will respond that this "one step at a time" decision is sound, because pregnant women are the only ones who can save the fetus. Whereas others can save the child in the lake, the woman is the sole possible Good Samaritan. Thus, it makes sense to visit the burden on her and not others. But it could turn out that you are the only one who can save the drowning child – or any child in need for that matter. Even in this simple case, American law *does not* impose such a burden to help.

Moreover, it's not at all clear to me why the pregnant woman has a monopoly on the opportunity to help the fetus. If the fetus cannot be removed without destroying it, admittedly, she is the only one who can carry the fetus to term. But this does not mean she has to shoulder all the costs. This doesn't mean she is the only one who can help. Why can't the state assist her by compensating her for the pregnancy? Or why can't the man who impregnated the woman be liable for such damages in an effort to mitigate or alleviate the woman's burden? So the pro-lifer will have to explain not only why she has imposed a duty to help exclusively on pregnant women but also why she refuses to compensate the woman who carries the child to term. After all, we pay even those whom we conscript to fight a war. Why is the pregnant woman treated differently?

Add insult to injury, the passerby that sees the drowning child in the lake, unlike the pregnant woman or the person attached to the famous violinist for nine months, suffers minimal hardship in being forced to save the child's life. Forcing the pregnant woman to carry a child to term exposes her to great physical burdens, burdens that the law is very reluctant to impose on others.[15] A woman must, for example, eat properly

---

[15] Regan 1979: 1579–1591.

avoiding many kinds of activities that could endanger the fetus. Vermont's forced Good Samaritan law, one of only a few such statutes in the United States, only compels help if it can be done "without danger or peril to" oneself or "interference with" other important duties.[16] It requires far less than what an abortion statute requires of women. The Texas abortion statute at issue in *Roe* only permitted an exception for "saving the life of the mother."[17] The comparison is stark and telling. Under the Vermont statute, you *need not* help if doing so will expose you to some non-life-threatening danger or interfere with other "important" duties.[18] The abortion statute, though, requires the pregnant woman to carry the fetus to term for nine months unless doing so threatens her very life.

While there may even be disagreement over whether the fetus is a person, there is no doubt that the innocent drowning child is one. In fact, the penalty for violating the Vermont statute – for failing to help – is a fine of no more than $100. Contrastingly, the statute overturned in *Roe* doled out a prison sentence of two to five years for anyone helping a woman procure an abortion.[19]

Perhaps the pro-lifer will respond that abortion cases far exceed those requiring Good Samaritanism. And since it's easier to force women to carry a fetus to term rather than force individuals to save drowning children, it makes sense to focus only on preventing abortion. But, and this is precisely the point, the debate is not carried out in these terms, terms that structure the controversy in a more constructive, democratic fashion. If the debate were carried out within the language of Justification rather than in the locution rights, opposing factions might be more likely to speak to one another rather than past one another. These assertions are not even floated in the debate. And, even if they are true, why can't a polity pass a law requiring individuals to help knowing that this law may be harder to enforce than one prohibiting abortion? Why can't the polity pass such a law so as to make clear that the concern is genuinely one of saving life? And again, if the pro-lifer concedes that such an obligation should, everything else being equal, be imposed on all, why is compensation not even discussed? Why is there no talk of compensating women for carrying this burden, a burden that the pro-lifer *apparently* concedes should be (ideally) imposed on all? Rather, the pro-lifer stakes her claim without even addressing these issues or questions suggesting that she does not operate within the framework of Justification I propose here.

Just this cursory assessment suggests that those against abortion may very well care about something other than minimizing harm. Perhaps

---

[16] 12 V.S.A. § 519 (a) (1968).   [17] *Roe* at 188.
[18] 12 V.S.A. § 519 (a) (1968).   [19] Ibid.: at 118.

those against abortion seek to oppress or subjugate women by requiring only women to bear this burden. Perhaps they desire to institute and sustain antiquated gender roles ensuring that women stay out of the work force. My justificatory constraint rules out these reasons. As Thompson correctly states:

> And it shows also that the groups currently working against liberalization of abortion laws, in fact working toward having it declared unconstitutional for a state to permit abortion, had better start working for the adoption of Good Samaritan laws generally, or earn the charge that they are acting in bad faith.[20]

This charge of "bad faith" arises because the current abortion debate is not concerned about minimizing harm in this way, about forced Samaritanism. Without facing up to the implications of its platform, the pro-life position, as it is currently articulated, seems to do something more than simply mitigate harm. Put glibly, it seems to care about something other than just life. Whatever it is, under my theory of Justification, a democratic polity's laws may not be based on it.

This is not because of a right to equality. The fact that women *qua* women are burdened is not doing the normative work. This would once again have us look to the individuals or group of individuals who are being burdened, asking, for instance, whether they are a suspect class. I will more directly criticize the doctrines of class and classification in Chapter 8. Rather, reconsideration of the abortion debate squarely turns on just the legislative purpose. For example, if merely redheads were required to offer aid, this would also point to an illegitimate purpose. The fact that only some are being irrationally burdened – no matter who they are – suggests an improper rationale, failing my account of limited government.

In this way, a turn to legislative purpose may create democratic common ground in this contentious debate. A democratic polity could decide that it wants to minimize harm to innocent life forcing others to aid or help those in fatal need. Or decide to compensate those that it does impose such a burden on. But, as it stands now, compelling only women to do so, without even a discussion of compensation – bracketing the issue of Samaritanism – suggests that something other than harm minimization is afoot. If the fetus is a person, the debate must be about the legitimacy of forcing members of the polity to be Samaritans. It must be about how far we are willing to compel individuals to go to save others – whether they are fetuses or a child in need. In so far as this is what is at stake in the abortion question, Justice Scalia is right to have the decision left to the relevant democratic polity.

[20] Thompson 1971: 64.

To be clear, my re-conceptualization of limited government does not seek to end debate on abortion. After all, rights are the conversation stoppers. The very fact that my framework encourages these kinds of questions in the abortion debate is reason to accept it rather than deem it misguided. It is precisely because Justification does not close off democratic possibilities – even opening up new ones – that I proffer it as a superior account of limited government. I seek to rethink limited government to encourage more room for deliberation. By rejecting talk of rights and channeling debate in the direction of Justification, we do just that.

So how is it that the pro-life position has avoided such discussions? Why is Regan and Thompson's rightful worry that laws against abortion are nothing other than a kind of forced Samaritanism not part of the much-heated debate? Again, I suggest that rights are the culprit. They seek to classify. By looking at how best to categorize the woman's act of removing the fetus, the rationale behind an abortion statute is regrettably overlooked. Our attention is diverted. It is problematically aimed at whether the woman's act is one of privacy or the right to life. Only by rejecting rights and turning to legislative purpose are we able to make sure that pro-lifers face up to the implications of their position. Talk of rights can more easily mask illegitimate rationales. A turn to the minimization of harm as the lodestar of state action gets us to think about the pro-life position as blatant forced Samaritanism, as a possible pretext for oppressing women.

The pro-choice supporters, on the other hand, see the right to choose as the only acceptable option. Their focus on bodily control blinds them to the fact that a democratic polity could force others to help. Again, Justification does not dictate substantive outcomes but only the reasons the polity may proffer in passing legislation. To be clear, as long as the polity genuinely acts only to prevent harm, it may regulate or even prohibit abortion.

Perhaps there are policies that the two sides could agree on. At a minimum, a debate along these terms seems more productive. A focus on harm minimization illuminates the debate, offering a space between the otherwise incompatible options usually proffered by it, a space that balances liberty and democratic decision-making.

There is certainly much more to be said on the abortion issue. For example, there are some pro-lifers who make exceptions for women who are raped. But, then, can these individuals still claim that a law against abortion with such an exception seeks to minimize harm to the fetus? Or does it seek to minimize harm to the woman, an important difference given the turn to legislative purpose? My discussion here is no way exhaustive. It highlights a normative framework that the current debate and its focus on rights have preemptively cut off.

In rejecting rights and making room for democracy, and this should now be evident, my theory of Justification importantly avoids the anti-democratic nature of rights. The constraints of demonstrability and consent do not attach to individuals but to the *democratic majority*. Individuals take a back seat under this method of limiting government. The democratic community and by implication its socially constituted members articulate the relevant political obligations. The polity, and not its individual members, is the normative player.

Thus, democracy is necessary to articulate *which* demonstrable harms the polity will minimize and *how* it will minimize them. The utilitarian cost/benefit analysis of only regulating harm is left with the democratic polity. We are not mere un-encumbered, rights-bearing selves. Many of our legal commitments including our duty not to murder do not arise from a pre-political, transcendent set of rights. A law prohibiting murder does not stem from a right to bodily integrity. Rather, the democratic process itself must generate these commitments. Locke's need for a pre-political right to life is unnecessary, needlessly discounting the fact that a democratic polity will on its own offer such protection. Using my account of Justification, our political obligations, far from transcending society, are imbedded in it.

Again, my constraint does not require the polity to prevent or minimize demonstrable, non-consensual harm. A democratic majority could decide *not* to prevent any harm at all. In turn, by rejecting rights and turning to Justification we stand to enliven democratic discourse and participation. The demos will have to decide what kinds of demonstrable harms to prevent and how to do so. Since we have rejected talk of rights – with their focus on substantive outcomes – the polity has no choice but collectively to decide what legislation to pass. The demos cannot pass the democratic buck precisely because we have repudiated the very language of rights that invites such quiescence. Rejecting such conversation stoppers means the demos must discuss issues rather than easily relegate them to courts.

A democratic polity need not, for example, compensate or prevent genetic harm. Presently, the United States does not have laws remedying it. Still, by turning to legislative purpose, the polity is free to regulate it. A democratic polity could institute an adversarial or inquisitional system, use juries or judges to decide guilt, decide not to permit plea-bargaining, adhere to a presumption of guilt, apportion certain harms to the tort law, or even fail to create a tort law at all or a host of other possibilities in minimizing harm or in administering a criminal justice system.

A prohibition on cruel and unusual punishment – another kind of right – is non-existent under my theory of Justification. The polity will decide how severe a punishment to impose. Could the polity, for instance, decide that jaywalking merits the death penalty? Or that a certain crime (randomly picked and changed every month – to cite one of many possible punishment schemes) gets the harshest penalty? The short answer is: yes. As long the democratic polity seeks to minimize demonstrable harm – genuinely contending that the punishment of death will in fact deter such crimes – it is free to legislate as it likes. Here the relevant debate will be about deterrence or what punishment system is most effective at minimizing harm. Conceding this, though, is no cause for alarm or even possible retreat to a regime of rights. These objections fail to realize that a majority of the polity must, in fact, decide to impose such a penalty. It is not surprising that, as far as I know, no contemporary, real world democratic regime has imposed the death penalty for a simple crime such as jaywalking.

The more relevant issue and the one the Supreme Court recently addressed in *Roper v. Simmons* (2005) involves sentencing juveniles convicted of murder to death. While the Court overturned such a practice (appealing to the Eighth Amendment's prohibition on "cruel and unusual punishments"[21]), germane to our discussion is their appeal to international norms of decency. The majority opinion cites such norms in interpreting the bounds of the Eighth Amendment. Justice Scalia, writing for the dissent, contends that such appeals to international standards are largely irrelevant, undercutting the democratic will of Americans.[22] I am sympathetic to Scalia's argument. Deciding whether juveniles should receive such a harsh punishment is within the range of options open to the democratic polity under my theory of Justification. Using Oakeshott's language, Justification does not dictate outcomes only the relevant constraints.

The democratic polity may very well choose to heed or incorporate norms from other polities – looking to the international sentiments on the permissibility of such punishment. But this is to be left to the individual democratic polity to decide. This informs our commitment to letting democracy do the work. The Court should not substitute its own judgment. To do so is to invite the republican worry that rights discount the value of democracy. Under my justificatory constraint, the Court would have no reason to overturn the practice considered in *Roper*.

Rejecting the rights to property, privacy, and religion

Integral to the conventional schedule of rights are the rights to property, privacy, and religion. These rights seem particularly salient in the conventional account of limited government. They are the paradigmatic

---

[21] U.S. Constitution Amendment VIII.   [22] *Roper*, dissenting at 622–628.

components of the private sphere. In rejecting them, the arguments above no doubt apply here as well. Still, I highlight the particular problems with these specific rights.

Property

Property can include physical objects, lands, organs, and body parts.[23] With no right to property, there is no presumptive right to any of these things. My theory does not assume a labor theory of value or a right to appropriation. Just as a polity could decide to fail to minimize physical harm at all – permitting everyone to grab another's organs – it could just as easily deem that no one can lay exclusive claim to any physical object or piece of land even if labored upon. Allowing others to take our organs, though possible under my theory of Justification, is highly unlikely. Again, since all (or at least a vast majority) will suffer under this state of affairs, the polity will have every reason to mitigate such harm and protect bodily integrity.

Similarly, it may choose to minimize the harm that arises from having objects you've acquired taken away by others. This kind of economic or monetary harm is something the polity may (but of course need not) seek to mitigate or prevent. In fact, the democratic polity may be so bent on minimizing economic harm, the loss of conventional property, that it opts for a classic, libertarian state. Nozick's vision of the state is no doubt a possibility under my account of limited government. Of course, even in such a regime there will be no right to property, only the majority's decision to prevent a particular harm. Alternatively, the majority could fail to recognize property whatsoever instituting a communistic state. All land and physical objects would belong to no one at all. This is unlike Nozick or Ackerman's account where the polity is forced to maintain a libertarian system or a robust welfare state, respectively. The polity has room to decide and negotiate, borrowing Nancy Fraser's term,[24] which redistribution paradigm to legislate. This informs democracy.

In this way, we permit the polity to mitigate or minimize harm by regulating the alleged economic sphere. Once property loses its special status given the rejection of categorization, allowing one to keep what one earns, for example, is simply one decision among many. It can always be

---

[23] See Calabresi and Melamed (1972) on the distinction between entitlements and alienability. The threshold question is what, if anything, are members of the polity entitled to – their organs, their labor, etc.? And then, under what conditions can they alienate them? I leave the polity to decide these issues of entitlement and alienability.

[24] Fraser 1997.

revisited and revised by the polity. Only when such property relations are reified independent of the democratic process do we run into trouble tying the hands of the democratic majority. With no private sphere to deem property special and beyond the regulation of the state, it is easier to imagine the democratic majority, in Waldron's language, acting in good faith to institute any number of regimes.[25]

This leaves adults to create any kind of contractual relationship they desire. The state will generally have no good reason to un-do them. Like the prostitution contract outlined above, questioning the consent turns out to be a sophisticated kind of paternalism. This emphasis on contractualism, though, is no cause for alarm. The objection that by leaving adults to contract as they see fit, we exacerbate and reinforce existent power relations[26] is inapplicable under a theory that rejects rights. That is, those who seek to characterize contractualism as an effective retreat to the private sphere – leaving such contracts beyond the scope of state regulation – fail to realize that consent and privacy can be de-coupled. We can honor consent, as my theory does, without rendering such consensual relations beyond the reach of the democratic polity.

The tension between contractualism and regulation arises only if one endorses a notion of rights. After all, the conventional characterization of anti-paternalism contends that we have a *right* to enter into various kinds of contracts or arrangements. We have a right to consent to anything. Obviously, this will push against a polity's decision to regulate such contracts.

But this is not my position. The reason I can enter into the slavery contract or any contract for that matter is *not* because I have a right to do so. It is not because I have a right to consent to any arrangement I desire. Rather, the polity has no good reason to tell me to do otherwise. It is the "good reason" that does the normative work. As long as the polity only seeks to minimize harm (this is what it means to have a good reason), it can pass a wide variety of laws, ones that regulate or even prohibit certain contracts.

Suppose, then, that the polity decides to mitigate economic inefficiency or to remedy structural inequality by redistributing wealth. No one has consented to these harms. They may simply be products of a free market system. The polity may decide to minimize such harms in various ways. First, the majority may decide to redistribute indirectly by passing minimum wage laws, maximum hours legislation, obligatory working conditions and the like. A polity may very well decide that forcing businesses to

---

[25] Waldron 1999.   [26] J. Cohen 2002, Shapiro 1999.

pay workers a certain wage either translates into more consumer spending that in turn generates a more efficient economy or mitigates structural inequality. Reasonable people may disagree about such claims, and again, rightly so. Rejecting rights, my account of limited government leaves these decisions "open to discussion."

Now setting obligatory working conditions or minimum wage laws may very well harm individual workers. Imagine a worker who desires to work for less than the minimum wage or under sub-par workplace conditions. Why can't she consent to being harmed? Wouldn't such laws prevent a worker from doing so thereby interfering with her interests? And isn't this blatant paternalism – the polity thinking it's in the best interest of the worker to garner a certain wage or work under particular conditions?

These questions fail to appreciate the crucial move in my argument. We must consider the polity's rationale for passing such laws not its effects. Take the example of drug use. The polity may not prohibit it on grounds that the activity is too dangerous for those engaging in it. This is a paternalistic rationale. The harm is consensual. But if the polity outlaws drugs to reduce the crime rate demonstrating a nexus between drug use and crime, the majority acts appropriately. Here the harm is not consensual. By seeking to minimize harm to *others*, the polity does not act in the best interests of the drug user.

If the rationale is to act in the best interests of the worker, the polity acts illegitimately. Similarly, if the polity prohibits the voluntary slave or prostitute contracts, because it finds their terms too harmful or severe, it acts improperly. But if the polity acts to mitigate overall economic inefficiency or inequality, it does not act paternalistically (just as it acts properly by prohibiting drug use to reduce crime). No one including the individual worker has consented to this harm. By setting its sights at reducing inefficiency or structural inequality instead of minimizing harm to the particular worker, the polity acts appropriately. The fact that these policies prevent the worker from consenting to sub-par conditions or a low wage is of no consequence. My justificatory constraint looks to the aim or purpose of the legislation not its effects.

Second, the polity may decide to mitigate harm directly. Rather than enact prophylactic measures by regulating certain contracts, the polity may institute policies such as stakeholding – giving each of its members a certain amount of money upon adulthood[27] – or a negative income tax. It is up to the democratic polity to decide how, if at all, to minimize market inefficiency or inequality. This ensures robust democratic flexibility.

---

[27] Ackerman and Alstott 1999.

Now in preventing harm, the polity may very well also decide to regulate the prostitution ("sexual") contract. If prostitutes are like workers,[28] perhaps the polity could require that sexual services garner a minimum fee. Alternatively, perhaps the polity decides that prostitution leads men to treat *all* women as sexual objects not just those who are prostitutes. This, in turn, leads to greater violence against women or exacerbates the gender salary gap – perhaps women are not treated seriously at work. This is a legitimate rationale on which the polity may act. The polity may act to remedy such social inequality. Again, it may not regulate or prohibit prostitution in order to act in the best interests of the prostitute herself. In that case, the harm at issue would be consensual. Yet, if the polity believes in good faith that prostitution leads to publicly ascertainable non-consensual harm – harming other individuals in various ways by reinforcing social hierarchy – it may prohibit the practice.

Regulation of the marriage contract may be another way of minimizing harm to women. Perhaps the polity can set up default rules that assets must be divided up in a certain manner or that half of the husband's wages during the marriage must be placed in the wife's separate bank account.[29] Perhaps the polity prohibits prenuptial agreements. After all, the wife, who decided not to work and stay at home with the kids, is potentially left with less earning power and fewer assets given her skill sets in the modern economy than her ex-husband.[30] She may be kept out of the workforce thereby perpetuating stereotypes that women are less capable than men, stereotypes that may very well be demonstrably harmful to *all* women. As long as the polity acts in good faith, it may regulate such contracts as well.

Prohibiting or regulating contracts may have beneficial consequences for others. As long as the polity seeks to bring about these consequences – rather than acting in the interests of the contracting party – it may do so. The fact that such policies may restrict the ability to make certain arrangements – the worker cannot work for a low wage, the wife cannot sign a certain prenuptial agreement, the drug user cannot use drugs – is not problematic, as long as the polity genuinely acts to minimize some non-consensual harm. None of these individuals can claim a rights-violation, because I have rejected rights. I repudiate the claim that the polity is forbidden from interfering with a certain set of activities or transactions. This problematically turns our attention away from the polity itself. Keeping our eye on legislative purpose permits the polity to regulate or prohibit anything.

But how do we know when the polity's reason is paternalistic – it thinks prostitution is a "bad" kind of activity – and when the rationale is

---

[28] Engels 1942 [1884], Jaggar 1980.   [29] Okin 1989: 182–183.   [30] Cf. Becker 1985.

legitimate – seeking to minimize non-consensual harm? One way of smoking out paternalism is examining what the law actually prohibits. If a law against prostitution is genuinely only about minimizing harm to women, it should not at all be concerned with male prostitutes, especially those who seek female clients. Prohibiting females from paying for sex does not implicate worries that women will be treated as sexual objects. Here it is men who are treated as objects. If anything, permitting female-Janes to solicit male prostitutes turns the conventional hierarchy of sexual objectification on its head. It may very well aid in mitigating the deleterious consequences of patriarchy. Consequently, if feminists seek to prohibit *all* prostitution, they must aim to do something more than simply minimize non-consensual harm. Perhaps they do seek to act in the best interests of the prostitute or to un-do her consent, rationales that fail my justificatory constraint.

The majority may also decide to minimize or remedy the harm the job applicant faces by being otherwise perfectly qualified. Such harm, unlike the alleged "moral harm" of gay sex or mixing of the races, is quite demonstrable. Though the prospective employee may have the necessary skills, she is rejected on the basis of a characteristic unrelated to job performance – race, sex, hair color, blood type, and the like – a rejection that leaves her without an economic livelihood. If the democratic polity decides to minimize such harm, it can do so in various ways. The polity may remedy such harm by creating a "surfer's paradise" with a universal basic income for all.[31] That way, even if the employer discriminates on such characteristics, the employee is not economically harmed. After all, all members of the polity get a wage. Alternatively, the polity may decide to pass non-discrimination laws that prohibit non-state employers from discriminating in this way.[32] Again, the fact that such harm occurs in the private sphere is of no normative significance once we reject the public/private distinction. As long as it only seeks to prevent harm, the polity may regulate *any* area or sphere.

It is not some right to equality of opportunity that is doing the work. If that were the case, the polity's only option would be to pass such non-discrimination legislation. A *right* to equality needlessly restricts democratic flexibility. It is *not* the discrimination by the employer *qua* discrimination that is objectionable under my theory of Justification. Remember, the "what" of my theory of Justification is state-action. Though government agencies are forbidden from engaging in such discrimination, because in doing so the state seeks to do something other

---

[31] Shapiro 1999: 184–186, Parijs: 1995.   [32] Shapiro 1999: 184–186.

than minimize harm, non-state actors may very well discriminate. Here the demonstrable harm is the economic suffering the job applicant faces by being otherwise qualified but jobless. The polity, in turn, may remedy this harm with a universal wage or such non-discrimination legislation. The higher the universal wage the more freedom the employer may have to discriminate. Though Ian Shapiro does not connect this "sliding-quantum" rule[33] to a rejection of rights, I suggest that a turn to harm minimization under-girds this democratic flexibility.

It makes no difference whether the activity is an economic transaction, a contractual arrangement, or sex in the bedroom. The kind of activity has no purchase in my account. I reject the appeal to classifications or spheres of non-interference. Again, I care only about the rationale underlying the legislation, ordinance, or regulation. It must only seek to minimize demonstrable harm. By rejecting rights, no arrangement, association, or activity is beyond the reach of the state. Libertarianism, communism, a robust welfare state, to name just a few, are all possible setups under my justificatory constraint.

Privacy

The New Deal called into question much of the special status of the economic sphere. Few contemporary scholars of political theory still adhere to treating such economic activities as beyond the scope of state regulation. Nevertheless, the maintenance of a right to intimacy – and thus adherence to some kind of private sphere – is a far more entrenched position.[34] But even though its limitations are evident, as the only game in town to protect sexual freedom and confidentiality, privacy's nagging staying power seems quite strong indeed.

The fact that the private sphere has historically included the family – leaving women and children vulnerable to non-consensual harm – is reason to reject it and the conventional account of limited government that accompanies it. By adopting my justificatory constraint, we can. Laws against physical abuse that make exceptions for husbands beating their wives may not stand. If the polity decides to minimize physical non-consensual harm (as it most probably will), it cannot irrationally limit the legislation's scope. A law that prevents abuse as long as it does

---

[33] Ibid.: 184.

[34] Judith Thompson (1975) seeks to collapse the right to intimacy into other rights such as the right to property, the right to "not be looked at" and the right "not to be listened to" (Thompson 1975: 304). But with nothing else, her "simplifying hypothesis" is still insufficient. It does not explain why certain laws that restrict sexual activity are illegitimate.

not occur in the home seeks to do something more than just prevent harm. Perhaps it also seeks to oppress women or endow husbands with greater control, rationales that violate the "only" requirement. The distinction between rape and abuse in the family and rape and abuse on the street has no purchase under my theory of Justification, a theory that repudiates the special or unique nature of the family. Requiring that the polity exclusively seek to prevent harm ensures that it does not make such irrational distinctions – tagging certain behavior as private and thus off limits to state regulation.

The private sphere (encompassing family, religious, and economic life) has a longer history than the right to privacy. In fact, case law has only recently recognized the constitutional right to privacy.[35] For my purposes they can be treated together – suffering from many of the same defects. Privacy can include "informational" and "decisional" privacy. The informational kind protects us from governmental disclosure of confidential information. Its decisional counterpart protects us from governmental intrusion in certain areas.[36] I move back and forth among these similar normative doctrines using "privacy" as a catchall phrase.

My justificatory constraint is also better at securing confidentiality and sexual freedom. First, there may very well be facts of my life that I do not want to share with others: the names of my sexual partners, my weight, my health, or my diary – to name just a few. Admittedly, there is nothing special about such information. I reject privacy. While privacy appealed to categorization to protect such interests – deeming them "intimate" or "personal" – I look to the rationales behind disclosing them. What good reason could the polity offer to force disclosure of such information? Certainly, it could compel disclosure to prevent fraud or misrepresentation. It could force companies to disclose their financial statements for potential investors. Without sufficient information, harm to such investors would be non-consensual. But the state will be hard pressed to release a list of those individuals who have certain sexually transmitted diseases. Release of such information will not aid in minimizing *non-consensual* harm. STDs are transmitted by consensual sexual intercourse.[37] Now the state may very well inform its members that there are such sexually transmitted diseases just as it informs investors about the financial status

---

[35] *Griswold v. Connecticut*, 381 U.S. 479 (1965) (the Court articulates the constitutional right to privacy by way of substantive due process).

[36] Turkington 2002.

[37] Laws may already be in place to prevent rape – thus, minimizing transmission by forced sex.

of companies. Otherwise, those engaging in such sex would not be consenting to a possible infection.

Second, sexual freedom is also secure. Unfortunately, the conventional liberal refrain of tolerance with its emphasis on categorization has been the longstanding mechanism to protect sexual freedom. We do not need it under my theory of Justification. We also do not need acceptance. These doctrines, the representatives of liberalism and republicanism, are generally seen as our only options. It is no wonder that political theory has been beset with two almost equally unpalatable positions. My theory of Justification offers a simple way out. It allows us to have our cake and eat it too. We permit gay sex and its straight counterpart for the very same reason, namely the state has no legitimate reason to prohibit either.[38] Correspondingly, my gay sex life, her one-night stands, and their monogamous straight relationship are all secure for the same reason. Under my theory of Justification (purged of privacy), neither is straight sex deemed valuable nor gay sex considered depraved but somehow tolerated. There is no gold standard of sexuality. The constraint of demonstrability ensures that all such sexual freedoms share the same fate: the state will be hard pressed to proffer a legitimate reason to prohibit any of them.

Why are sodomy laws or laws prohibiting redheads from sleeping with blonds irrational or arbitrary? Simply put, these laws do not seek to prevent demonstrable harm. The polity's reason for passing such laws has nothing to do with harm prevention. We need only recognize that a sodomy law fails just like a law regulating the sexual activity of redheads and blonds. Once we realize the implications of this claim – and this is the take home point, rights turn out unnecessary. No longer must I characterize my behavior as private in order to gain protection under a right to privacy regime.

Moreover, by distinguishing between those activities that allegedly occur in private – such as sex – and those that do not – such as marriage – freedom can perversely be guaranteed in the former but taken away in the latter. Rejecting rights, there is no presumptive normative difference between the acts of sex and marriage. The concern ought to be the state's reason for doing something. Just as the polity will be forced to appeal to the minimization of some non-demonstrable harm to prohibit sodomy, it will have to proffer a similarly illegitimate reason to bar same-sex marriage. The fact that marriage is traditionally a union between a single man

---

[38] This does not necessarily mean that the state may not ban copulation on the street. Such activity could constitute a nuisance like the traffic nuisances outlawed in *Railway Express*. Or perhaps health reasons would justify a prohibition on "public" sex. Admittedly, if individuals have sex in a deserted park, there may not be any legitimate reason to ban it.

and a single woman will not do. Claiming that same-sex marriage will destroy the institution of marriage seems baseless. Such protests seem just as silly as Devlin's claim that permitting gay sex will un-do government. Both are unequivocal examples of morals legislation and thus fall together. Constraining democratic decision-making in line with my theory of Justification is liberty enhancing, rendering the right to privacy unnecessary.

Religion

But still deep seated is the commitment to the special status of religion or culture – the belief that religious or cultural practices should be treated differently than the practices of other associations. We should reject this contention, one that also shields harm from state regulation under the pretext of protecting religion. In particular, it leaves children in these religious or cultural groups vulnerable to harm. Again, the location of the demonstrably harmful activity – the bedroom, the workplace, or the church – makes no difference to the overall goal of harm minimization.

Still, rejecting the right to religion has great impact on identity politics or multiculturalism in general. After all, most students of multiculturalism[39] accept the (often unstated) premise that religious and cultural affiliations are importantly different from their voluntary counterparts. These scholars care about race, gender, sexuality, religion and the like. Most of the debate focuses on how to define such categories or what more categories to include.

The doctrinal issue that is rarely discussed is why aren't the following associations/preferences included among the multicultural list: membership in the local chess club, being a Rotarian (member of the Rotary Club), being a PTA (Parent Teacher Association) parent, or belonging to a political association – to name just a few? How, then, are these groups to be distinguished away? Often, multicultural theorists appeal to domination or oppression to define their categories.[40] Iris Marion Young, in fact, contends that groups that experience one or more of the following – exploitation, marginalization, powerlessness, cultural imperialism, and violence – are worthy of consideration by multiculturalism.[41] Such experiences are not applicable to the Rotarian or the member of the PTA. Unlike racial and sexual minorities, Rotarians or PTA members have not been discriminated against in this way.

---

[39] See, e.g., Fraser 1997, Kymlicka 1995, Shachar 2001, Taylor 1994, Young 1990.
[40] Fraser 1997, Young 1990.   [41] Young 1990: 48–63.

However, once we adopt my justificatory constraint, we have no need for deploying these claims of identity. The polity has no good reason to institute racial segregation or limit marriage to one man and one woman. The unfortunate emphasis on categorization seems to imply that segregation is unjust because it discriminates against blacks, or that sodomy laws are wrong because they affect gays. Even multiculturalists would agree that segregation on other grounds – hair color, blood type, PTA status, number of letters in your first name – is also problematic, an argument I flesh out in more detail in Chapter 8. Thus, it is not the group that is central in this argument but once again the rationale underpinning the forced segregation. Simply put, such laws cannot be appropriately justified. They are irrational. On the face of it, they seek to do something other than minimize demonstrable, non-consensual harm.

If the polity has passed legislation minimizing physical harm, it will be hard pressed to exclude select minorities from its scope. It will be hard to make distinctions among different kinds of people while *exclusively* minimizing physical harm. Invariably such distinctions would seek to do more than just minimize harm – perhaps oppress one group or elevate another. It does not matter whom such violence is visited upon. In fact, if it turns out that pornographic pictures, negative stereotypes in the media, or social symbols cause non-consensual demonstrable harm, the polity may very well decide to regulate, counteract, or even prohibit such material. Appeal to identity politics is simply unnecessary.

In fact, Fraser advocates the necessity of recognition – a core claim of identity politics – with the example of gays and lesbians, "the despised sexualities."[42] However, here too my theory is sufficient to do the work. Generally, the state will have no good reason to prohibit what consenting adults do or to limit marriage to opposite sex couples. The whole panoply of laws that discriminate against gays is repudiated by the constraint of demonstrability. Nevertheless, Fraser claims that overcoming "homophobia and heterosexism requires changing cultural valuations (as well as their legal and practical expressions) that privilege heterosexuality, deny equal respect to gays and lesbians, and refuse to recognize homosexuality as a legitimate way of being sexual."[43] But a turn to the polity's reason for acting permits the majorities to remedy "misrecognition"[44] by dismantling social structures that may very well lead to demonstrable harm. And it can do so without appeal to claims of group differentiation. As long as our attention is on the polity's rationale for acting, we need not speak in the language of identity politics. In fact, the preoccupation with creating

---

[42] Fraser 1997: 16–23.   [43] Ibid.: 18–19.   [44] Fraser 1997, Taylor 1994.

certain standards and then either forcing groups to assimilate them or reluctantly permitting deviations[45] is non-existent under my account of limited government. Again, my theory of Justification rejects such assimilation. It articulates no standard or norm of sexuality.

The very language of group classification is non-existent with a turn to legislative purpose. Much like Fraser's ideal of transformation where there is no such differentiation, my theory of Justification also "deconstructs" such groups. They are obsolete under it. According to Fraser's own argument, in such a world identity politics has no purchase.

Suppose the multiculturalist turns her attention to the need for a religious exemption. She seeks to accommodate the demonstrable disadvantage that befalls the member of a group in attempting to follow a polity's general laws or regulations. Imagine the polity passes the following law: All those traveling on airplanes or entering government buildings must remove any and all kinds of headgear. In passing such legislation, the polity seeks to prevent individuals from concealing weapons. The multiculturalist contends that the Sikh, who wears a turban for religious reasons, ought to gain an exemption or accommodation from such a law. Suppose further that a mere hat wearer – someone that simply enjoys wearing hats – also petitions to gain an exemption. Obviously, the multiculturalist will object to giving the hat wearer an exemption. After all, multiculturalism maintains there is something special about the religious activity as opposed to the mere preference.

By repudiating categorization, my account treats all associations as similarly situated.[46] It does not matter whether the activity is donning a turban because you are a Sikh, deciding to wear a hat on a sunny day, choosing not to eat meat for religious reasons, or fasting to make a statement to your friend. Distinguishing activities on account of their religious, economic, or private character is not sufficient to warrant varying treatment under my regime of Justification. Such attempts problematically appeal to rights.

The only peg on which to hang such a distinction is the issue of consent. As long as the Sikh and the hat wearer have chosen to engage in their illegal behavior, the polity has no grounds on which to grant either an

---

[45] Young 1990: 158–168.

[46] Sandel (1996: 61–65) criticizes the neutral state for treating religious groups as mere voluntary associations. Under this voluntary paradigm, religion is not taken seriously. Again, my theory of Justification cannot take religion more seriously than another association or preference. Sandel would have us view such religious obligations as un-chosen. As I argue below the polity could treat religious practices as un-chosen disadvantages but doing so is not without its problems, a consideration Sandel does not entertain.

exemption. By entering the airplane or government building both choose to engage in an activity that violates the law. Attempts to distinguish these kinds of behavior on the basis of anything other than consent run afoul of my justificatory constraint. The Sikh's only option, then, is to claim that wearing a turban constitutes an un-chosen disadvantage.[47] Being unable to enter the building or airplane, the Sikh is effectively disadvantaged. The multiculturalist must argue that given his upbringing the Sikh had no or very little choice in wearing the turban. The hat wearer, on the other hand, chooses to put on a hat. Assuming we can make this distinction between chosen and un-chosen practices, the appeal to disadvantage is the only viable way to justify special treatment for religion.

The polity may very well place emphasis on this alleged lack of choice, offering the Sikh an exemption. But what about those who suffer from an analogous disadvantage? Brian Barry considers the counter-example of the individual with expensive tastes who because of her upbringing feels compelled to always have the finest foods, wines, and caviar.[48] She too suffers from a disadvantage like the Sikh. If the polity cannot justify this "one step at a time" measure – accommodating the Sikh but not the *bon vivant* – it may have to exempt both. If the rationale is truly about minimizing harm in this way, the *bon vivant* may need special meals at the state university. In any case, the decision will be rightly left to the democratic majority.

Still, characterizing the religious or cultural practice as un-chosen has the additional drawback of reifying and essentializing it, making democratic deliberation in such groups difficult. One consequence of placing religion in the private sphere – as beyond the reach of state regulation – is to render it static, unchanging, and unitary. By viewing culture and religious affiliations as voluntary, contingent, and constructed such affiliations are open to revision and deliberation.[49] Benhabib even characterizes religious and cultural affiliations as requiring "voluntary ascription." She, like Tocqueville, seems to view all associations as voluntary.[50] Even if the polity were willing to exempt all those who are so disadvantaged, doing so would run the risk of ossifying the cultural practice rendering it inhospitable to reflexive democratic contestation.[51]

---

[47] Kymlicka 1995: 108–115.   [48] B. Barry 2001: 34–35.

[49] Benhabib 2002, Parekh 2000.   [50] Tocqueville 2000 [1835]: 239–242.

[51] It is not even clear that the practice of wearing a turban is historically and religiously central to Sikhism. In fact, there are many self-proclaimed Sikhs who are "clean-shaven" who do not wear turbans (McLeod 1989). There is a dilemma in justifying the religious exemption. On the one hand, contemporary theory has come to see religious affiliations and practices as contingent, open-ended, and freely constructed. On the other hand, in order to justify different or special treatment for such groups we must view these affiliations as un-chosen, static, and not freely constructed. We cannot have it both ways (Bedi 2007).

Failure to realize the connection between justification and rights

The problem with rights is easily identified. It is easy to see why the conventional account of limited government is flawed. Rejecting it and rights, though, seems far more difficult. Scholars have failed to realize that specifying the appropriate legislative purpose renders them obsolete. To the contrary, those sympathetic to Justification also needlessly appeal to rights or some version of the private sphere. Ackerman,[52] Habermas,[53] Rawls,[54] and Oakeshott[55] all make some gesture to the necessity of such doctrines.

Rawls, for instance, overlooks the relationship between his theory of Justification and the public/private divide. Rawls contends that public reason "tries to elaborate a reasonable conception for the *basic structure alone*."[56] In limiting the scope of state power to only "political, social, and economic institutions" (the basic structure),[57] Rawls fails to see the redundant nature of this limitation. Though he correctly identifies Justification as prohibiting appeals to certain moral and religious viewpoints to justify legislation (coming close to articulating my justificatory constraint), he problematically still maintains the private sphere, a sphere that is obsolete under his own argument. Once he rightly limits government by limiting the reasons or rationales on which it may act, he no longer needs to carve out those areas, interests, spheres, or classifications off limits to state regulation. There is no reason to limit the application of public reason or Justification. Given the appropriate constraint, the kind of activity implicated – is it part of the "basic structure"? – is irrelevant.

Even the critics of this kind of Justification fail to notice the relationship between this argument and rights. Sandel repudiates neutrality, the forefather of my theory of Justification, but fails to realize how the right to privacy is obsolete under its very terms: "The principle that government must be neutral among conceptions of the good life *finds further* constitutional expression in the area of privacy rights."[58] Sandel then goes on to

---

[52] Ackerman (1980: 372) ("Indeed, it is the very point of Neutrality to permit each citizen to defend his rights *without* requiring him to convince his fellows that his personal good serves the common good").

[53] Habermas (1996: 313) ("Certainly the intimate sphere must be protected from intrusive forces and the critical eyes of strangers, but not everything reserved to the decisions of private persons is withdrawn from public thematization and protected from criticism").

[54] See the discussion of Rawls in this chapter.

[55] Oakeshott (1975: 183) ("The idea of 'public' distinguished from 'private', where all wants, choices, performances, satisfactions, property, and agency are recognized to be private and to be the responsibility of the chooser, the doer, or the owner, and all performances and all ownership are 'public' in respect of being required to subscribe to the conditions specified in *respublica*, and in no other respect").

[56] Rawls 1996: 13 (emphasis added).   [57] Ibid.: 11.

[58] Sandel 1996: 91 (emphasis added).

spend an entire chapter articulating the problem of tolerance inherent in the right to privacy.[59] Privacy is incorrectly assumed to be *integral* to this theory of Justification. If the state must be neutral to conceptions of the good, we do not need privacy.

Benhabib also rails against the neutral state and by implication my theory of Justification for its tendency to re-privatize issues. "As sensitive as one may be to the traditional liberal fear that unlimited public conversation might erode those few constitutional guarantees we can rely upon, the reprivatization of issues that have become public only generates conceptual confusion, political resentment and moral outrage."[60] I agree with almost everything Benhabib has to say here. Most of her criticism, though, has mischaracterized Justification (or rather failed to appreciate this account of limited government) simply because she has neglected to purge from it the unnecessary public/private sphere distinction.[61] Under my theory of Justification, there is no limitation to the scope of state power. Once the private sphere has been rejected, the very idea that there can be a privatization of issues under such a theory is impossible.

Benhabib's deliberative democratic project also views "all social practices and activities" as possible "subjects for *public discussion and expression*."[62] Similarly, no issue is beyond the reach of my theory of Justification. Everything is on the agenda to be discussed and debated. There are no "gag rules" that remove certain subjects from the dialogue.[63]

The only limitation is on how the democratic polity goes about justifying its decision. My theory of Justification captures the project of deliberative democracy advocated by Benhabib and others. It does so by channeling democracy (the deliberative project) into deciding *which* demonstrable, non-consensually harmful activities to minimize and *how* to do so. The "conceptual confusion, political resentment, and moral outrage" Benhabib speaks of are avoided.

But then why are rights so entrenched political doctrines? Why have we not already endorsed my theory of Justification? I suspect that this has much to do with the historical rise of democracy. Since national, absolutist regimes arose first to be followed by democracy, the state was initially seen as opposed to the interests of its citizens.[64] Rather than locate the problem in the non-democratic nature of the regime, rights were deployed to protect us from the

---

[59] Ibid.: 91–119.   [60] Benhabib 1992: 99.

[61] Interestingly, in a footnote Benhabib (1992: 115 fn. 20) does offer an interpretation of the neutral state (specifically, Ackerman's account) as constraining *only* the grounds "one can put forward in justifying one's conception of the good without, however, excluding such conceptions from being aired in public." This is similar to the mechanism of Justification I defend here.

[62] Benhabib 2002: 120.   [63] Holmes 1997.   [64] Anderson 1974, Mill 1989 [1859].

absolutist state. Locke wrote during the time of monarchy – arguing against the divine rights of kings in his *First Treatise of Government*.[65] His vision of government as premised on natural rights trades on the historical reality that the democratic majority's interests did not coincide with that of the state. The state at that time was not to be trusted – it was a monarchy, hence the conventional social contract. The methodology of carving out those interests or areas off limits to the state no doubt represented a distrust of it. Consequently, this distrust was at its core a dissatisfaction with the fact that self-government – rule by the demos – was not a reality. The conventional account of limited government assumed a non-democratic government. The hesitation with articulating an *affirmative* constraint – the minimization of demonstrable, non-consensual harm – as under-girding state action may very well stem from the fact that historically polities were non-democratic. The state was seen as opposed to the interests of its members.

In fact, in *Federalist* #84, Alexander Hamilton makes this very point when he argues against the need for a bill of rights to the 1787 Constitution:

> It has been several times truly remarked, that bills of rights are in their origins, stipulations between kings and their subjects, abridgements of prerogative in favor of privilege, reservations of rights not surrendered to the prince. Such as the Magna Charta. ... Such was the *petition of right* assented to by Charles the First. ... Such also was the declaration of right presented by the lords and commons to the prince of Orange in 1688. ... It is evident, therefore, that according to their primitive signification, they [bills of rights] have no application to constitutions professedly founded upon the power of the people, and executed by their immediate representatives and servants. (*Federalist* #84 1961 [1788]: 578)

Under this explanation, it is no wonder that there is no necessary connection, as Berlin implies, between democracy and rights. Rights arose first to be followed by democracy. As a historical matter, the question of "who governs" came after. With democratic institutions undeniably in place, the baggage of rights seems to have unfortunately traveled with us.

Why, then, do we insist on rights as *the* protector of our liberties, as if we were still living in an age of monarchies and rights were "trumps" we could flail in their despotic direction? Gone are those days – as even Hamilton writes. Yet the same amulets that we deployed in those days have grafted onto our own democratic times. Why use rights against our democratically elected governments when we can demand that they *justify* themselves instead? With the demise of absolutism and the non-negotiable status of democracy, we can reject rights. With the turn to democracy, we can rightly turn to reasons. Doing so affirms and reinforces our commitment to democratic rule. This argument is not just one of ideal theory.

---

[65] Locke 1988 [1690].

Part III

Justification in practice

6   Rejecting the constitutional rights
       to property and religion

I argue in the last and third part of my book that American constitutional law has moved in the direction of my theory of Justification rejecting the rights of the private sphere and should continue to do so. Properly understood, I argue that Supreme Court case law informs the re-conceptualized account of limited government proffered in Part II. In this Part, we revisit my argument but through the lens of constitutional decision-making. The Court already engages in the practice of looking to legislative purpose.[1] In deciding the constitutionality of statutes, regulations, or laws, it ascertains and evaluates their intent, purpose, or goal. Such an inquiry stands at the core of my theory of Justification. However, the Court also cares about rights. I concede that constitutional law can never entirely purge the language of rights. Particular clauses, the Bill of Rights and various other amendments to the Constitution no doubt create or affirm certain enumerated rights, rights that undoubtedly attach to individuals. Though, it should be noted that the original 1787 Constitution did not contain a bill of rights. Again, Alexander Hamilton argued against including one, suggesting, in fact, that such a schedule of rights is "not only unnecessary" but "dangerous."[2] But this is not the Constitution we have today, one where rights are an ingrained feature of the constitutional landscape. Thus, my constitutional argument is not nearly as broad or as comprehensive as my political theory one.

I make the more modest argument in this chapter and the next that the Court has rejected the core rights of the private sphere: property, religion, and privacy. It has done so by solely examining whether the rationale

---

[1] Cf. David Beatty 1994. "The ambition of this essay is to show that if, instead of thinking of bills of rights as guaranteeing individuals will be able to act in certain ways and have specific interests recognized by the state, we see them as entrenching basic principles of rationality and proportionality – of necessity and consistency – into the framework of government, the differences among legal theorists which have threatened the objectivity and determinacy of law will for the most part disappear" (Beatty 1994: 16). He goes on to write that "[i]ssues of justification and not interpretation are what judges struggle to resolve" (Beatty 1994: 21).
[2] *Federalist Papers* #84 1961 [1788]: 579.

under-girding legislation seeks to do something other than minimize demonstrable harm. It has in this way moved towards my account of limited government.

In a way, the Court's jurisprudence, then, is more evolved than conventional political theory. The Court must actually contend with its institutional, historical, and practical role as a component of a separated system of powers. Because the Supreme Court must maintain its institutional authority and legitimacy, it cannot always thwart *actual* majorities. It must invariably permit some democratic decision-making. Whereas political theorists can confidently stick to rights even at the cost of democratic flexibility – there is no real world consequence in doing so – the Court must be cognizant of its role in an actual democratic system. Unsurprisingly, the Court has partially turned to my theory of Justification.

The Court is a paradigmatic enforcer of such a theory. Unlike other branches of government, the Court gives reasons, rationales, explanations, and arguments for its decisions. Its alleged a-political status, the life-tenure of its members, and its adherence to the rule of law place it in an ideal position to decide when the state has compromised equality and freedom. Yet, in choosing to invalidate a democratically enacted law or statute, the Court must also permit a wide range of democratic flexibility.

Contemporary constitutional jurisprudence looks to reasons as well as rights. It does so by conducting a more exacting scrutiny of those laws that encroach upon a fundamental right or invoke a suspect class/classification. As a general rule, the Court protects liberty by way of two distinct branches: fundamental rights and equal protection. In *U.S. v. Carolene Products Co.* (1938), a central New Deal case repudiating the conventional autonomous economic sphere, the Court articulates this constitutional division of labor in its famous footnote: the Court should be wary "when legislation appears on its face to be within a specific prohibition of the Constitution, such as those of the first ten Amendments" (fundamental rights) or when it discriminates against "discrete and insular minorities" (suspect class/classification – equal protection).[3]

Under the first branch, those laws that presumptively infringe a constitutional right such as the right to free speech or the right to privacy trigger heightened, more exacting scrutiny. Under the second, equal protection, branch, laws get higher scrutiny when they presumptively invoke a suspect class or classification. When this happens, the Court makes it more difficult for the democratic polity to pass such laws. It requires that the polity proffer a more compelling reason.

---

[3] *Carolene Products* at 153, fn. 4.

But laws that violate no such right or do not invoke a suspect class or classification merely get rational review. A paradigmatic example is a law regulating highway speed limits. In these cases, the Court does not tie the hands of the polity. Here it is easy for the legislature to pass such laws. With rational review, democratic flexibility is at its peak. With heightened scrutiny, it's at its nadir. As one scholar suggests, heightened scrutiny is strict "in theory and fatal in fact" while rational review is "minimal scrutiny in theory and virtually none in fact."[4] In other words, the law will probably be upheld under rational review but struck down under heightened scrutiny.[5] (Notable exceptions where legislation passed such strict scrutiny include affirmative action[6] and the Japanese internment during World War II.[7]) The more a law is scrutinized, the more it frustrates democratic decision-making. So as to trigger heightened scrutiny, constitutional litigants who desire to invalidate a law strive to characterize it as violating a fundamental right or invoking a suspect class/classification.

In adjudicating the balance between the rights of the individuals and the collective interests of the democratic majority, this constitutional division of labor purports to secure freedom and equality. A law that prevented only blacks from having oral sex would presumably violate equal protection (equality). Alternatively, suppose a law prohibited *everyone* from having oral sex. This law does not seem to violate equal protection. It does not discriminate against a suspect group. Rather, it infringes a right to privacy (freedom). In this way, the two branches represent distinct, but complementary, doctrines. One picks up the constitutional slack of the other – with equal protection securing equality and rights ensuring freedom.

I argue that this conventional bi-furcated analysis and its accompanying heightened scrutiny are problematic and unnecessary. The Court need not appeal to rights or suspect classes/classifications to ensure liberty. It should turn its *complete* attention to legislative purpose. The Court should adopt one standard of review rejecting the use of higher scrutiny. In line with the re-conceptualized account of limited government proffered in Part II, a re-conceptualized *rational review* is sufficient to do the liberty work while permitting democratic flexibility.

By rational review, I do not mean some hypothetical reason. The Court should not ask whether there is a possible rational reason for the law – this

---

[4] Gunther 1972: 8.
[5] For a good discussion of the instances where the Court has struck down laws on rational review grounds alone, see Farrell (1999).
[6] *Grutter v. Bollinger* (2003).   [7] *Korematsu v. United States* (1944).

is too permissive. I interpret the test as ascertaining the polity's *actual* reason or rationale for passing a law – a kind of rational review with bite.[8] Fulfilling Justification requires determining whether that reason is rational, whether the polity truly seeks only to prevent harm.

In line with Part II of this book, this Part also makes dual claims. By rejecting the pathology of categorization – whether it be rights or a concern with class or classification – turning instead to the minimization of demonstrable harm, we better ensure equality and freedom (the first claim). At the same time, we permit greater democratic flexibility (the second claim). By leaving individuals and groups out of the constitutional equation looking only to legislative purpose, we better balance and fulfill the values of liberty and democracy.

In framing my argument, I concede from the outset that constitutional law does not entirely accept my theory of Justification. In going from ideal theory to the law, two things are lost in translation. First, as mentioned before, I do not contend that constitutional law rejects all rights. I make the more limited argument that it has carried out the project of Part II for only economic, religious, and intimate activities – the rights of property, religion, and privacy. Second, the constraint of consent undoubtedly plays a central role in my theory rejecting much paternalistic legislation. But currently, case law does not endorse the condition of non-consent. It accepts paternalism. For example, laws against suicide are constitutional.[9] After all, constitutional law views paternalistic laws as legitimately securing the health and safety of the members of the polity. However, I do suggest that constitutional law has moved to accepting the constraint of demonstrability – rejecting morals legislation. In this Part, then, I speak of the minimization of demonstrable harm. Constitutional jurisprudence is better off accepting even this partial construction of my justificatory constraint.

In this chapter, I focus on the Court's rejection of the right to property and religion leaving privacy for the next chapter. I purposely approach

---

[8] See, e.g., *Bankers Life & Cas. Co. v. Crenshaw*, 486 U.S. 71 (1988) ("[A]rbitrary and irrational discrimination violates the Equal Protection Clause under even our most deferential standard of review," at 83). *Nordlinger v. Hahn*, 505 U.S. 1 (1992) (under rational review "the relationship of the classification to its goal is not so attenuated as to render the distinction arbitrary or irrational," at 11); *Romer v. Evans*, 517 U.S. 620 (1996) (employing a kind of rational review with bite to invalidate Colorado's homophobic amendment); *Tuan Anh Nguyen v. INS*, 533 U.S. 53 (2001) (Justice O'Conner, dissenting, "Rational basis review … is much more tolerant of the use of broad generalizations about different classes of individuals so long as the classification is not arbitrary or irrational," at 76); *Lawrence v. Texas* (2003) (Justice O'Conner, concurrence, affirming a more "searching form of rational review," at 508).

[9] *Washington v. Glucksberg* (1997) (holding that due process right to privacy does not include the right to suicide).

these traditional areas of the private sphere in that order: the rejection of property being the least novel or controversial and the rejection of privacy being the most.

Rejecting the rights to property and contract

The substantive due process clause of the Fourteenth Amendment[10] is the primary textual provision protecting the right to property and the right to contract. I argue that in the 1930s, the New Deal Court rejected this appeal to substantive due process. It re-negotiated the public/private divide by permitting regulation of the economy and repudiating the rights to property and contract that conventionally accompany it. The Court, as I suggest, rejects such rights permitting the democratic polity to regulate the economy as it sees fit.

Lochner v. New York (1905) represents the classic, conventional picture of the autonomous economic, private sphere and the pathology of carving up those areas off limits to state interference. In this case, the state of New York passed a law mandating certain working conditions and a maximum 60-hour working week for bakers. New York sought to regulate the bakery profession, exercising its collective power to legislate a particular economic theory. In thwarting a democratic decision, the Court declared such maximum hours legislation unconstitutional. In implicitly upholding the pre-political commitment to an economic sphere (and its accompanying right to property/contract), the Court reasoned that the statute interfered with "the right of contract between the employer and employees."[11] It was held unconstitutional.

Just as Nozick sees rights as side-constraints attaching to individuals prohibiting the state from upsetting a historical pattern, so too does the *Lochner* Court. It refuses to upset or constrain consensual economic dealings. Constraining democratic flexibility, the *Lochner* Court does not permit the polity to un-do such patterns. Nozick's thoroughgoing libertarianism and its robust endorsement of an economic sphere stand as the normative justification for *Lochner*.

Lochner, much like Locke, implicitly sees the right to property as natural, as beyond the scope of state regulation. The polity may not seek to minimize economic harm, because doing so encroaches upon a pre-political interest of the individual. For the libertarian, economic disparities are legitimate, independent of the political process. They stand in

---

[10] "[N]or shall any State deprive any person of life, liberty, or property, without due process of law ... ." U.S. Constitution Amendment XIV § 1.

[11] *Lochner* at 53.

an economic sphere beyond the range of state power. In invalidating a democratically enacted law seeking to regulate the economy, *Lochner* undercuts democracy's ability to define our normative obligations.

Moreover, and this is a purely constitutional difficulty, the textual basis for such a right was found in the due process clause of the Fourteenth Amendment. Under the due process clause, no state can "deprive any person of life, liberty, or property, without due process of law."[12] Compare this with other amendments such as the First Amendment ("Congress shall make no law ... abridging freedom of speech"), Second Amendment ("the right of the people to keep and bear arms shall not be infringed"), and Sixth Amendment ("the accused shall enjoy the right to a speedy and public trial"). In each of these cases, the text states that there is a right, interest, or area that government may not infringe or violate. Such amendments do not say anything about process. For instance, the First Amendment does not read: "Congress shall make no law ... abridging freedom of speech *without due process*."

But the Fourteenth Amendment in discussing life, liberty, and property does qualify such interests with the language of "due process." In other words, as a textual matter, the state may deprive you of life, liberty, or property as long as it affords you due process of law. Though due process by its very terms speaks of procedure ("process") and not substance, *Lochner* parlays the term to include the right to contract. "The right to purchase or to sell labor is part of the liberty protected by this amendment."[13] *Lochner* treats this clause in the Fourteenth Amendment as guaranteeing certain substantive rights like the right to free speech or the right to bear arms. It takes language that invokes procedure in order to generate a non-procedural right, here the rights to property and contract.

Scholars have criticized this right for lacking a textual basis in the Constitution. In fact, this kind of judicial reasoning is pejoratively referred to as Lochnerism.[14] John Ely contends that locating such rights in due process turns out too open-ended, leaving such a technique vulnerable to the vicissitudes of the moment.[15] As Ely goes on to state, "that attitude, of course, is precisely the point of the *Lochner* philosophy, which would grant unusual protection to those 'rights' that somehow *seem* most pressing, regardless of whether the Constitution suggests any special solicitude for them."[16] This textual difficulty and the charge of Lochnerism will appear again in discussing the modern privacy cases and their grounding of the right to privacy in the oxymoronic doctrine of substantive due process.

---

[12] U.S. Constitution Amendment XIV.   [13] *Lochner* at 53.
[14] Abraham 1990, John Ely 1980.   [15] John Ely 1973.   [16] Ibid.: 939.

In any case, with the New Deal and Franklin D. Roosevelt's threat to pack the Court, the Court reversed its position, abandoning the private sphere's conventional commitment to the rights of property and contract. It rejected them, allowing the democratic polity flexibility in passing economic legislation. Though the Court never explicitly overruled *Lochner*, it effectively did so in a series of cases such as *Nebbia v. New York* (1934), *West Coast Hotel Co. v. Parrish* (1937), and *United States v. Carolene Products Co.* (1938). In *Nebbia*, for instance, the Court upheld a New York law that regulated minimum and maximum retail prices. Contra *Lochner*, the *Nebbia* Court reasoned that:

neither property rights nor contract rights are absolute; for government cannot exist if the citizen may at will use his property to the detriment of his fellows, or exercise his freedom of contract to work them harm. Equally fundamental with the private right is that of the public to regulate it in the common interest.[17]

The Court sought to repudiate the economic sphere rejecting the trumping rights of property and contract that accompany it. The "private character of business," as the *Nebbia* Court reasoned, "does not necessarily remove it from the realm of regulation of charges and prices."[18] By rejecting the allegedly special nature of the economy, the Court permits the polity to pass such economic legislation. It turned its attention away from individuals to the polity's rationale to regulate "in the common interest." As long as the polity seeks to minimize harm – secure the health and safety of its members – the Court rightly leaves the decision with the democratic majority. Here the Court limits government by limiting the reason or rationale on which the polity may act instead of carving out those areas, interests, or spheres – such as the economic sphere – off limits to state regulation.

In *West Coast Hotel*, the Court addressed the constitutionality of Washington's minimum wage law. Declaring a victory for leaving the democratic polity to decide such issues, *West Coast Hotel* upheld the regulation spelling the demise of the absolute right to contract and the autonomous economic sphere. "In dealing with the relation of employer and employed, the Legislature has necessarily a wide field of discretion in order that there may be suitable protection of health and safety."[19] In accord with my theory of Justification, the Court looks to the rationale of the legislation. In fact, in *West Coast Hotel* the Court appealed to the unequal bargaining position of the parties to support this kind of state action. Conceding that the parties are competent to contract, it held that in such relationships the "parties do not stand upon an

---

[17] *Nebbia* at 510.   [18] Ibid.: at 535.   [19] *West Coast Hotel* at 393.

equal ... footing."[20] Though my argument in ideal theory rejects this kind of paternalism, constitutional law does not. It does not require that harm be non-consensual. Important for the argument here is that in *West Coast Hotel* – contra *Lochner* – the Court did acknowledge that the polity may regulate or prevent harm in the economic sphere.

Carolene Products consummated the collapse of the libertarian, laissez-faire economic sphere. Here the Court upheld a Congressional prohibition on the shipment of certain skimmed milk compounds. In deeming that economic legislation gets mere rational review the Court held that:

> [T]he existence of facts supporting the legislative judgment is to be presumed, for regulatory legislation affecting ordinary commercial transactions is not to be pronounced unconstitutional unless ... it [does not rest] upon some rational basis.[21]

Again, *Carolene Products* contemplates heightened scrutiny only for those statutes that discriminate against fundamental rights or particular minorities. By implication, then, the rights to property and contract are *not fundamental*. These conventional commitments of the private economic sphere are not specifically secured by the Constitution. They do not warrant higher scrutiny, tying the hands of the polity. Like their religion counterpart to be explored below, there is nothing special about them. As long as the state seeks to protect health and safety – acts "upon some rational basis" – the Court ought not to intervene.

The above cases strike a blow to the due process right to property. The more recent *Kelo v. City of New London* (2005) expands the state's power of eminent domain under the Fifth Amendment. In part that amendment reads: nor "shall private property be taken for public use, without just compensation."[22] The Court has dealt a further blow to property[23] by substantially gutting the "public use" limitation of the takings clause. Here too it rejects the conventional account of limited government sanctioning wide democratic flexibility.

In *Kelo*, the city of New London approved a development plan to increase tax revenue and revitalize an economically distressed city. Part of the plan gave land to a private non-profit entity that would in turn develop it.[24] When certain private owners were unwilling to sell their parcels of land, the city initiated condemnation proceedings.[25] The

---

[20] Ibid.: at 394.   [21] *Carolene Products* at 152.   [22] U.S. Constitution Amendment V.
[23] Roderick Walston suggests that with the New Deal's evisceration of the right to property, the takings clause becomes particularly important in protecting such a right (Walston 2001).
[24] *Kelo* at 2658.   [25] Ibid.: at 2660.

issue before the Court was whether this taking (though compensated) met the public use requirement of the Fifth Amendment, whether it constituted a case of eminent domain. Even though the land would be given to a private entity, the Court upheld the takings reasoning that the city had robust democratic discretion in regulating property that would serve the public interest. After all, the appeal to public interest constitutes an appropriate ground on which the polity may act. The Court reasoned that legislatures have "broad latitude in determining what public needs justify the use of the takings power."[26]

The dissenting opinion laments the further rejection of the sanctity of private property. "Under the banner of economic development, all private property is now vulnerable to being taken and transferred to another private owner, so long as it might be upgraded – i.e. given to an owner who will use it in a way that the legislature deems more beneficial to the public – in the process."[27] The Cato Institute, a conservative think tank, echoes this concern in a Cato Supreme Court Review. Writing the Review, James W. Ely, Jr. contends that *Kelo* represents a further lamentable elaboration of the New Deal "constitutional hegemony that radically weakened traditional judicial solicitude for economic rights."[28] By permitting broad regulation of property under both the due process clause and the takings clause, the Court effectively rejects this conventional commitment of the private sphere.

With these decisions comes an implicit acceptance of Justice Oliver Wendell Holmes' dissent in *Lochner*. As argued in Chapter 5, the democratic polity must decide what, if any, demonstrable harms to minimize. Holmes endorses such democratic flexibility in economic matters reasoning that:

[A] Constitution is not intended to embody a particular economic theory, whether of paternalism and the organic relation of the citizen to the state or of laissez faire. It is made for people of fundamentally differing views, and the accident of our finding certain opinions natural and familiar, or novel, and even shocking, ought not to conclude our judgment upon the question whether statutes embodying them conflict with the Constitution of the United States.[29]

Reasonable people will disagree about such economic harm, and rightly so. Holmes values democracy. He implicitly understands that there is nothing special about property or the economic private sphere. Accordingly, the Court subjects laws that regulate the economy to rational review not heightened scrutiny. Constitutional jurisprudence permits the polity to redistribute resources or place conditions on contract formation.

---

[26] Ibid.: at 2664.   [27] Ibid.: at 2671, dissenting.
[28] James Ely 2005: 40.   [29] *Lochner* at 76, dissenting.

Lochner's overturning of a democratic decision to regulate contracts forecloses such democratic flexibility needlessly affirming the conventional focus on rights. Indicating an acceptance of my theory of Justification, Holmes' dissent entertains the very range of options that such a theory of limited government creates – libertarian, welfarist, communistic, etc. Admittedly, by rejecting rights, I also reject any affirmative right to welfare or equality. The polity need not redistribute wealth. It could opt for a laissez-faire theory of economics. The point is that this decision must be left to the polity, a decision that the Court in *Lochner* took away from the New York legislature. As a historical matter, it was the right to property that thwarted attempts to redistribute wealth or regulate the economy. American legal history suggests that we need only repudiate such a right rather than impose an affirmative one.

Constitutional law's rejection of the special status of property is not a novel claim. Admittedly, scholars disagree about the Framers concern over property. Some contend that the Lockean pre-political commitment stood at the center of the Founding[30] while others push for a less materialistic, more republican vision of the Early Republic.[31] However, whatever may have been the intent of the Framers, the Court's modern evisceration of economic rights opening the way for substantive democratic flexibility is widely acknowledged. Even if scholars disagree about whether constitutional law should have taken this turn, the current state of the law is not in dispute. Ackerman, for instance, argues that this turn away from the right to property was an affirmation of a higher law-making moment, refashioning the constitutional baseline.[32] Others lament such New Deal decisions suggesting a return to the natural rights approach of *Lochner*.[33] Douglas Ginsburg, a conservative jurist on the District of Columbia Court of Appeals, characterizes the conventional, right-to-property-based *Lochner*-era Constitution as the "Constitution-in-Exile"[34] conceding that current doctrine rejects such a right. Justice Clarence Thomas, one of the most conservative members of the Court, contends that the "Court's dramatic departure in the 1930s from a century and a half of precedent" was a "wrong turn."[35] Even if they disagree about the soundness of this departure and its ensuing deference to democratic decision-making, all agree that current constitutional doctrine has effectively repudiated the right to property.

---

[30] Beard 1913, Hartz 1955.   [31] Bailyn 1967, Wood 1969, cf. Skinner 1997.
[32] Ackerman 1998: 312–344.   [33] Arkes 1995, Epstein 1988, Siegan 1980.
[34] D. Ginsburg 1995: 83.
[35] Justice Thomas' concurrence in *U.S. v. Lopez*, 514 U.S. 549 (1995) (holding that Gun Free School Zones Act exceeded Congress' commerce clause power).

I, on the other hand, applaud such a rejection, because such economic decisions are, under my theory of Justification, rightly left to the polity. The democratic polity may choose to institute any number of economic regimes.

Rejecting the right to religion

Though the Court's repudiation of the economic component of the private sphere is widely recognized – even if criticized – rejection of the special status of religion seems less obvious.[36] In the remaining part of this chapter, I argue that case law generally rejects the special, unique status of religion. The Court appropriately turns away from a focus on the religious observer and her right to religion, looking instead to the democratic polity's reason for enacting the regulation.

I argue that just as there is nothing special about the economy – the Court permits regulation of it – constitutional law also fails to offer religion any special solicitude. Religion is like any other association, group, or preference deserving no more and no less protection. As far as the Constitution is concerned the Sikh is the same as the hat wearer, the Christian the same as the Rotarian.

The ensuing cases, then, set out two complementary rules. First, if a law is facially neutral – it just so happens to burden a wide range of groups one of which is religion – no exemptions or accommodations are constitutionally required. In these instances, the Court rightly defers to the democratic will even when religion is burdened. Religion gets no extra constitutional protection. Second, if non-religion is offered some benefit or exemption, then that benefit must be offered to religion. Here the Court invalidates those laws that single out religion for unfavorable treatment. Such legislation obviously seeks to do something other than merely protect health and safety therefore failing constitutional muster. These cases represent the Court's concern with legislative purpose rather than with individuals or groups.

Religion is neither more important nor less important than its associative or preference counterpart. As a matter of constitutional law, religion cannot be advantaged or disadvantaged vis-à-vis other associations or preferences.[37] I suggest that this both permits substantive democratic flexibility as well as ensures that the polity does not promote or advance

---

[36] *Pace* Carter 1993, Sandel 1996, Tushnet 2001.

[37] Vincent Phillip Munoz (2003) proffers a similar principle calling it a theory of "non-cognizance." The law should not be cognizant of religion. He argues that a proper understanding of James Madison's "Memorial and Remonstrance" reveals the principle that "the state may neither *privilege* nor *penalize* religious institutions, religious citizens, or religiously motivated conduct as such" (Munoz 2003: 17) (emphasis added). These dual

religion. First, I look to the Court's jurisprudence on religion (and primarily the free exercise clause) in articulating these dual claims, claims that constitute the Court's rejection of the right to religion. Second, I contend that this rejection is neither novel nor a cause for constitutional alarm given that the First Amendment protects all associations – religion and non-religion.

Religion no more important than non-religion

Laws invariably impinge on religious activity or make such activity more difficult. The Court has been reluctant, though, to require that the democratic majority specially accommodate religion. As long as laws are facially neutral, the Court has generally held that the free exercise clause of the First Amendment ("Congress shall make no law ... prohibiting the free exercise [of religion]"[38]) does not require accommodation.[39] In doing so, the Court rightly defers to the democratic polity.

For example, in upholding the Sunday Closing Laws,[40] the Court acknowledged that such laws could disadvantage some religions. Here the claimants were Orthodox Jews. Their faith already required that they abstain from all manner of work from Friday night to Saturday night. Because their shops had to be closed on Saturday for religious reasons, the law threatened their ability to earn a livelihood by prohibiting them from opening on Sunday. Even though the law so burdened the claimants, the Court held that this did not rise to a free exercise violation. The Court concluded that the purpose of such laws no longer retained their religious character. On the contrary, these closing laws sought to offer the weekly laborer a day of rest and repose to improve overall productivity.[41] Given an appropriate legislative purpose, the effect on religion was *not* constitutionally material. The Court refused to offer the religious practice any more protection.

claims constitute the core of my argument regarding the Court's rejection of the special status of religion, a rejection that may very well accord with the Madisonian vision. See also Eisgruber and Sager (2007).

[38] U.S. Constitution Amendment I.

[39] These exemptions are, in the language of Kymlicka (1995: 30–31), polyethnic rights.

[40] *Braunfeld v. Brown*, 366 U.S. 599 (1961) and *McGowan v. Maryland*, 366 U.S. 420 (1961).

[41] *Braunfeld* at 607 ("[W]e cannot find a state without power to provide a weekly respite from all labor and, at the same time, to set one day of the week apart from the others as a day of rest, repose, recreation, and tranquility – a day when the hectic tempo of everyday existence ceases and a more pleasant atmosphere is created, a day which all members of the family and community have the opportunity to spend and enjoy together, a day on which people may visit friends and relatives who are not available during working days, a day when the weekly laborer may best regenerate himself. This is particularly true in this day and age of increasing state concern with public welfare. legislation"); *McGowan* at 444–445.

Similarly, in *Goldman v. Weinberger* (1986), an Orthodox Jew in the Air Force was not allowed to wear his yarmulke while on duty. The military's dress code policy forbade the wearing of any kind of non-authorized headgear – including religious ones. He sued claiming that the Air Force regulation violated his right to the free exercise of his religion. In rejecting Goldman's claim, the Court once again reasoned that free exercise does not constitutionally obligate the government to accommodate or exempt religion.[42] The state is not required to treat religion any differently. The dress code was legitimate, because the rationale underlying it sought to ensure "hierarchical unity" by minimizing the harm of "individual distinctions."[43] In other words, the "uniformity sought by the dress regulations" was a neutral goal that could impinge on such religious activity.[44] It did not matter that the law burdened religion. Its rationale or justification was proper.

The dissenting opinion in *Weinberger* concedes that if Goldman merely wanted to "wear a hat to keep his head warm or cover a bald spot[,]" no accommodation would be constitutionally required.[45] The dissent, then, invokes the private sphere's traditional commitment to religion – treating religion differently from its non-religion counterparts. If a mere preference were at issue instead of a religious practice, the dissent would easily reject the claim for exemption.

Because *Weinberger* repudiates the special, unique status of religion, the majority opinion fails to make this conventional distinction between religion and non-religion, between a yarmulke and a mere preference for a hat. By doing so, wearing a yarmulke has the same constitutional status as wearing a hat. The Court refuses to engage in classification or categorization – seeing the former as special and the latter as a mere preference.

Goldman could still wear his yarmulke in non-military settings. The military regulation only prescribed appropriate headgear while on duty. The Sunday Closing Laws also only economically disadvantaged religion. Neither of these laws prohibited the religious activity outright. However, the Court considered just such a law in *Reynolds v. U.S.* (1879) (held that free exercise did not exempt Mormon bigamy from criminal laws against it) and *Employment Division, Dept. of Human Resources v. Smith* (1990) (held that free exercise did not exempt Native American religious use of peyote from a law against controlled substances). In these cases, the religious activity was not merely disadvantaged. Here a facially neutral law prohibited the activity entirely.

---

[42] *Weinberger* at 509–510.   [43] Ibid.: at 508.
[44] Ibid.: at 509.   [45] Ibid.: at 503, Justice Brennan, dissenting.

In considering the possibility of religious exemptions from the law, the *Reynolds* Court focuses on the right question of "whether those who make polygamy a part of their religion are excepted from the operation of the statute."[46] Squarely answering in the negative, the Court claims that to allow such an exemption would un-do the very purpose of government. "To permit [an exemption for Mormons] would be to make the professed doctrines of religious belief superior to the law of the land, and in effect to permit every citizen to become a law unto himself. Government could exist only in name under such circumstances."[47] In this way, the Court fails to treat religion differently from non-religion or a mere preference, reasoning quite stridently that doing otherwise jeopardizes the existence of the state. Once again focusing on the legislative purpose, the *Reynolds* Court reasons that a democratic polity may very well decide that laws against polygamy minimize the harm of patriarchy and "despotism."[48]

Smith also looks to the legislative purpose of the law instead of its effects. At issue in *Smith* was a criminal prohibition on controlled substances, a prohibition that included peyote. Justice Scalia, writing for the Court, held that the law's rationale is to minimize "socially harmful conduct."[49] As this is a legitimate purpose, the constitutionality of the law does not depend on its effects on religion:[50]

It would doubtless be unconstitutional, for example, to ban the casting of "statues that are to be used for worship purposes," or to prohibit bowing down before a golden calf.

Respondents in the present case, however, seek to carry the meaning of "prohibiting the free exercise [of religion]" one step further. They contend that their religious motivation for using peyote places them beyond the reach of a criminal law that is not specifically directed at their religious practice, and that is concededly constitutional as applied to those who use the drug for other reasons.[51]

These "other reasons" simply include non-religious ones. Just as someone may not smoke peyote for fun or "kicks," she may not do so for religious reasons – or so the Court suggests. Focus on the religious observer – the Orthodox Jew or the Native American – is not relevant, only the legislative purpose.

In response to *Smith*, Congress passed the Religious Freedom Restoration Act of 1993 (RFRA).[52] This act declared that religion is an "unalienable right" that may not be burdened without a compelling justification. In singling out religion, Congress no doubt sought in very clear language to deem it more important than non-religion, than a mere preference. RFRA stands as an attempt to reaffirm the private sphere's

---

[46] *Reynolds* at 166.   [47] Ibid.: at 167.   [48] Ibid.: at 166.   [49] *Smith* at 885.
[50] Ibid.: at 885.   [51] Ibid.: at 878.   [52] H.R. 1308.

commitment to the right to religion, to its special status. However, the Court struck down the Act in *City of Boerne v. Flores* (1997) arguing that it went beyond the remedial powers granted to Congress under the Fourteenth Amendment. Effectively, Congress could not in such a broad manner alter the constitutional floor. For our purposes, the decision reaffirms the principle that, as a matter of constitutional law, religion is no more important than non-religion.

Yet, the democratic majority may, if it so desires, pass more modest accommodation legislation. As general matter, the Constitution sets the floor leaving states and the federal government to fashion more inclusive laws. Whereas the free exercise clause *does not* require exemptions, the government may, in some circumstances, choose to offer them. This rightly leaves the democratic polity with needed flexibility. In *City of Boerne*, the federal government had gone too far in enacting RFRA. However, in *Cutter v. Wilkinson* (2005) the Court upheld the Religious Land Use and Institutionalized Persons Act, a more modest measure under the spending and commerce clauses prohibiting government from imposing a substantial burden on the religious activity of inmates in prisons. The federal government's conscientious objector exemption also privileges religion over a mere preference (*U.S. v. Seeger* (1965)), 10 U.S.C. 774 (a)–(b) permits an exemption for religious apparel responding to *Weinberger*, and Title VII exempts religious groups from the prohibition on religious discrimination. These represent instantiations of democratic flexibility. By failing to afford religion any special status, the Court rightly leaves the polity to decide whether to provide such affirmative accommodation. The Court affords democracy a substantive role. Similarly, by rejecting property, the Court permits the polity to institute any number of economic regimes.

However, the Court reins in such democratic decision-making when it goes too far in accommodating religion, privileging religion over non-religion. In these cases, the Court examines the legislative purpose deeming it constitutionally improper. The Establishment Clause[53] provides the corresponding text. If legislation seeks to unconstitutionally promote religion, it obviously does something other than merely minimize harm. For example, in *Thorton v. Caldor* (1985) and *Texas Monthly, Inc. v. Bullock* (1989), the Court struck down on establishment grounds a Connecticut statute that provided Sabbath observers with an absolute and unqualified right not to work on their day of Sabbath and a Texas sales tax exemption for religious periodicals, respectively.

---

[53] U.S. Constitution Amendment I "Congress shall make no law respecting an establishment of religion …"

In these two cases, religion was so advantaged as to run afoul of the establishment clause. In *Thorton*, the Court held that the Connecticut statute did not have a secular purpose. By imposing on employers "an absolute duty to conform their business practices to the particular religious practices of the employee" the statute advances religion.[54] In smoking out this improper legislative purpose, the concurring opinion realizes that the exempting statute does not afford non-religious practices similar accommodation.[55] As long as we articulate the only legitimate rationale on which the state may act – the prevention of demonstrable harm – we can be confident that the Court will overturn such laws that privilege religion.

Similarly, in *Texas Monthly*, the Court invalidated a Texas law that gave a sales tax exemption only to religious periodicals. The exclusive nature of the tax – like its counterpart in *Thorton* – suggested that an illegitimate legislative purpose was afoot. The rationale was not secular.[56] As the Court reasoned, Texas could not claim that it sought to subsidize, by an exemption, the community's cultural and intellectual character, an otherwise legitimate rationale. Since the exemption applied only to religion and no other cultural or intellectual groups, this could not have been the purpose.[57] Consequently, these kinds of law fail constitutional muster. In line with my account of limited government, they fail to embody the secular rationale of minimizing harm.

Contrastingly in *Walz v. Tax Commission of City of New York* (1970), the Court upheld a New York law under the establishment clause that granted a tax exemption for "religious, educational or charitable purposes."[58] Here, unlike *Thorton and Texas Monthly*, the legislation did not seek to advance religion. The Court reasoned that the New York law did not single

out one particular church or religious group or even churches as such; rather, it has granted exemption to all houses of religious worship within a broad class of property owned by nonprofit, quasi-public corporations which include hospitals, libraries, playgrounds, scientific, professional, historical, and patriotic groups.[59]

Because the law exempted other non-profit groups including religion, the "legislative purpose of [the] property tax exemption is neither the advancement nor the inhibition of religion."[60] The Establishment Clause was not violated in this case, because religion was treated like any other non-profit association. It was not considered more important.

However, the notable exception to this constitutional principle is *Wisconsin v. Yoder* (1972). Here members of the Amish order sought exemption from a Wisconsin law that required compulsory school attendance until the age of

---

[54] *Thorton* at 709–710.   [55] Ibid.: concurring at 711.   [56] *Texas Monthly* at 15.
[57] Ibid.: at 15–16.   [58] *Walz* at 666–667.   [59] Ibid.: at 673.   [60] Ibid.: at 672.

sixteen. The Court held that free exercise *required* an exemption. The ruling is clearly incongruous with the cases above. Here the Court constitutionally required the government to offer an exemption to religion. Whereas other parents could not exempt their children from the school attendance rule, the Court deemed that the Amish must be allowed to do so.

There is no question that the law was facially neutral. It served the state's educational goals. By requiring education until the age of sixteen, Wisconsin clearly sought to prevent the harm of having uneducated citizens.[61] The Court recognized that "[p]roviding public schools ranks at the very apex of the function of a State."[62] Certainly, the Court would not have required that Wisconsin accommodate non-religion. Suppose parents wanted to remove their children from school for reasons having nothing to do with religion. The Court would have no doubt rejected such a claim. Its anomalous treatment of religion is at odds with the cases above. Here the Court problematically looks to the individual interest instead of keeping its constitutional eye on just the legislative purpose. With a clearly permissible rationale, the effect on religion should not be constitutionally relevant. The Court's free exercise of jurisprudence establishes the principle that religion is no more important than non-religion.

The case seems particularly striking given the role of children. After all, one of the problems with the private sphere's commitment to religion is the domination of minorities within it. In *Smith* and *Reynolds*, the parties affected were all adults. Adults were seeking to have their religious activities exempted. Though adults certainly brought the case in *Yoder* – they no doubt had standing – the exemption they sought applied directly to their children, children whose interests were seemingly ignored. Justice William Douglas' dissent focuses on this very issue – worrying that such an exemption could end up trumping the interests of the children:

If the parents in this case are allowed a religious exemption, the inevitable effect is to impose the parents' notions of religious duty upon their children ... As the child has no other effective forum, it is in this litigation that his rights should be considered.[63]

As Douglas suggests, we see the tendency of the private sphere to shield from state regulation harm that occurs to the vulnerable internal minorities of minorities – here the children of the Amish.

Needless to say, I find the holding not only a deviation from the Court's general jurisprudence on free exercise but also a mechanism by which to reinforce the private sphere's domination of vulnerable minorities. On the constitutional side, subsequent cases have interpreted *Yoder*'s holding as

---

[61] *Yoder* at 213.   [62] Ibid.   [63] Ibid.: at 242, dissenting.

arising from a hybrid claim of free exercise and the right to raise your children as you see fit.[64] Subsequent cases suggest that unlike *Smith* and *Reynolds*, free exercise and another right (here a right to parenting) are at play in *Yoder*.

This hybrid claim, though, makes little sense. Apparently, religion is no more important than non-religion, unless it also implicates another constitutional right. But the right of parents to instruct their children[65] would apply to non-religion as well. If non-Amish parents sought to exempt their children from the compulsory Wisconsin attendance law, the Court would have certainly rejected their claim. The state's interest would trump the right to parenting. How can this right, then, breathe life into a right to religion that the Court has already rejected?

Conceding that *Yoder* is hard to distinguish constitutionally from *Smith* and *Reynolds*, I consider it inconsistent with the Court's general repudiation of the right to religion. By once again touting the right to religion, the Court frustrates democratic decision-making. Undoing the educational goals of the state, it required that Wisconsin offer an exemption for the Amish. In contending that the Court has rejected the special status of religion, *Yoder* stands as a glaring exception.

Religion no less important than non-religion

In treating religion like any other preference or association, constitutional law also mandates that religion not be given worse treatment. The flipside of not advantaging religion is not disadvantaging it. The next series of cases outline the Court's rule that if non-religion is exempted from a law or treated in a particular way, the Constitution requires that religion be treated in a similar fashion. After all, if there is nothing special about religion, there is no presumptive reason to treat it worse, to treat it any differently. In line with the account of limited government proffered in Part II, this symmetry informs an inquiry regarding legislative purpose.

The principle arises in *Sherbert v. Verner* (1963) and its companion unemployment compensation cases.[66] *Sherbert* held that a denial of unemployment benefits on account of religion violated the free exercise clause. In *Sherbert*, the appellant was a member of the Seventh-Day Adventist

---

[64] See, e.g., *Smith* at 881. ("The only decisions in which we have held that the First Amendment bars application of neutral, generally applicable law to religiously motivated action have involved not only the Free Exercise Clause alone, but the Free Exercise Clause in conjunction with other constitutional protections.")

[65] *Pierce v. Society of Sisters*, 268 U.S. 510 (1925).

[66] *Thomas v. Review Board*, 450 U.S. 707 (1981); *Hobbie v. Unemployment Appeals Commission*, 480 U.S. 136 (1987). In *Thomas* and *Hobbie*, like *Sherbert*, the law at issue made some kind of exemption for non-religion.

church. Her religion required that she not work on Saturday, the day of her Sabbath. She sought jobs in South Carolina only to be turned down, because she refused to work on Saturday. Consequently, she filed for unemployment benefits under the South Carolina Compensation Act. She was denied such benefits. The relevant portion of the statute, as quoted by the Court, read that a "claimant is ineligible for benefits [i]f ... he has failed, without good cause ... to accept available suitable work when offered him by the employment office or the employer."[67] Thus, the statute offered some kind of relief to individuals – even if on an individualized, discretionary basis informed by "good cause." Since the law permits exemptions for non-religion, free exercise requires that it must accommodate religion as well.

For example, in *McDaniel v. Paty* (1978), the Court held that under the free exercise clause Tennessee could not bar ministers or priests from serving as delegates to the state legislature. The law treated religion as less important than non-religion. After all, the Tennessee constitutional provision did not disqualify anyone else on grounds of non-religious membership or preference. By singling out religion, Tennessee unconstitutionally disadvantaged religion. There is no justification for such disparate treatment. As the Court remarked, "the American experience provides no persuasive support for the fear that clergymen in public office will be less careful of anti-establishment interests or less faithful to their oaths of civil office than their unordained counterparts."[68] The rationale for such legislation was to "stick it to" religion. In *Sherbert* and *McDaniel* the Court invalidated laws that treated religion as less worthy of protection than non-religion, holding that the legislative purpose was illegitimate.

In *Smith*, the Court articulates the principle that religion is no less important than non-religion:

a distinctive feature of unemployment compensation programs is that their eligibility criteria invite consideration of the particular circumstances behind an applicant's unemployment: "The statutory conditions [in *Sherbert* and *Thomas*] provided that a person was not eligible for unemployment compensation benefits if, 'without good cause', he had quit work or refused available work. The 'good cause' standard created a mechanism for individualized exemptions." [citations omitted] [As our] decisions in the unemployment cases stand for the proposition that where the State has in place a system of individualized exemptions, *it may not refuse* to extend that system to cases of "religious hardship" without compelling reason.[69]

In other words, if the law contemplates an exemption for non-religion, the state may not deny this possibility to religion. Doing so is arbitrary.

---

[67] *Sherbert* at 401.   [68] *McDaniel* at 629.   [69] *Smith* at 884 (emphasis added).

Religion is like any other preference. It can neither be advantaged – given an exemption where none is offered – nor disadvantaged – denied an exemption where others are explicitly offered.

Subsequent cases bear out this principle that religion is no worse than non-religion.[70] For example, the Court affirms it in *Church of the Lukumi Babalu Aye, Inc. v. City of Hialeah* (1993). Here members of the Santeria religion began setting up a church in the city of Hialeah. Knowing that the adherents of this religion practice ritual animal slaughter, the city council passed a series of ordinances that outlawed animal slaughter permitting a number of exemptions. The Court struck down the ordinances as violating the free exercise clause. Here the law was not facially neutral, because it treated religion as less important than non-religion. The law made sure to exempt certain non-religious activity from the slaughter prohibition – much like the "good cause" exception in the unemployment compensation statute. The ordinances in *Lukumi* left only religion, and specifically the practices of Santeria, vulnerable to sanction. For example, one of the ordinances, as the Court points out, defines sacrifice as "to unnecessarily kill … an animal in a public or private ritual or ceremony not for the primary purpose of food consumption."[71] Consequently, the law privileges killing animals for food over killing them for religious reasons.

Another of the ordinances, outlawing animal slaughter, specifically exempts certain "licensed [food] establishment[s]."[72] In permitting exemptions only for non-religious reasons – such as the raising and killing of livestock – the ordinance fails constitutional muster. Here the very language of the statute disadvantaged religion, privileging non-religion.[73] The Court concluded that the purpose of the law was the "suppression of the central element of the Santeria worship service."[74] The Court's focus was not on the Santeria group – the conventional analysis – but rather on the polity's purpose in enacting the statute, a purpose that was illegitimate.

Thus, and this is the crucial point, we do not need the right to religion to protect us from such liberty-compromising laws. By simply realizing that the purpose of the city ordinance was to do something other than prevent harm, the Court is able to strike it down. Likewise, in *Sherbert* and the unemployment cases, the statute was unconstitutionally read to exclude religious exceptions when it clearly permitted non-religious ones. We do not need to latch onto the special status of religion and its attachment to

---

[70] Duncan 2005: 1185–1189.   [71] *Lukumi* at 535–536.   [72] Ibid.: at 536.
[73] "To determine the object of a law, we must begin with its text, for the minimum requirements of neutrality is that a law not discriminate on its face" (*Lukumi* at 533).
[74] Ibid.: at 535.

individuals or groups to secure liberty. A look only at the legislative purpose does the necessary work.

Appealing to the line of cases stemming from *Sherbert*, the *Lukumi* Court held that since such ordinances are not facially neutral, they are unconstitutional. The ordinances "devalue [...] religious reasons for killing by judging them to be of lesser import than nonreligious reasons. Thus, religious practice is being singled out for discriminatory treatment."[75] The Court holds that there is nothing special about religion. If that is the case, there is no presumptive rational reason to treat it worse than non-religion.

That having been said, the case of *Locke v. Davey* (2004) – much like its *Yoder* counterpart – represents an unfortunate deviation from this principle. Here the state of Washington created a scholarship program to aid academically gifted students with postsecondary education expenses. In accordance with its state constitution, the law did not permit the recipient to use the scholarship to pursue a devotional theology degree. Joshua Davey desiring to use the money to pursue such studies challenged the law. Surprisingly, the Court held the law constitutional. Distinguishing the case from *Lukumi*, the Court reasoned that here the "disfavor of religion (if it can be called that) is a far milder kind" imposing neither "criminal nor civil sanction on any type of religious service or rite."[76] Moreover, unlike *Sherbert*, it does not require the student to "choose between [his] religious beliefs and receiving a government benefit."[77] *Davey* could have used the money to pursue a non-religious degree.

But such arguments are flawed and do not fit with the cases above. Put simply, the severity of the burden and the choice the law forces one to make seem constitutionally irrelevant. The only relevant inquiry is the legislative purpose. In fact, the circumstances in *Smith* were far worse: there the law was far more burdensome and the choice more stark. The statute upheld in *Smith* prohibited the religious practice entirely, even making it a crime. *Davey*'s reasoning cannot be squared with *Smith*'s. The *Davey* Court assumes that there is something different, unique about religion. Otherwise, if religious instruction were like any other kind of instruction, there is no good reason for the state of Washington to disadvantage only it. *Davey*'s logic treats religion differently.

In his dissent, Justice Scalia points out that the majority violates the principle of *Lukumi* and by implication *Sherbert*:

When the State makes a public benefit generally available, that benefit becomes part of the baseline against which burdens on religion are measured; and when the

---

[75] Ibid.: at 537.   [76] *Davey* at 720.   [77] Ibid.: at 720–721.

State withholds that benefit from some individuals solely on the basis of religion, it violates the Free Exercise Clause.[78]

Again, rejecting the right to religion entails that it is no less and no more important than non-religion. *Davey*, as Scalia rightly argues, violates the former criterion. It cannot be reconciled with the Court's overwhelming repudiation of the right to religion. I consider *Yoder* and *Davey* wrongly decided.

Free exercise clause obsolete

Rejecting the special status of religion, though, need not be cause for constitutional alarm. Mark Tushnet argues that appeal to other constitutional provisions of the First Amendment – speech and association – picks up any constitutional slack rendering the free exercise clause obsolete.[79] By treating religion like any other association, associative freedom can do much of the constitutional and normative work.[80] My theory of Justification permits any association (religion and non-religion) to organize itself in the particular way it sees fit. If adults choose to join an organization that is racist, sexist, or homophobic, as a general matter, the state has no good reason to intervene. Limiting democratic government, by limiting the reason or rationale on which it may act, renders the right to religion obsolete. The Catholic Church may decide not to accept women or openly gay men into the priesthood just as the Ku Klux Klan may decide not to accept non-white members. The right to religion is unnecessary.

Moreover, there is a constitutional peg on which to roughly hang this argument, namely the right of expressive association. As Tushnet argues, the line of cases leading to *Boy Scouts of America v. Dale* (2000) permits associations to exclude members on bases that are inconsistent with the association's message even if such exclusion would otherwise be illegal.[81] In *Dale* the Court effectively held that the Scouts are homophobic, permitting them to exclude gays. "[P]ublic or judicial disapproval of a tenet of an organization's expression does not justify the State's effort to compel the organization to accept members where such acceptance would derogate from the organization's expressive message."[82] But if such exclusion is *not* inconsistent with the association's message, the association may not exclude. Such was the fate of the Jaycees who sought to exclude women from their membership. In that case, the Court held that exclusion of women was not central to the group's message.[83] Hence, the group could not so exclude.

---

[78] Ibid.: at 726–727, dissenting.   [79] Tushnet 2001.   [80] Cf. Kukathas 2003.
[81] Tushnet 2001: 85.   [82] *Dale* at 661.
[83] *Roberts v. United States Jaycees*, 468 U.S. 609 (1984).

Similarly, we need not view the fact that statutory language[84] and case law[85] exempt religious associations from Title VII non-discrimination laws as a religious issue at all but rather one of expression.[86] Just as the Scouts may exclude gays so too may the Catholic Church exclude women from ministerial positions. As Tushnet concedes: "the precise scope of the right of expressive association remains to be determined. At a minimum, it provides a constitutional basis, other than the Free Exercise Clause, for exempting church employees from coverage of state non-discrimination laws."[87]

Cass Sunstein, for example, finds the anomalous treatment of religion from the scope of anti-discrimination law a "puzzle" since other criminal and civil laws no doubt apply to religious associations.[88] He says that according to this asymmetry "it is unproblematic to apply ordinary civil and criminal law to religious institutions, but problematic to apply the law forbidding sex discrimination to those institutions."[89] He finds such an exemption difficult to justify invariably implicating problems of multi-culturalism. After all, his essay appears in a volume addressing the question "Is Multiculturalism Bad for Women?" For Sunstein, this seems to represent a case of treating religion differently from non-religion. That is, he sees this as an instance where religion is afforded special status. However, realizing that such exemptions apply on grounds of expression solves the apparent puzzle removing it from the troublesome confines of multiculturalism. Since all associations, religious and non-religious, may exclude on the basis of their expressive message, this is no longer an issue of religion. Rather, it is a more straightforward First Amendment concern. The question is not whether multiculturalism is bad for women but rather: Is the very notion of expression – and its inherent doctrine of exclusion – bad for women and other groups? An affirmative answer to this question seems easier to swallow. Such exclusion may very well be an inevitable cost to freedom of association. Ultimately, Sunstein's puzzle does not involve a distinction between religion and non-religion.

The asymmetry simply arises from the fact that other illegal activities – notably crimes such as rape and murder – *are not* considered (and perhaps may not be) integral to an association's expression. However, exclusion of women and gays from the priesthood or of non-whites from the Ku Klux

---

[84] § 702 of Title VII, 42 U.S.C. 2000e-1(a).
[85] See, e.g., *Alicea-Hernandez v. Catholic Bishop*, 320 F.3d 698 (7th Cir. 2003), *EEOC v. Roman Catholic Diocese of Raleigh*, 213 F.3d 795 (4th Cir. 2000) (affirming the ministerial exemption that exempts non-discrimination laws from covering employment relationships between religious associations and their "ministers").
[86] Tushnet 2001: 85–86.   [87] Ibid.: 85.
[88] Sunstein 1999, cf. Barry 2001: 169–176.   [89] Sunstein 1999: 86.

Klan does seem important to the message of such groups. Effectively, talk of exemption and the problem of religion in particular are misleading and unnecessary, since all groups – the Catholic Church and the Boy Scouts, for example – may constitutionally exclude under the doctrine of expressive association. The Court has rejected the right to religion, deeming it no more and no less important than non-religion. Religion's alleged special status is not even constitutionally necessary.

7   Rejecting the constitutional right to privacy

By looking entirely to the rationale of the law we also do not need the right to privacy. The normative arguments of Part II find constitutional life in the Court's privacy jurisprudence. *Lawrence v. Texas* (2003), the recent Supreme Court case deeming gay sodomy laws unconstitutional, is the central component of this argument. I contend that a resuscitated rational, single-tier of review is sufficient to do the constitutional work. I argue that a repudiation of morals legislation – legislation that seeks to minimize some non-demonstrable harm – renders the right to privacy and the ensuing need for more exacting scrutiny obsolete.

Like "neutrality," "morals legislation" is on its face a misleading term. Of course, all laws are based on some kind of morality. Caring only about demonstrable harm is a moral stance. By morals legislation, I do not mean all legislation based on morality. That would be an easily defeated position. Rather morals legislation or mere morality is proxy for the refusal to endorse the condition of demonstrability. Morals legislation is legislation that does not pick out some publicly ascertainable harm. Rather, it is legislation whose justification rests on some non-demonstrable harm: gay sex is disgusting or wrong, marriage between individuals of different hair colors is sinful and the like. I argue that rejecting such rationales, requiring that the state only minimize *publicly ascertainable* harm, opens the way for the rejection of privacy.

This chapter is in three parts. First, I review the Court's modern right to privacy cases articulating the relationship among the substantive due process right to privacy, morals legislation, and rational review. I show that we no longer need privacy as long as the state eschews such legislation. Second, I argue that the Court in *Lawrence* generally adopts this argument declaring unconstitutional legislation that seeks to minimize non-demonstrable harm. Specifically, *Lawrence* holds that morals legislation fails rational review paving the way for the constitutional rejection of the problematic and unnecessary right to privacy. Third, I argue that this turn away from privacy toward legislative purpose is also apparent in the Court's abortion jurisprudence.

The relationship among the right to privacy, morals legislation and rational review

Now a general right to privacy can mean (and this is not an exhaustive list) my right to keep my thoughts to myself, my right not to have my home searched, my right not to have my appearance used without my consent, or my right to sleep with whomever I choose. A right to privacy can be seen, among other things, in tort law, in Fourth Amendment jurisprudence, and in the right to property.[1]

My focus is on "decisional privacy," the privacy that protects individuals from government interference in certain "intimate" areas of their lives such as those dealing with sexual or reproductive choices. It finds constitutional substance in *Griswold v. Connecticut* (1965) a case that overturned a ban on contraceptive use for married people. In *Griswold*, the Court articulated the modern right to privacy by appealing to a penumbra of constitutional clauses: "The present case, then, concerns a relationship lying within the zone of privacy created by several fundamental constitutional arrangements."[2] In drawing an implicit right to privacy from such clauses as the right to association in the First Amendment, the Third Amendment's "prohibition against the quartering of soldiers 'in any house' in time of peace without the consent of the owner," and the Fourth Amendment's "right of the people to be secure in their persons, houses, papers, and effects,"[3] the Court grounded this right in the due process clause of the Fourteenth Amendment.[4] Because the contraceptive ban interferes with this right to privacy, the Court applied heightened scrutiny. It invalidated the law reasoning that it could not pass such an exacting standard.[5]

In addition to the problem of tolerance (explored in Part I), there is also a legal difficulty with the right to privacy. Its constitutional version seems to lack a secure textual basis. After all, *Griswold* looks to a constitutional penumbra – rather than an explicit provision – in drawing out such an implicit right. It grounds this right in the oxymoronic doctrine of substantive due process. Like its property counterpart in *Lochner* the modern right

---

[1] In their seminal article on privacy, Warren and Brandeis (1890) primarily discuss these conceptions of privacy.

[2] *Griswold* at 485.   [3] Ibid.: at 484.   [4] Ibid.: at 481–482.

[5] The Court reasoned that the legislation "[could not] stand in light of the familiar principle" that a state purpose "to control or prevent activities constitutionally subject to state regulation may not be achieved by means which sweep unnecessarily broadly." Ibid.: at 485 (quoting *NAACP v. Alabama*, 377 U.S. 288 (1964)). In *Eisenstadt v. Baird* 405 U.S. 438 (1972), the Court, strictly on equal protection grounds, held that since the right to privacy allowed married couples the ability to use contraception, the right extended to unmarried couples as well.

to privacy has little textual basis in the Constitution. *Griswold* attempts to distinguish *Lochner* by reasoning that the contraceptive ban does not touch "economic problems, business affairs, or social conditions" but rather the "intimate relation of husband and wife and their physician's role in one aspect of that relation."[6] But if the Court has rejected the private sphere's commitment to the special status of property, what is so special about the bedroom? What makes privacy so different? If the Court is willing to look only at legislative purpose when it comes to the economy, why shouldn't it do the same for privacy? In fact, as we saw in Chapter 2, the "private" nature of the marital relationship – like its economic counterpart – has shielded harm from state regulation. The appeal to substantive due process leads us to the problem of Lochnerism. We are faced with the difficulty that constructing such rights turns out a generational phenomenon.

Securing sexual freedom by the right to privacy seems constitutionally sticky. Those who look to the right to privacy are stuck between a constitutional rock and hard place. Either concede that *Lochner* was rightly decided thereby permitting the use of substantive due process to generate the privacy right or give up the appeal to due process relinquishing privacy.

I argue that this is a false constitutional dilemma, a dilemma that is easily avoidable. Simply put, we can reject the problematic right to privacy by simply prohibiting morals legislation. This allows us also to reject *Lochner*. Doing so requires re-conceptualizing rational review in line with my theory of Justification. Traditionally, rational review requires that the regulation serve a legitimate purpose.[7] The Court views the conventional police powers of the state as sufficient for meeting this purpose.[8] Specifically, legislation passes rational review if enacted to protect the "health, safety, and *morals* of the general public."[9]

For example, in upholding an Indiana statute prohibiting all-nude dancing in public establishments, the Court in *Barnes v. Glen Theatre, Inc.* (1991) stated that the purpose of the statute was to protect "societal order and morality."[10] The Court went on to write that the "traditional police power of the States is defined as the authority to provide for the public health, safety, and morals, and we have upheld such a basis for legislation."[11] Since the statute did not encroach upon constitutionally protected activities, the Court did not evaluate the law under strict

---

[6] *Griswold* at 481.
[7] Rational review also requires that the regulation be rationally related to the legitimate purpose. But as long as one adopts the "only" requirement of my justificatory constraint, we have no need for examining how finely or broadly tailored the statute is.
[8] The Tenth Amendment of the U.S. Constitution affirms the police powers of the states.
[9] Brest *et al.* 2006: 430 (emphasis added). See also *Lochner* (1905).
[10] *Barnes* at 568.   [11] Ibid.

scrutiny. In other words, mere morality (some kind of non-demonstrable harm), not just health and safety, has served as a legitimate justification for legislation under rational review.[12]

As a doctrinal matter, the right to privacy and its ensuing heightened scrutiny are our only defense against morals legislation. This is borne out by the theory of tolerance. Society may find a particular activity offensive such as sodomy or contraceptive use, even though it demonstrably harms no one. These minority behaviors deviate from the majoritarian standard. But as long as such an activity occurs in "private" – the bedroom, for instance – society should tolerate it. In a right to privacy regime, legislation that does seek to regulate such "private" activity triggers heightened scrutiny. Such exacting scrutiny generally rules out such privacy-encroaching laws. We need the right of privacy, if the state may legislate morality – if it may seek to do something other than prevent demonstrable harm.

This regime of tolerance was expanded in *Roe v. Wade* (1973) to include the right to abort a fetus. In that decision, the Court reiterated the holdings of the other cases, reasoning that while the "Constitution does not explicitly mention any right of privacy[,] ... the Court has recognized that a right of personal privacy, or a guarantee of certain areas or zones of privacy does exist."[13] The Court further held that this zone is "broad enough to encompass a woman's decision whether or not to terminate her pregnancy."[14] The Court acknowledged, though, that "some state regulation in areas protected by the right to privacy is appropriate."[15] It is just that when fundamental rights are implicated, the "regulation[s] limiting these rights may be justified only by a 'compelling state interest,' and ... legislative enactments must be narrowly drawn to express only the legitimate state interests at stake."[16] The Court ultimately held that there was no compelling state interest to warrant the privacy infringement at least during the first trimester. Given the presence of possible harm to the fetus, abortion is different from the other modern privacy cases, cases where there is no such demonstrable harm. For that reason, I treat abortion and its relation to privacy separately at the end of this chapter.

In any case, *Roe*, like *Griswold*, did not consider the law under rational review. Since both regulations – the prohibition on contraceptive use and the prohibition on abortion – interfered with the right to privacy, the Court applied strict scrutiny. Privacy is our defense against morals legislation. By

---

[12] See *Griswold* at 498. Justice Goldberg's concurrence admits that the "discouraging of extra-marital relations" is a *"legitimate* subject of state concern," ibid. (emphasis added).
[13] *Roe* at 152.   [14] Ibid.: at 153.   [15] Ibid.: at 154.   [16] Ibid.: at 155.

way of strict scrutiny, it sweeps under the rug private behavior that, though not harmful, is deemed "deviant" by the majority. In *Griswold*, for example, the "deviant" behavior was the use of contraception in the bedroom. Unfortunately, case law does not explicitly articulate this relationship. As a result, constitutional theory has not noticed that a repudiation of morals legislation renders the right to privacy obsolete. Like the theorists of Justification explored in Part II, legal scholars and jurists have failed to see the connection between the right to privacy and the prevention of demonstrable harm. It comes as no surprise that few politicians, scholars, and judges are willing to reject the right to privacy. If the state may only seek to minimize demonstrable harm, we *do not* need privacy.

We do not need heightened scrutiny, if the following rationales for state legislation immediately fail a re-conceptualized rational review: the virtuous path of monogamy; God deems gay sex, and even certain kinds of heterosexual sex, a sin; oral sex between men (or blonds and redheads for that matter) is disgusting. They do not pick out any demonstrable or publicly ascertainable harm. With this justificatory constraint, we have no need for the problematic right to privacy. We need not search the Constitution for some enigmatic right. We can circumvent the problematic pedigree of *Lochner*. We need simply proclaim that the state may only regulate the health and safety of its members. The appeal to health and safety (without morality) is nothing other than the minimization of demonstrable harm. Re-conceptualizing rational review by dropping morality from the traditional police powers of the state is sufficient to secure our liberty avoiding the need for privacy or appeal to substantive due process.

Evidence of the Court's blindness to this relationship between morals legislation and privacy is apparent in *Bowers v. Hardwick* (1986). Though *Bowers* has now been overturned, I spend time analyzing it so as to point out this constitutional blind spot, a blind spot that has hobbled a clear understanding of privacy jurisprudence. Seeing where *Bowers* went wrong is crucial in articulating a better constitutional principle. Following *Griswold*, *Eisenstadt*, and then *Roe*, it seems reasonable that the Court would have placed gay sex within the zone of privacy, within the scope of tolerance. Even if a polity may characterize certain consensual sexual behavior as offensive, privacy ought to permit such harmless activity that occurs behind closed doors. This is the very purpose of tolerance. In *Bowers*, however, the Court held that the right of privacy could not protect gay sex between consenting adults in the bedroom.[17] It upheld a facially

---

[17] *Bowers* at 186.

neutral Georgia sodomy statute interpreting it as primarily affecting gays.[18] The *Bowers* Court commits two mistakes: one, it refuses to afford gay sex protection under the right to privacy; and two, it reaffirms the old constitutional principle that mere morality (the prevention of non-demonstrable harm) alone can justify laws under rational review. While *Bowers* is undoubtedly the most haunting decision of the modern right to privacy cases, it is, for our purposes, also the most illuminating.

Bowers found that gay sex did not trigger the right to privacy. By appealing to, among other things, early American history and the common law's proscription against gay sex, it held that such activity was not a part of the due process right to privacy. For conduct to qualify as a fundamental right under due process, it must be "deeply rooted in this Nation's history and tradition" or "implicit in the concept of ordered liberty."[19] The Court concludes that sodomy is not such an activity.

Thus, the conventional criticism of *Bowers* is its narrow reading of the scope of privacy.[20] Even though the statute was facially neutral – applying to sodomy between individuals of the same and opposite sex – the Court goes out of its way to frame the issue as whether there is a fundamental right for "homosexuals to engage in sodomy."[21] Following Justice Scalia's practice of evaluating the constitutional status of an activity by focusing on its most specific level of characterization,[22] the *Bowers* Court did just that – asking not if there was a right for consenting adults to sleep with whom they choose or a right to be left alone, but rather if there was a right to gay sex. As Laurence Tribe and Michael Dorf contend the "majority describes the right narrowly [about gay sex], the dissent broadly [about the right to be left alone]."[23] The level of generality, then, directly implicates whether gay sex is protected with a narrow reading upholding the statute and a broader one invalidating it. Under this criticism, the majority poses the wrong question needlessly making the case about gay sex.

This problem of scope more generally stands as a reason to reject rights and their fetish for categorization. This is clearest in the reflexive conception of rights criticized in Chapter 2. Permitting the democratic polity to reflect on the scope and meaning of such rights invites a *Bowers* kind of move. The majority could read rights narrowly so as to jeopardize equality and freedom.

---

[18] Ibid.: at 187.   [19] Ibid.: at 193.   [20] Tribe and Dorf 1990.   [21] *Bowers* at 190.
[22] *Michael H. v. Gerald D.*, 491 U.S. 110 (1989) (holding that there is no constitutional due process right of a biological father to "a child adulterously conceived").
[23] Tribe and Dorf 1990: 1066.

I agree with this common charge against *Bowers*. But it does not do justice to the opinion's faulty reasoning. Even interpreting the question as one of gay sex, the Court should have invalidated the sodomy statute! The opinion goes wrong in failing to realize that the alleged "deviant" nature of gay sex pushes for its very protection under a regime of privacy. The right to privacy and its corresponding regime of tolerance have deep-seated roots. After all, Locke's *Letter Concerning Toleration*, published anonymously for the first time in 1689, stands as testament to the historical pedigree of the liberal principle of tolerance.[24] The protection from the right to privacy is no doubt "deeply rooted." By its very nature, however, such a right protects behavior that is "deviant" and abnormal, that is not deeply rooted or popular. Such activities are deviations from the norm. Simply put, if an activity *were* deeply rooted in our nation's history and tradition such as procreative sex within the bounds of marriage, there would be no need for the right to privacy. Acts that are so rooted and implicit in the concept of ordered liberty seem anything but private.

In fact, it is as if the Court requires that the majority tradition and culture *accept* gay sex before the right to privacy will apply. This seems to turn the right to privacy and the regime of tolerance on its very head. In *Griswold*, no one claimed that contraceptive use has a deeply rooted past. Rather, tolerance (the right to privacy) itself has the long pedigree. The principle may be deep seated but the activities it seeks to protect invariably are not. This is the function of such a right. The Court admits that gay sex is a "victimless crime."[25] In no part of the *Bowers* opinion does the Court contend that gay sex is harmful or leads to harm. Rather, the Court admits that purely "majority *sentiments*" (emphasis added) regarding morality are all that stand beneath such a proscription.[26]

Under the Court's own reasoning gay sex is a non-demonstrably harmful, but nevertheless "offensive" practice carried out in the bedroom by a *minority*. This is the paradigmatic kind of activity that the right to privacy ought to protect – that we ought to tolerate. Thus, it would be a mistake to criticize the *Bowers* opinion simply for arguing that the case is about the abnormal and non-traditional status of gay sex – narrowing the characterization of the relevant activity. Even if gay sex is a "deviant" sexual practice that takes place behind closed doors, such a conclusion deems it suitable and proper for protection under the right to privacy. If it were not, privacy would not be needed.

I reject tolerance, because the protection it offers is not genuinely equal. Still, *Bowers* should have at least gone this far. Having bizarrely cut off the appeal to privacy, *Bowers* also rejects appeal to rational review. Since gay sex

---

[24] Locke 2003 [1689].   [25] *Bowers* at 195.   [26] Ibid.: at 196.

does not fall within the zone of privacy (an argument that seems to fail on its own terms), the *Bowers* Court considers the sodomy statute under rational review. Significantly, in the last paragraph of its decision, the Court states:

> Even if the conduct at issue here is not a fundamental right, respondent asserts that there must be a rational basis for the law and that there is none in this case other than the presumed belief of a majority of the electorate in Georgia that homosexual sodomy is immoral and unacceptable. This is said to be an inadequate rationale to support the law. The law, however, is constantly based on notions of morality, and if all laws representing essentially moral choices are to be invalidated under the Due Process Clause, the courts will be very busy indeed. Even respondent makes no such claim, but insists that majority sentiments about the morality of homosexuality should be declared inadequate. We do not agree, and are unpersuaded that the sodomy laws of some 25 states should be invalidated on this basis.[27]

Bowers validates the state's ability to legislate morals. It fails to endorse the condition of demonstrability. It allows the state to minimize harm that is not publicly ascertainable. The Court's suggestion that the law is "constantly based on notions of morality" misses the point of Justification where the harm must be demonstrable. Perhaps this flawed reasoning, like Bork's proposal critiqued earlier, implies that the polity may pass legislation to minimize emotional disgust. But such a rationale is ruled out by Justification. *Bowers* fails to realize that even though most, if not all of us, would consider it wrong to murder, this is not the reason we prohibit the activity. Rather a polity prohibits it, because the very act of murdering is harmful. The sodomy statute at issue, however, was based solely on society's disapproval of homosexuality, or at least gay sex, *not* on the rationale that such sex was itself harmful. The *Bowers* decision, then, stands for the proposition that such justifications are permissible. The decision in *Lawrence* must be read in light of this.

Lawrence's repudiation of morals legislation

Lawrence represents the crux of my constitutional argument in this chapter. While lip service has been paid to the decision's revolutionary character,[28] most scholars have failed to realize its true conceptual import.[29] The decision in *Lawrence* must be seen as reacting to the

---

[27] Ibid.

[28] Barnett (2003) and Chapman (2004) argue that the revolutionary character of the decision stems from the Court's switch from a fundamental-rights-based analysis to a more liberty-centered approach. While their arguments are not wrong, they miss the more important relationship between morals legislation and privacy. After all, liberty is the value to be promoted. The question is how best to realize it. I argue that by repudiating morals legislation and rejecting the right to privacy we better ensure freedom.

[29] Though Goldberg (2004b) and Rubenfeld (2005: 184–190) realize that the decision could call into question morals legislation, they fail to connect this to the right to privacy.

Bowers' rationale, as eschewing morals legislation allowing for the rejection of the right to privacy.

The facts of *Lawrence* were as follows. Police officers from Harris County in Houston, Texas, entered an apartment on a report that there was a weapons disturbance.[30] The officers observed two men, John Lawrence and Tyron Garner, engaging in a sexual act.[31] The two were arrested and convicted under Texas Penal Code 21.06, which made it a crime for a person of one sex to engage in oral or anal sex with someone else of the same sex. The defendants appealed their convictions on due process and equal protection grounds.[32] The Court of Appeals for the Texas Fourteenth District affirmed the convictions, basing its decision on the controlling status of *Bowers*.[33] The Supreme Court reversed. Writing for the majority, Justice Anthony Kennedy overturned both parts of *Bowers*.[34] First, the majority held that sodomy is protected under the constitutional right to privacy. Second, and far more interestingly, it held that a law fails rational review if based solely on morality.

The *Lawrence* opinion must be read in light of *Bowers*. The Court says as much when it "conclude[s] [that this] case requires us to address whether *Bowers* itself has continuing validity."[35] Justice Kennedy spends most of the opinion arguing that sodomy deserves protection under the right to privacy. On the privacy prong of the argument he re-appraises the notion that the proscription against sodomy has longstanding roots. In countering the *Bowers* reasoning, *Lawrence* observes that not only was there an "absence of legal prohibitions focusing on homosexual conduct"[36] in early American history, but also sodomy laws were, in fact, rarely enforced "against consenting adults acting in private."[37] The Court comments that it "was not until the 1970's that any State singled out same-sex relations for criminal prosecution, and only nine States have done so."[38]

Lawrence counters the assertion in *Bowers* that history has condemned this type of activity (admittedly, failing to realize the internal problem with the *Bowers* decision). Even before *Bowers*, the Wolfenden Report in 1957 recommended to the British Parliament the "repeal of laws punishing

---

[30] *Lawrence* at 562.   [31] Ibid.: at 563.   [32] Ibid.   [33] Ibid.

[34] Justice Kennedy was joined by Justices Stevens, Souter, Ginsburg, and Breyer. *Lawrence* at 561. Justice O'Conner concurred in invalidating the statute but refused to join in the overturning of *Bowers*. Ibid.: at 579 (O'Conner, J., concurring). O'Conner put forth a novel rational review plus argument. Ibid.: at 579–581. She argued that morality cannot be used in rational review analysis when there is a prima facie equal protection claim, as was the case here – the sodomy statute only applied to gay sex. The majority refused to entertain the equal protection argument. Justice Scalia dissented, joined by Justices Rehnquist and Thomas.

[35] *Lawrence* at 575.   [36] Ibid.: at 568.   [37] Ibid.: at 569.   [38] Ibid.

homosexual conduct."[39] Additionally, the European Court of Human Rights, five years before *Bowers*, held that sodomy laws were invalid under the European Convention of Human Rights.[40] As a post-*Bowers* decision, the *Lawrence* opinion cites *Planned Parenthood v. Casey* (1992) as reaffirming "the substantive force of the liberty protected by the Due Process Clause."[41]

But the decision does more than merely "tinker" with the right to privacy regime inherited by *Bowers*. The Court reconsiders the role of morality in rational review analysis. While appeal to morality has traditionally satisfied rational review, *Lawrence* declares otherwise. Toward the end of the opinion, Justice Kennedy quotes Justice John Paul Stevens' dissent in *Bowers*. The *Lawrence* decision explicitly relies on Stevens' words to invalidate the gay-specific sodomy statute:

> Our prior cases make two propositions abundantly clear. First, the fact that the governing majority in a State has traditionally viewed a particular practice *as immoral is not a sufficient reason for upholding a law prohibiting the practice*; neither history nor tradition could save a law prohibiting miscegenation from constitutional attack. Second, individual decisions by married persons, concerning the intimacies of their physical relationship, even when not intended to produce offspring, are a form of "liberty" protected by the Due Process Clause of the Fourteenth Amendment. Moreover, this protection extends to intimate choices by unmarried as well as married persons.[42]

This is the crux of the *Lawrence* decision. It expands the right of privacy to include gay sex but, more importantly, it deems the minimization of non-demonstrable harm an insufficient basis for legislation. The state may not legislate merely on grounds of morality. Claiming simply that homosexuality is wrong or an improper lifestyle is not a good reason to prohibit it. The ruling accepts the condition of demonstrability.

By quoting Stevens' dissent, the *Lawrence* Court heralds in a new understanding of rational review. The opinion states that morality is "not [a] sufficient reason for upholding a law prohibiting the practice [of sodomy]."[43] It does not say that laws that interfere with fundamental rights such as the right to privacy may not be based on morals. In fact,

---

[39] *Lawrence* at 572–573.   [40] Ibid.: at 573.

[41] *Lawrence* at 573. The majority avoided application of the Equal Protection Clause. The statute in *Lawrence* specifically outlawed gay sex (the one in *Bowers* outlawed sodomy between same-sex couples and opposite sex ones). If, as the *Lawrence* Court realizes, it were to "hold the statute invalid under the Equal Protection Clause some might question whether a prohibition would be valid if drawn differently, say, to prohibit conduct both between same-sex and different-sex participants" (ibid.).

[42] *Lawrence* at 577–578 (quoting *Bowers* at 216 (1986) (Stevens, J., dissenting)) (emphasis added).

[43] *Lawrence* at 577.

the Court states that the gay sodomy statute furthers no "legitimate state interest."[44] This is undoubtedly the language of rational review – applying to all regulations. The majority could have said that the statute furthers no "compelling state interest" thereby leaving the door open for morality (the appeal to non-demonstrability) to justify non-fundamental-interest-violating laws, but it did not. It thus gave rational review new life.

This reading is supported by Justice Scalia's perceptive dissent. Justice Scalia focuses on the real import of the decision when he writes that most "of the [majority] opinion has no relevance to its actual holding – that the Texas statute 'furthers no legitimate state interest which can justify' its application to petitioners under rational-basis review."[45] Justice Scalia believes that the majority opinion renders suspect laws "against fornication, bigamy, adultery, adult incest, bestiality, and obscenity."[46] In so far as these laws do not seek to prevent demonstrable harm, Scalia may be right. However, and we will revisit this issue below, as long as an appropriate justification can be given, namely the minimization of harm, they may pass rational review. Even if Scalia may exaggerate the ramifications of the holding, I do agree with his understanding of it.

By recognizing that most of the majority opinion is irrelevant to its holding, Scalia also seems to imply that the Court could have avoided the discussion of privacy altogether. Certainly, the legislation in *Griswold* fails the constraint of demonstrability. After all, it is the minimization of some non-demonstrable harm, a belief that sex, for instance, should be carried out within the bonds of marriage for procreative purposes, that no doubt led to the *Griswold* regulation. We would not have been burdened with the problematic right to privacy if the Court, in any of the modern sexual freedom cases, had simply proclaimed, as the *Lawrence* court finally did, that morals legislation is impermissible. Constitutional law can limit government not by carving up those areas, interests, or spheres off limits to state regulation like the private sphere. It can simply deem legislation illegitimate that seeks to do something other than minimize demonstrable harm. A sodomy law is just as arbitrary, just as silly as a law banning sex between redheads and blonds. Privacy turns out to be obsolete.

Why, then, did the *Lawrence* Court even acknowledge that gay sex falls within the zone of privacy? Why did it not articulate this new standard of rational review and leave it at that? The Court's intention could have been one of strategy. Just five months after *Lawrence* was decided, the Massachusetts Supreme Judicial Court, under the Massachusetts Constitution, invalidated the state's refusal to grant marriage licenses to

---

[44] Ibid.: at 578.   [45] Ibid.: at 586, dissenting.   [46] Ibid.: at 599, dissenting.

same-sex couples.[47] It was the marriage issue that the *Lawrence* majority was worried about. If the majority had not also expanded the right to privacy, if it had simply said we no longer need privacy and had invalidated the sodomy law under rational review, the ban on same-sex marriage would seem blatantly illegitimate. By choosing to additionally decide the issue on privacy grounds, the majority gives the *semblance* that the decision does not implicate behavior outside the bedroom. The Court says as much when it disingenuously writes that this case "does not involve public conduct or prostitution. It does not involve whether the government must give formal recognition to any relationship that homosexual persons seek to enter."[48]

Yet, if the majority's purpose were truly to limit the holding to intimate activities, it did not have to further hold that morality serves no legitimate state interest. It could have simply kept the constitutional attention on the right to privacy – focusing on the individual. It did not need to turn its attention to legislative purpose giving teeth (bite) to rational review. And, as we saw above, it is this re-conceptualized rational review that Ginsburg invokes in her dissent in *Gonzales*. The *Lawrence* Court did not have to go as far as it did in order to strike down sodomy laws. By its very reasoning it implicates much more. It goes beyond tolerance.

Admittedly, the language of privacy occupies a primary role in the Court's opinion. From the very start, Justice Kennedy writes that liberty protects us from intrusion in "private places."[49] Later he writes that the due process clause protects "private conduct"[50] focusing on individuals and their protected interests or behavior. Most of the opinion makes this conventional right to privacy argument. Conceding that, I'd like to suggest that the argument on privacy is a dog and pony show, or at the very least it should be read as such. Justice Kennedy spends almost seven of the eight pages of the *Lawrence* opinion demonstrating that gay sex implicates the right to privacy. Gay sex, like the use of contraceptives, falls within the zone of privacy. Having put those at ease who fear the day when the prohibition on same-sex marriage is declared unconstitutional, Kennedy, in the last page of the decision, squarely turns to the rationale underlying the sodomy law, deeming it illegitimate. Spelling the end of morals legislation, he opens the way for the rejection of privacy.

Not distracted by the show, Justice Scalia quite rightly points out:

If moral disapprobation of homosexual conduct is "no legitimate state interest" for purposes of proscribing that conduct … what justification could there possibly be

---

[47] *Goodridge v. Dep't of Public Health*, 440 Mass. 309 (Mass. 2003). I explore this decision in more detail in the next chapter.
[48] *Lawrence* at 578.   [49] Ibid.: at 562.   [50] Ibid.: at 564.

for denying the benefits of marriage to homosexual couples exercising "[t]he liberty protected by the Constitution"? Surely not the encouragement of procreation, since the sterile and the elderly are allowed to marry. This case "does not involve" the issue of homosexual marriage only if one entertains the belief that the principle and logic have nothing to do with the decisions of the Court. Many will hope that, as the Court comfortably assures us, this is so.[51]

Scalia is absolutely correct that there is no justification for the ban on same-sex marriage, because this would invariably involve the minimization of some non-demonstrable harm. He chides the majority for it. I see it as a bold step forward for liberty, dropping the baggage of privacy. Although the majority could have been more forthright and candid with its decision, perhaps the gratuitous right to privacy argument was necessary for other justices to sign on to the opinion. Maybe the justices, like most theorists, fail to realize that a right to privacy is obsolete under a repudiation of morals legislation. In fact, though Justice Thomas dissents in *Lawrence*, he admits that the sodomy law is an "uncommonly silly law."[52] But Thomas refuses to side with the majority, because he cannot locate in the text of the Constitution a "general right to privacy."[53] Thus, he fails to see that he does not need privacy as long as he turns to the state's reason for enacting the legislation, a reason that fails rational review. After all, if rational review is to mean anything, it means that a law may not be based on a rationale that is, as he frankly admits, "uncommonly silly."

We ought to interpret *Lawrence* as laying the foundation for the ultimate rejection of the right to privacy. As more cases arise under this new conception of rational review, I hope constitutional scholars and litigants will realize that the right to privacy is no longer needed. *Lawrence* is groundbreaking, not because it holds that gay sex implicates the right to privacy. The right to privacy argument should have carried the day in *Bowers*. The classic limited government mantra "what you do in your bedroom is your business" should have worked in 1986. Permitting gay sex seems a paradigmatic instance of tolerance. The true power of *Lawrence* stems from its focus on legislative purpose and not individual "private" acts. *Lawrence* accepts the condition of demonstrability deeming unconstitutional all laws that seek to minimize non-demonstrable harm.

Now Rubenfeld finds my reading of *Lawrence* unpersuasive.[54] Sharing some of the concerns of Scalia, Rubenfeld contends that if the opinion truly repudiates morals legislation, it calls into question laws against prostitution, bigamy, polygamy, obscenity, and even racial discrimination

---

[51] Ibid.: at 605, dissenting (citation omitted).   [52] Ibid.: at 605, dissenting.
[53] Ibid.: at 605–606, dissenting.   [54] Rubenfeld 2005: 184–190.

in the workplace. He maintains that legislating against these activities invariably requires appeal to morality thus finding them indistinguishable from their sodomy counterparts. For example, racial discrimination would "certainly be unconstitutional under a principle that the state may not legislate morality. Discrimination inflicts no force or fraud on anyone."[55] According to Rubenfeld, *Lawrence* cannot stand for the proposition that morals legislation is unconstitutional. Doing so would have too far-reaching implications for the present state of constitutional law, or so Rubenfeld suggests.

Yet, similar to the criticism of neutrality, this kind of objection invariably creates a straw man to defeat easily. A repudiation of morals legislation is not a rejection of legislation based on morality. That would be an easily refuted position. Rather, *Lawrence* prohibits legislation that seeks to minimize non-demonstrable harm. Demonstrability is the condition doing the necessary distinguishing work. Rubenfeld's criticism – like Scalia's – fails to realize this important point. Sodomy laws can certainly be distinguished from prohibitions against prostitution, bigamy, polygamy, and obscenity. Feminists have argued that the latter four can lead to the domination and harm of women[56] – a claim that certainly cannot be made in regard to gay sex. Admittedly, such harm may be consensual. However, conceding that case law does not fully endorse my theory of Justification – permitting the minimization of *consensual* harm – *Lawrence* does endorse the condition of demonstrability. This is sufficient to alleviate Rubenfeld's concerns.

As a result, laws that prohibit discrimination in the workplace such as Title VII are most certainly aimed at minimizing publicly ascertainable harm. Rubenfeld simply misses the point that such laws aim to do just that. Having an employer discriminate against you on account of your race demonstrably harms you, leaving you without a job or a livelihood. It seems a bit much to claim that this kind of injury is a harmless activity like consensual sodomy. Perhaps Rubenfeld needlessly focuses on the "right to equality" as under-girding such non-discrimination legislation. Yet, as pointed out in Chapter 5, the harm here is the fact that the prospective employee has no job – not some idea that the employee's rights have been violated. Consequently, the polity has various options in deciding how to minimize this harm, such as pass non-discrimination legislation or institute a universal wage. Whereas sodomy laws do something other than minimize demonstrable harm, laws like Title VII seem entirely inapposite, minimizing harm for which we can publicly proffer evidence. Rubenfeld

---

[55] Ibid.: 189.   [56] See, e.g., A. Dworkin 1981, Okin 1999, Pateman 1988.

and Scalia mischaracterize the meaning of morals legislation by failing to realize that demonstrability stands at the core of this distinction.

In fact, in carefully analyzing the Court's review of alleged morals legislation, Suzanne Goldberg contends that even before *Lawrence*, morals legislation was already headed out the door.[57] She suggests that my reading of *Lawrence* is not as radical as Rubenfeld or Scalia would have us believe. For example, in *Reynolds v. U.S.* (1878) and *Paris Adult Theatre I v. Slaton* (1973), the Court partially appealed to demonstrable harm in permitting regulation of bigamy and obscene movies in theatres, respectively.[58] The *Reynolds* decision, as Goldberg interestingly points out, never once uses the word "morality." In that decision the Court argues that "polygamy leads to the patriarchal principle, which, when applied to large communities, fetters the people in stationary despotism, while that principle cannot long exist in connection with monogamy"[59] thereby looking not simply to offensiveness or majority sentiments.

Similarly, in *Paris Adult Theatre I*, the Court noted that this case "goes beyond whether someone, or even the majority, considers the conduct depicted as 'wrong' or 'sinful'."[60] In articulating the reasons for regulation of obscene materials in commerce and public accommodations (such as movie theatres), the Court cites a report suggesting a correlation between "obscene material and crime."[61] It contends that although "there is no conclusive proof of a connection between antisocial behavior and obscene material, the legislature [...] could quite reasonably determine that such a connection does or might exist."[62] If that is indeed the actual reason, the legislature may regulate obscenity. *Paris Adult Theatre I* reasoned that "States have the power to make a morally neutral judgment that public exhibition of obscene material, or commerce in such material, has a tendency to injure the community as a whole, to endanger the public safety, or to jeopardize ... the States' right ... to maintain a decent society."[63]

Contrastingly, this was not the language of *Bowers* where the majority's moral disapproval was deemed sufficient *on its own* to uphold sodomy laws. The *Bowers'* opinion did not at all contend that the regulation of gay sex entailed a state interest in averting "antisocial behavior" or "public safety." In upholding sodomy laws, *Bowers*, unlike *Reynolds* and *Paris Adult Theatre I*, did not rely on even a *partial* appeal to the minimization of publicly ascertainable harm. Again, *Bowers* admits that only the "sentiments" of the majority stood behind Georgia's sodomy statute.

---

[57] Goldberg 2004b.   [58] Ibid.: 1261–1281.   [59] Ibid.: 1264 (quoting *Reynolds* at 166).
[60] Ibid.: 1269 (quoting *Paris Adult Theatre I* at 69).   [61] *Paris Adult Theatre I* at 58.
[62] Ibid.: at 60.   [63] Goldberg 2004b: 1270 (quoting *Paris Adult Theatre I* at 69).

Repudiating morals legislation, accepting the constraint of demonstrability, need not lead to Rubenfeld or Scalia's slippery slope. In fact, case law may already endorse this justificatory constraint.

Still, reading *Lawrence* as overturning the sodomy statute on the basis of rational review alone – declaring morals legislation unconstitutional – may very well call into question the ban on same-sex marriage, and rightly so. It is only this result that Kennedy's opinion disingenuously tries to protect against. Under my reading, the ban on same-sex marriage must fall. Eventually (I hope), the right to privacy will become obsolete, carrying no constitutional purchase. I see *Lawrence*, then, as a "mid-course correction" case setting the stage for the eventual turning away from the right to privacy.[64] As more cases arise on the Court's docket the relationship between morals legislation and privacy will become more apparent. *Lawrence* has taken the bold step of ushering in a new constitutional regime in which the right to privacy is obsolete.

Abortion jurisprudence's turn away from privacy

Further evidence of the Court's rejection of the constitutional right to privacy is its abortion jurisprudence. Having shown that privacy is unnecessary to ensure sexual freedom, a similar argument is available in abortion case law. In Part II, I argued that a turn to legislative purpose rejecting the right to privacy informs a more fruitful, democratic debate about abortion. Here I suggest that the Court's analysis of abortion has moved in a similar direction. Specifically, whereas *Roe v. Wade* (1973) squarely grounds a woman's ability to choose in the framework of privacy, *Planned Parenthood v. Casey* (1992) does so by appeal to an undue burden standard.[65] Whereas *Roe* looks to the individual, *Casey* seems to look to legislative purpose.

As a preliminary matter, the Court has never held that the fetus is a person under the Fourteenth Amendment.[66] But the state may still have an interest in potential life. The crucial issue in *Roe* and *Casey* is how the Court strikes the balance between it and concerns of liberty.

In *Roe*, the Court held that the woman's ability to choose rested within the ambit of the right to privacy. It reasoned that such a right is "broad enough to encompass a woman's decision whether or not to terminate her pregnancy."[67] The Court did recognize that the state has some interest in the potential human life as well as the health of the mother. Justice Harry

---

[64] Ackerman (1998: 356) uses the term to describe *West Coast Hotel* (1937) – representing the first phase of the repudiation of *Lochner* (1905).
[65] Shapiro 2001.   [66] *Roe* at 156.   [67] Ibid.: at 153.

Blackmun's opinion proposes a three-part structure. The Court held that up to the first trimester, the state could not regulate abortion. Subsequent to this and up to viability, the state may regulate it as long as such regulations are reasonably related to maternal health. After viability, the state could go so far as prohibiting abortion altogether except where necessary for the "preservation of life or health of the mother."[68]

If the right to privacy is taken to include the right to reproductive freedom, *Roe* seems the natural and logical outgrowth of *Griswold*. Dworkin makes this very argument, contending that procreative autonomy stands at the center of both decisions, because abortion "cannot be distinguished from contraception by supposing that a decision about the former is less serious; on the contrary, it is more."[69] Both, then, concern the ability to control reproduction. The "intimate and personal" nature of the decision to use contraception in *Griswold* pushes for *Roe*'s right to abort, a decision that seems more about bodily control, more about the intimate and personal.[70]

The constitutional and conceptual link between the right to privacy (as articulated in *Griswold*) and *Roe* is strong.[71] For example, during his confirmation hearings, Chief Justice Roberts refused to come down one way or the other on how he would decide the abortion issue, deeming it very much alive and thus inappropriate to discuss directly.[72] However, in questioning him about abortion or *Roe*, many committee members made sure to ask Roberts about the right to privacy as affirmed in *Griswold*.[73] Senator Sam Brownback, a Republican member of the committee, even remarked that it "is noteworthy to me that a supermajority of committee members have asked you [Roberts] about privacy and leading up to questions on *Roe*" (*sic*).[74] The Senate saw the right to privacy as necessary to the central holding of *Roe*. Rejecting the right to privacy meant a certain repudiation of *Roe*. After all, the conventional debate over abortion looks to individuals or groups – characterizing the activity as falling in one category or another.

---

[68] Ibid.: at 164–165.   [69] R. Dworkin 1993: 107.

[70] Ibid.: 106.   [71] Shapiro 2001: xxii–xxvi.

[72] 9.13.2005, Judiciary Committee Hearings. In response to Senator Arlen Specter's question regarding "any erosion of precedent as to *Roe*," the now Chief Justice Roberts replied: "Well, again, I think I should stay away from discussions of particular issues that are likely to come before the court again. And in the area of abortion, there are cases on the courts docket, of course. It is an issue that does come before the court" (Senate Judiciary Confirmation Hearings) (2005 WL (Westlaw) 2214702 (F.D.C.H.)).

[73] 9.12-15.2005, 2005 WL (Westlaw) (2204109, 2214702, 2229899, 2229890, 2237049, 2237054, 2250085) (F.D.C.H.).

[74] 9.14.2005, 2005 WL (Westlaw) 2229890 (F.D.C.H.).

With *Casey*, however, privacy – with its fetish for characterization – does not seem so necessary. In explicitly rejecting *Roe's* trimester framework,[75] the *Casey* Court affirmed a woman's ability to choose but did so by focusing on whether the abortion law imposes an undue burden on her: "Only where state regulation imposes an undue burden on a woman's ability to make this decision does the power of the State reach into the heart of liberty protected by the Due Process Clause."[76] At issue in the case were three laws allegedly burdening a woman's right to abort: a husband notification requirement, an informed consent provision, and a parental consent requirement with judicial bypass. The Court held that while the first was unconstitutional the second two were not.

Now *Casey*, like *Roe*, speaks in the language of rights. It asks whether the laws at issue unduly burden a woman's right to choose. I concede that *Casey* does not entirely repudiate the emphasis on individuals, on the woman's right to abort. Still, it rightly also looks to legislative purpose suggesting that a prohibition on abortion means that an improper rationale is afoot. In making his argument, Justice Kennedy, one of the authors of the opinion, replaces talk of privacy with talk of legislative purpose much in line with his opinion in *Lawrence*.[77] The *Casey* Court reasons that:

[T]he liberty of the woman is at stake in a sense unique to the human condition and so unique to the law. The mother who carries the child to full term is subject to anxieties, to physical constraints, to pain that *only she must bear*. That these sacrifices have from the beginning of the human race been endured by woman with a pride that ennobles her in the eyes of others and gives to the infant a bond of love cannot alone be grounds for the State to insist that she make the sacrifice. Her suffering is too intimate and personal for the State to insist, without more, upon its own vision of the woman's role, however dominant that vision has been in the course of our history and our culture.[78]

The Court recognizes that women are singled out to bear this kind of sacrifice for "the State." Constitutional law does not require others to be such forced Good Samaritans.[79] In this way, the state seeks to foist upon women its "own vision of [their] role." As the Court goes on to say, the "ability of women to participate equally in the economic and social life of the Nation has been facilitated by their ability to control their reproductive lives."[80] *Casey* turns the constitutional attention away from the individual woman to the rationale or reason underlying an abortion statute finding it suspect.

---

[75] *Casey* at 873.   [76] Ibid.: at 874.   [77] Cf. Barnett 2003.
[78] *Casey* at 852 (emphasis added).   [79] West 2005: 128–130.   [80] *Casey* at 856.

Justice Ginsburg and Ian Shapiro read this as a move from privacy to equality.[81] Rather than focus on privacy, the Court moves in the direction of equal protection.[82] Failing to afford women the right to abort is a kind of sex discrimination – or so the equality argument goes.[83] The Court's language of equality and the emphasis on rejecting sexist conceptions of the social role of women buttress this claim. While this interpretation is not entirely wrong, I suggest that the focus should not be on sex discrimination but rather on the rationale underlying a law against abortion. Though each analysis in this case amounts to the same thing, the sex discrimination claim needlessly invokes and brings into play the problematic doctrines of suspect class and classification, doctrines I criticize in the next chapter.

As outlined in Part II, only women are forced to prevent this kind of harm. The burden of helping is only imposed on them. *Casey*'s emphasis on the burden rather than a right exemplifies this turn away from privacy toward legislative purpose. This is the crucial implication of *Casey*. In his partial concurrence to *Casey*, Justice Blackmun, in line with much of the majority opinion, states that by "restricting the right to terminate pregnancies, the State conscripts women's bodies into its service, forcing women to continue their pregnancies, suffer pains of childbirth, and in most instances, provide years of maternal care."[84] Realizing that only women bear this burden, he remarks that the "State does not compensate women for their services; instead it assumes that they owe this duty as a matter of course."[85] Blackmun's words have two implications. First, under his argument, if compensation were given to women who were forced to carry the fetus to term, the right to privacy and the accompanying right to abort would seemingly be unnecessary. Again, we conscript bodies for military service, but still provide compensation. Second, because the state currently does not provide such compensation, maintaining that women owe this duty "as a matter of course," abortion laws seek to do something other than only minimize harm. Hence, their legislative purpose is suspect. Blackmun implicitly realizes that as a general matter American law does not force others to help or aid in this way. He rightly suggests that abortion laws force only women to be Good Samaritans. And thus, the rationale underlying such laws is suspect. The *Casey* Court, then, cares less about the alleged "private" (or personal)

---

[81] R. Ginsburg 1992, Shapiro 2001.
[82] Interestingly, in *Geduldig v. Aiello*, 417 U.S. 484 (1974) and *General Electric Co. v. Gilbert*, 429 U.S. 125 (1976) the Court held that pregnancy discrimination was not a form of sex discrimination under the equal protection clause.
[83] Balkin 2005, Siegel 2005, West 2005.   [84] *Casey* at 929, concurring in part.   [85] Ibid.

nature of the abortion decision with its focus on bodily control (à la Dworkin) and more about the appropriate legislative purpose.

***

In this way, the Court has rejected the core rights of the private sphere – property, religion, and privacy. In doing so, it has also turned to Justification, specifically re-conceptualizing rational review to accord with the constraint that the state may only seek to minimize demonstrable harm. Properly understood, American constitutional law informs the re-conceptualized account of limited government proffered in Part II. But constitutional law must go farther.

The last two chapters argued that the Court has taken a turn to the central features of my theory of Justification rejecting the rights of property, religion, and intimacy that accompany the private sphere. Here I extend my argument to the Court's equal protection analysis. This chapter examines the best way to understand equality, and in particular, the Fourteenth Amendment's language of "equal protection."[1] Current constitutional jurisprudence interprets this language to mean that laws that invoke certain classes or classifications – such as race or sex – get heightened scrutiny. I argue that this focus on categories or groups is flawed. In line with my theory of Justification, we better ensure equality by simply adopting one standard of review asking if the legislation seeks only to minimize harm.

I concede that the Court *has not* moved in this direction. In fact, legal scholars[2] have not even suggested an abandonment of the conventional equal protection approach for a single, unified level of rational review. I take up this task here. Under current case law, laws discriminating on the basis of race,[3] alienage,[4] and national origin[5] get strict scrutiny: where the Court asks if the law is narrowly tailored to serving a compelling state purpose. Laws discriminating on the basis of sex[6] get intermediate

---

[1]   U.S. Constitution Amendment XIV § 1 ("No State shall ... deny to any person within its jurisdiction the equal protection of the laws").

[2]   *Pace* Goldberg 2004a. Goldberg rejects the multi-tiered approach offering a revised single standard of review. She cites language from opinions by Justices Marshall, Stevens, Powell, and Rehnquist suggesting "discomfort" with the conventional rational/intermediate/strict tiers of scrutiny (ibid.: at 518–525). However, she finds that their alternatives are unable to offer a comprehensive solution (ibid.). In refashioning her own positive single level of review, she initially asks whether a "plausible, nonarbitrary explanation exists for why the burdened group has been selected to bear the challenged burden" (ibid.: at 533). Like Pettit's theory (fn. 34, Ch. 3), this re-conceptualization fails to specify the meaning of arbitrary.

[3]   See, e.g., *Loving v. Virginia*, 388 U.S. 1 (1967).

[4]   See *Graham v. Richardson*, 403 U.S. 365 (1971).

[5]   See, e.g., *Oyama v. California*, 332 U.S. 633 (1948), *Korematsu v. United States*, 323 U.S. 214 (1944).

[6]   See, e.g., *Craig v. Boren*, 429 U.S. 190 (1976).

scrutiny: where the Court asks if the law is substantially related to serving an important governmental purpose. Rational review – that all other laws get – asks if the law is rationally related to serving a legitimate purpose.

Analyzing these different tests is not my concern here. Rather, I look at the *grounds* for triggering heightened scrutiny – whether intermediate or strict. In other words, what principles under-gird the Court's threshold decision to engage in higher scrutiny? I show that the Court's equal protection logic is perverse. We do not need to engage in higher scrutiny flagging certain classes or classifications as suspect. Doing so brings us back to the problematic focus on individuals or groups. I argue that like rights, we should reject such doctrines exclusively focusing once again on legislative purpose. This, in turn, permits much-needed democratic flexibility.

To that end, this chapter is in three parts. First, I argue that the Court's current approach to equal protection with its use of heightened scrutiny is internally inconsistent, because it perverts the rationales of anti-differentiation and anti-subordination. Second, I show that even on their own such rationales fail to ensure equality and freedom. Instead, we are better off abandoning such doctrines and simply asking if the legislation seeks to minimize demonstrable harm. Third, I suggest that this re-conceptualized rational review in line with my re-conceptualized account of limited government proffers a more democratic role for judicial review.

The Court's perverse equal protection logic

The Court's equal protection doctrine triggers heightened scrutiny when a law invokes a suspect classification or a suspect class. These two approaches to equality are, borrowing Ruth Colker's language: anti-differentiation (a focus on suspect classification) and anti-subordination (a focus on suspect class).[7] As a general matter, anti-differentiation maintains that the law should not treat individuals differently on the basis of morally irrelevant characteristics such as race, sex, sexual orientation, blood type, hair color and the like. Thus, anti-differentiation (AD) values formal equality. It cares about the rights of individuals. It holds that the law should not employ certain classifications. Such classifications make no normative and hence no legal difference. The law should not take them into account. Michael W. McConnell, a conservative judge on the Tenth Circuit of Appeals, characterizes the AD rationale in just this way: "The

---

[7] Colker 1986.

principle of equal protection of the laws can be understood as a rule of strict formal equality, requiring all citizens to be treated without regard to race or other 'morally irrelevant' distinctions."[8]

Though now overruled by *Grutter v. Bollinger* (2003) (holding that diversity is a compelling purpose for university affirmative action programs), *Hopwood v. Texas* (5th Cir. 1996) (holding that diversity is not a compelling purpose), a Fifth Circuit Court of Appeals decision, reasoned that the "use of race, in and of itself ... is no more rational on its own terms than would be choices based upon the physical size or blood type of applicants."[9] According to AD, an individual's race, sex, sexual orientation, hair color, blood type, and the like should not dictate varying treatment under the law.

On the other hand, an anti-subordination (AS) understanding of equality looks to remedying certain kinds of domination or harm. It aims to alleviate the subordinated status of particular minorities or classes. Rather than looking to the individual, it is a group-focused approach.[10] It looks to the rights of groups. As Colker writes (contending that the Court should adopt such an interpretation), anti-subordination seeks to "eliminate the power disparities between men and women, and between whites and non-whites, through the development of laws and policies that directly redress those disparities."[11] This approach eschews an individual-based outlook relying instead on remedying group powerlessness. Instead of a focus on classifications, AS looks to class – to the particular minority group. Very much in line with the identity theorists explored in Chapter 5, AS identifies vulnerable minorities or groups such as blacks, gays, and women arguing that laws must occasionally invoke certain classifications to remedy powerlessness. According to this approach, individuals may very well need to be treated differently on the basis of race, sex, or sexual orientation in order to do the necessary anti-subordination work.

The crux of my argument entails realizing that beneath the distinction between AD and AS is case law's distinction between classification and class. Classifications include race, sex, hair color, sexual orientation, and blood type – a focus on the rights of the individual. Their respective classes would be blacks, whites, men, women, redheads, blonds, gays, straights, type O, type AB negative, etc. – a focus on the rights of groups. AD contends that when a law categorizes on the basis of a suspect *classification*, it should trigger heightened scrutiny. Contrastingly, AS triggers such scrutiny only when the law discriminates against a suspect *class* or group. To summarize, AD worries that legislation will categorize on the

[8] McConnell 1997: 1282; cf. Rawls 1971: 14.   [9] *Hopwood* at 945.
[10] Colker 1986; see also Balkin and Siegel 2003.   [11] Ibid.: 1007.

basis of race, sex, sexual orientation, hair color, blood type, etc., while AS seeks to mitigate or remedy the subordinated status of minorities such as blacks, gays, and women.

The Courts' earlier equal protection cases invoke both AD and AS. For example, in *Strauder v. West Virginia* (1879) (invalidating a law that categorically excluded blacks from a grand or petit jury) the Court spoke to both principles. It reasoned that the Fourteenth Amendment grants to blacks the "right to exemption from unfriendly legislation against them distinctively as a colored" as well as an "exemption from legal discriminations, implying inferiority in civil society ... and discrimination which are steps towards reducing them to the condition of a subject race."[12] Here the focus is on the suspect class – blacks. Such a law treats them as inferior. In fact, the use of "unfriendly" suggests that remedial ("friendly"), race-conscious legislation may very well be permissible.[13] This is, after all, the AS position. It permits categorization on the basis of race as long as such a thing is done to remedy subordination. But the Court also states that the Fourteenth Amendment "was against discrimination because of race or color."[14] Here the appeal is to classification, a notion of formal equality that presumably prohibits discrimination against any racial group – white or black.

Justice John Marshall Harlan's dissent in *Plessy v. Ferguson* (1896) (upholding state-mandated racial segregation) also articulates principles of AD and AS. In upholding the principle of formal equality, he writes:

But in view of the constitution, in the eye of the law, there is in this country no superior, dominant, ruling class of citizens. There is no caste here. Our constitution is color-blind, and neither knows nor tolerates classes among its citizens.[15]

The focus here is on race – black or white. The law is meant to be "color-blind." Yet, in contending that such racial segregation is unconstitutional, Justice Harlan also appeals to AS, articulating claims of group powerlessness and domination. Refuting the contention that the segregation law equally affects blacks and whites, Harlan reasons that:

Every one knows that the statute in question had its origin in the purpose, not so much to exclude white persons from railroad cars occupied by blacks, as to exclude colored people from coaches occupied by or assigned to white persons.[16]
(...)
What can more certainly arouse race hate, what more certainly create and perpetuate a feeling of distrust between these races, than state enactments which, in fact, proceed on the ground that colored citizens are so inferior

---

[12] *Strauder* at 308.   [13] Brest *et al.* 2006: 355.   [14] *Strauder* at 310.
[15] *Plessy* at 559, dissenting.   [16] Ibid.: at 557, dissenting.

and degraded that they cannot be allowed to sit in public coaches occupied by white citizens?[17]

Here the focus isn't so much that the law categorizes according to race but that it specifically injures blacks. These passages of his dissent focus on the suspect class – blacks.

Similarly, in *Loving v. Virginia* (1967) (invalidating anti-miscegenation laws), the Court makes a dual argument: protesting the law's maintenance of "White Supremacy" (a worry about subordination) and its restriction based solely on "racial classifications" (a worry about formal inequality).[18] The *Loving* Court appeals to the principles of AS and AD. *Brown v. Board of Education* (1954) (held that racial segregation in public schools was unconstitutional) also looks to class and classification. In focusing on the class, it held that racial segregation harmed blacks, generating "a feeling of inferiority as to their status among the community."[19] Still, *Brown* frames the constitutional question by asking whether segregation in public schools "solely on the basis of race" is equal – focusing on the classification.[20]

In these four cases the legislation in question not only picked out, in Rawls' language, a morally irrelevant characteristic – race – but also discriminated against a subordinated minority – blacks. It is not surprising that these opinions looked to AD and AS in grounding their arguments. Both the rights of individuals and the rights of groups were violated. In other words, maintaining formal equality and remedying powerlessness were both clearly relevant. Either principle can trigger heightened scrutiny, because both class and classification can do the work in these cases.

However, AD and AS diverge with group-based affirmative action programs. Under AD such programs are presumptively problematic. The non-minority is being categorized according to an irrelevant characteristic such as race or sex. Since AD cares about the rights of individuals, these programs seem illegitimate. Under AS, though, such group-conscious programs would not receive heightened scrutiny. The group being disadvantaged – whites or men – would not be a suspect class. This is because whites do not need protection from the democratic process. They are not "discrete and insular groups" in the same way as blacks. They are not a democratic minority.[21] Consequently, there is no presumptive problem in discriminating against them.

This divergence is evident in the Court's race-based affirmative action cases. In *Regents of the University of California v. Bakke* (1978), the Court analyzed, for the first time, an affirmative action program that benefited a

[17] Ibid.: at 560, dissenting.   [18] *Loving* at 11–12.   [19] *Brown* at 494.
[20] Ibid.: at 493.   [21] John Ely 1980.

minority by disadvantaging a non-minority. At issue was a quota system at the University of California at Davis Medical School that accepted certain students from "disadvantaged" minority groups under a special admission program distinct from its general admission counterpart. Allan Bakke, a white male applicant whom the school rejected, instituted the legal action. At the time of his rejection, four unfilled minority quota spots were still available. Bakke argued that the group-conscious program was unconstitutional. The Court agreed holding that the university had violated equal protection. In subjecting the program to heightened scrutiny, the Court dismissed the AS rationale. It explicitly rejected the contention that since white males "are not a 'discrete and insular minority' requiring extraordinary protection from the majoritarian political process[,]" strict scrutiny should not apply.[22] The Court refused to distinguish between malicious and benign discrimination. "It is far too late to argue that the guarantee of equal protection to all persons permits the recognition of special wards entitled to a degree of protection greater than that accorded others."[23] The Court repudiates a concern with group rights.

Similarly, in *Adarand Construction, Inc. v. Pena* (1995) the Court invalidated a federal provision providing additional compensation in government contracts to contractors who hired minority subcontractors. (In *City of Richmond v. J. A. Croson Co.* (1989), the Court had rejected Richmond's similar proposal requiring contractors to use a certain percentage of minority subcontractors.) Echoing the AD approach and its focus on individuals rather than groups, the *Adarand* Court reasoned that the Fourteenth Amendment "protect[s] persons, not groups."[24] Once again, the Court champions AD and its focus on the rights of individuals.

The most recent affirmative action case, *Grutter v. Bollinger* (2003) seems to confirm the AD approach. Though *Grutter* upheld University of Michigan's affirmative action, non-quota-based program on grounds that diversity constitutes a compelling purpose, the Court still subjected the program to heightened scrutiny. Here, too, the petitioner was white alleging unconstitutional discrimination. Reaffirming the AD principle *Grutter* quotes from *Adarand* stating that "governmental action based on race – a group classification long recognized as in most circumstances irrelevant and therefore prohibited – should be subjected to detailed judicial inquiry."[25] In *Parents Involved in Community Schools v. Seattle School District, et al.* (2007), Chief Justice Roberts, writing for the Court, invalidated two school district plans that assigned students to schools

---

[22] *Bakke* at 290.   [23] Ibid.: at 295.   [24] *Adarand* at 227.   [25] *Grutter* at 326.

based on race to ensure racial diversity. The Court subjected the law to strict scrutiny. Affirming the AD approach, Roberts reasoned that "[t]he way to stop discrimination on the basis of race is to stop discriminating on the basis of race."[26]

The notion that such a classification (race) is irrelevant stands at the core of AD's adherence to formal equality. With such cases, scholars argue that the Court has endorsed AD repudiating AS.[27] Assuming that democratically enacted affirmative action programs are presumptively valid – as I do – some scholars no doubt lament the Court's adherence to AD. The formal equality principle calls into question such remedial legislation. By subjecting such remedial race-conscious laws to higher scrutiny, the Court makes it harder for the democratic polity to pass such legislation. It needlessly constrains democratic decision-making.[28]

Unlike AD, AS seeks to remedy group power differentials, and this may very well require categorizing an individual on the basis of an otherwise allegedly irrelevant characteristic. For example, to help the position of blacks as a group, the law may very well have to disadvantage or harm individual whites. The upshot of AS is that it permits such remedial legislation. It deems such legislation presumptively valid.

But, and this is the disadvantage with such an approach, under AS a characteristic may be morally irrelevant – eye color or blood type – but not define a disadvantaged group – those with blue eyes or type AB negative blood. Legal distinctions that discriminated against such groups would not trigger AS concerns. AS protects only those groups that occupy some kind of subordinated status in society. For example, a law that regulated the sexual activity of blonds or redheads would not violate the principle of AS. Blonds and redheads have not suffered a history of discrimination. After all, according to AS, suspectness arises not from an argument of moral irrelevance but from a group's subordinated status. At the very least, one would have to go outside the principle of AS to strike such a law down. Adherence to only AS, then, may very well be insufficient from an equality perspective. AD, on the other hand, would take issue with a law discriminating against blonds or redheads. Such a law invokes an irrelevant classification – hair color.

---

[26] *Parents Involved* at 41.   [27] See, e.g., Colker 1986, Nemko 1998, Hutchinson 2003.
[28] According to Winkler (2006) the total survival rate for race-conscious laws subjected to strict scrutiny in federal courts between 1990 and 2003 was only 27 percent (Winkler 2006: 839).

Consequently, AD and AS have distinct advantages and disadvantages:

AD:
> – *Advantage*: All morally irrelevant characteristics are presumptively invalid.
>
> – *Disadvantage*: Deems remedial legislation (affirmative action programs) presumptively invalid.

AS:
> – *Advantage*: Remedial legislation is presumptively valid.
>
> – *Disadvantage*: Some morally irrelevant characteristics may be presumptively valid.

Ideally, we want the conceptual advantages of both with none of the disadvantages. But, and this is the take home point, the Court's perverse logic ends up generating the disadvantages with none of the advantages. Current equal protection jurisprudence fails to endorse AD or AS.

Though the classification and class analyses are conceptually distinct, the Court collapses them. For instance, hair color may be a suspect classification – a morally irrelevant characteristic that the law ought not to invoke in treating individuals differently. However, blonds may not be a suspect class. After all, they do not occupy a subordinated status in society. They have not suffered a history of discrimination. The Court perverts AS and AD by conflating the class analysis with its classification counterpart.

The Court articulates the criteria for suspect classes only to have such an analysis improperly inform the list of suspect classifications. In *Carolene Products* (1938), the Court explains that legislation that affects "discrete and insular groups" may very well "call for a correspondingly more searching judicial inquiry."[29] Through the years, the Court has elucidated various criteria in determining suspectness, in cashing out the meaning of discrete and insular.[30] Two of the most important criteria include a history of discrimination[31] and immutability.[32] For example, in *Frontiero v. Richardson* (1973) (invalidating a federal statute that treated the spouses of servicewomen differently from the spouses of servicemen), the Court held that women count as a suspect class. The Court reasoned that sex is an immutable characteristic "determined solely by the accident of birth"

---

[29] *Carolene Products* at 153.

[30] See, e.g., Chemerinsky 2005: 653, Sullivan 2001: 647 (indicia of suspectness include political powerlessness, the history of discrimination, immutable characteristics, and relevancy between classification and governmental purpose).

[31] See, e.g., *City of Cleburne v. Cleburne*, 473 U.S. 432 (1985) at 441; *San Antonio v. Rodriguez*, 411 U.S. 1 (1973) at 28; *Frontiero v. Richardson*, 411 U.S. 677 (1973) at 677, 684–85.

[32] See, e.g., *Cleburne* (1985) at 440–444; *Frontiero* (1973) at 685–687.

and on the basis of it, women have suffered a history of discrimination.[33] If the characteristic – like race or sex – is immutable and those sharing it have suffered discrimination on account of it, the Court seems to treat the classification as suspect. But these indicia only outline the relevant suspect *class* – not the classification. The Court perverts AD by incorporating into it a principle of AS. After all, even though AD views hair color as a suspect classification, the Court fails to deem it as one. This is because strangely the Court looks to a suspect class analysis to generate its list of suspect classifications.

To truly take AD seriously, the Court would have to give heightened scrutiny to *all* morally irrelevant characteristics. Yet, case law only deems race, sex, alienage, and national origin as suspect classifications. Under the Court's logic, laws that classify according to hair color, eye color or blood type will not get heightened scrutiny. Such laws would only get rational review. But these may be just as arbitrary as their race and sex counterparts. If the Court truly cares about formal equality and that's the reason such laws trigger heightened scrutiny, all such irrelevant classifications should get similar treatment. According to an advocate of AD, the fact that race has been used in the past to oppress and subjugate cannot be the reason for triggering higher scrutiny. If that were the case, as a conceptual matter, AD would undermine its operating assumption, namely that only the morally irrelevant status of such a characteristic pushes for higher scrutiny. Formal equality must deem race a questionable classification, because of its normative irrelevance – not because blacks or any other minority may currently be powerless or subordinated. The argument of powerlessness is the province of AS.[34]

But since this is clearly not the approach the Court takes, it fails to fully endorse AD. Because the Court determines the list of suspect classifications by engaging in a suspect class analysis – looking, for instance, to a history of discrimination on the basis of an immutable characteristic – it does not completely adhere to formal equality. It perverts AD's central assumption by looking instead to AS's core claim of powerlessness. By

---

[33] *Frontiero* at 686.

[34] In her dissent to *Gratz v. Bollinger*, 539 U.S. 244 (2003) (a companion case to *Grutter* invalidating Michigan's undergraduate affirmative action program for not being narrowly tailored), Justice Ginsburg seems to suggest, in line with the AS approach, that the suspectness of race arises not from its irrelevance but from its historical use to discriminate against blacks. Though she confuses class with classification, she writes: our "jurisprudence ranks race a 'suspect category,' not because [race] is inevitably an impermissible classification, but because it is one which usually, to our national shame, has been drawn for the purposes of maintaining racial inequality" (*Gratz*, dissenting at 301). In this way, at least at a conceptual level, the AS approach defines suspectness by appeal to historical discrimination and powerlessness rather than by a concern with "moral irrelevance."

failing to treat other clearly morally irrelevant characteristics as suspect, its equal protection logic deems such classifications – hair color, blood type, physical size – as presumptively valid. As a result, the Court's logic undercuts the salient advantage of AD, namely its *prima facie* repudiation of laws that take into consideration such arbitrary factors. The Court claims adherence to AD, yet ends up incorporating part of the AS approach through the back door.

I say "part of," because the Court explicitly denies the need for remedying subordination. It refuses to fully endorse AS deeming affirmative action presumptively invalid. By only deeming those classifications suspect that entail suspect classes while *simultaneously* touting the merits of formal equality, the Court turns AS and AD on their heads. It subjects race-based affirmative action programs to heightened scrutiny, but fails to offer such scrutiny to laws that invoke other allegedly irrelevant classifications. Ultimately, it protects neither group rights nor individual ones.

The Court's logic perversely suffers from the disadvantages of AD and AS but none of the advantages. Put differently, the Court fails to fully endorse either principle – getting the worst of both worlds. Equal protection doctrine arose, as a historical matter, in those cases where both class and classification were at play. With the rise of race-based affirmative action, the Court has been unable to conceptually disentangle AD and AS, undermining both. It has been unable to separate classification from class, problematically combining the two.

This perverse logic is clearest in considering a law that segregated individuals on the basis of hair color. The Court's failure to deem hair color a suspect classification exposes the perversity of current equal protection doctrine. Under the Court's alleged formal equality approach such a law would be presumptively valid! It would only get rational review. But this exposes the Court's flawed conception of AD. Under AD, as long as the characteristic is morally irrelevant – such as race or hair color – legislation invoking it should be treated as suspect. Because the Court's equal protection analysis deems only some irrelevant classifications as suspect, it fails to fully realize formal equality simultaneously refusing to endorse AS. It claims to champion the rights of individuals but determines the scope of these rights by looking to the rights of groups.

Ultimately, we need an interpretation of equal protection that can reject morally irrelevant characteristics *as well as* permit affirmative action programs. Doing so requires that we reject both the rights of individuals and the rights of groups, turning our attention to legislative purpose. Adhering to the minimization of demonstrable harm as the lodestar of reviewing legislation does the job. If we simply ask – under one standard of review – whether the legislation seeks to minimize demonstrable harm we gain the advantages but none of the disadvantages of AS and AD. For instance, what is the reason behind race-based segregation, anti-miscegenation laws, a prohibition on same-sex marriage, sodomy laws, and state-mandated segregation based on hair color or blood type? In other words, what does the state seek to do in enacting such laws? As suggested in Part II, the state's reason would fail my theory of Justification. The rationales behind such legislation have nothing to do with demonstrable harm minimization. The state seeks to simply oppress, subjugate or do something other than minimize harm. *Brown* should have simply held that the racial segregation is irrational. We need not worry about whether the law infringes a group right or a more individual-regarding one. We need not engage in a more searching scrutiny precisely because the Court can reject such nefarious legislation on rational review grounds. A turn to legislative purpose, a re-conceptualized account of limited government, is sufficient.

In his concurrence in *City of Cleburne v. Cleburne* (1985) (invalidating a zoning law that discriminated against the mentally challenged under rational review), Justice Stevens suggests that racist legislation is irrational obviating heightened scrutiny to invalidate:[35]

> It would be utterly irrational to limit the franchise on the basis of height or weight; it is equally invalid to limit it on the basis of skin color ... We do not need to apply a special standard, or to apply "strict scrutiny," or even "heightened scrutiny," to decide such cases.[36]

As Stevens rightly implies, we do not need to find suspectness – e.g., a history of discrimination against a group – in order to invalidate such nefarious legislation. Such laws are irrational, because they seek to do something other than minimize demonstrable harm. We need not look to groups to invalidate such laws. Unfortunately, this is not the current constitutional principle with regard to race (after all, this language appears in a concurring opinion).

We should reject the doctrines of suspect class and classification and their accompanying tiers of scrutiny. These racist laws along with the ones in *Loving* seek to do something other than minimize harm. Consequently, the Court should have simply declared them irrational. Even scholars fail to realize that racial segregation fails not because it invokes a suspect classification or class (because of AD or AS) triggering heightened scrutiny, but simply because the state has no good rational reason to institute

---

[35] Goldberg 2004a: 518–525; fn. 1.   [36] *Cleburne* at 454, concurring.

it.[37] Erwin Chemerinsky, a notable exception to the tendency to quickly dismiss rational review as insufficient, argues in a mock *Brown* argument celebrating the decision's 50th birthday that:

[b]ecause the differences between the races are irrelevant to the state's goal of achieving optimal educational opportunities for children, the state-mandated segregation fails the reasonableness test [citation omitted], Kansas's decision to mandate segregation in public schools violates equal protection because it fails even the most deferential rational basis test.[38]

Since such segregation seeks to do something other than minimize harm, it must fail constitutional muster. Higher scrutiny is unnecessary.

The appeal to the doctrines of class and classification with their accompanying heightened scrutiny frustrates democratic deliberation. The debate over affirmative action seems incommensurable only because each side attempts to characterize or classify the activity – treating individuals of one race differently than those from another – as either violating an individual right or upholding a group right. These doctrines – formal equality versus anti-subordination – fail to look at the rationale behind legislation. Racial segregation is impermissible, simply because the state has no good reason to institute it. It is just as irrational as segregating redheads from blonds. Doing so does not attempt to prevent demonstrable harm.

But a democratic polity has good reason to pass affirmative action programs. Adopting the prevention of harm has the crucial upshot of simultaneously permitting affirmative action programs. With no heightened scrutiny to stand in its way, the polity may easily pass such legislation. While racial segregation laws are irrational, even silly, affirmative action laws are not. Affirmative action does seek to prevent demonstrable harm.[39] In fact, the Court in *Grutter* articulated a series of publicly ascertainable harms including: the deleterious effects of racial stereotyping, a lack of cooperation among racial groups, and even the frustration of national security. The Court reasoned that a diverse student body in the context of higher education promotes "cross-racial understanding" that "helps to break down racial stereotypes, and enables [students] to better

---

[37] Certain legal scholars rewrite *Brown* but fail to do so by contending that there is no rational reason for segregation. Rather, they largely look to principles of AD or AS to do the necessary work. (Balkin 2001: Introduction.)

[38] Chemerinsky 2003.

[39] In fact, Rubenfeld makes a similar argument suggesting that affirmative action, unlike racial segregation, proffers a legitimate purpose (Rubenfeld 1997). However, his argument fails to positively articulate the appropriate legislative purpose. By failing to do so, his argument is "incomplete" (Alexander 1998: 2681).

understand persons of different races."[40] The Court noted that without such racial diversity the military – which recruits from colleges and universities – would be less likely to achieve its "principle mission to provide national security."[41]

The affirmative action debate, then, *should not* be about whether helping racial minorities is a kind of racial discrimination like segregation. This obscures what is really at stake, namely what is the relevant harm and how best can we minimize or mitigate it. Without a doubt, comparison to segregation and other such legislation has no place in the affirmative action debate. Its unfortunate presence stems from an adherence to classification/class, to the methodology of rights. After all, such a methodology pits non-discrimination – we may not discriminate on the basis of race – against affirmative action. Focusing on the class or classification – deploying the claims of identity – needlessly deems such race-conscious policies dubious. Turning entirely to legislative purpose, rejecting the rights to formal equality and anti-subordination with their focus on individuals or groups better informs the debate. It makes clear that while state-mandated racial segregation is arbitrary, race-conscious legislation is not.

My theory of Justification leaves the polity to decide what demonstrable harms to minimize and how to do so. It may decide to institute a race-conscious affirmative action program to remedy the aforementioned harms. Alternatively, the polity may decide not to pass such legislation. Affirming the maxim-testing feature of Justification, constitutional law *does not require* such group-conscious programs just as it does not require maximum hours legislation. The point is that once the democratic polity has decided to remedy a demonstrable harm, the Court must not un-do that decision. Use of the doctrines of suspect class or classification is not necessary. Unlike racial segregation, remedial legislation is rational – minimizing some kind of publicly ascertainable harm. A simplified, single standard of review is sufficient to do the necessary work balancing equality and freedom – invalidating racial segregation – with the need for democratic flexibility – permitting affirmative action.

Anti-differentiation and anti-subordination jeopardizing equality and freedom

Perhaps the above argument rests too much on the Court's abuse of AD and AS. Leaving the Court's interpretation of AD and AS aside, are these principles on their own able to ensure equality and freedom? Perhaps my

[40] Ibid.: at 330.   [41] Ibid.: at 331.

move to the minimization of demonstrable harm as underlying equal protection is premature. After all, instead of repudiating the principles of AD and AS, why not endorse them fully? Even assuming as much, I argue that neither of these principles is sufficient to ensure liberty. Like the exhortations to equality explored earlier, these principles share the same fate of proving either too much or too little. We are better off sticking with legislative purpose – repudiating the focus on groups or individuals.

Both the formal equality approach and anti-subordination turn out to be over- and under-inclusive. With regard to the over-inclusive charge, each approach calls into question laws that we believe the polity ought to be able to pass. Again, it may be worth asking why murderers facing punishment may not claim a violation of equality. Laws distinguish between murderers and non-murderers, restraining the liberty of the former. But exactly what makes this characteristic – the fact that you murdered someone but I didn't – morally relevant? Admittedly, no one takes this seriously as a violation of AD. But why not? What makes our allegiance to equality in this case suddenly inapplicable? If our concern is with disadvantaged groups – minorities in the democratic process – why can't murderers count as such a group?

Consider this example. Jim Crow advocates would have maintained that race is a morally and hence legally relevant characteristic. They would have considered racial segregation laws just as legitimate as laws against murder. Now I do believe that we can treat murderers differently from non-murderers but not segregate individuals on account of their race or restrict their sexual behavior. But the appeal to AD does not explain why. The claim of relevance seems un-instructive. If we are willing to violate formal equality to punish murderers, what is so wrong with doing so to restrict sexual behavior or even to segregate?

In fact, why isn't the class of murderers suspect in line with AS? Murderers may very well meet the legal indicia of suspectness: there is evidence to suggest that some people are predisposed to violent behavior;[42] and it is certainly the case that murderers have suffered from a history of discrimination (though most would prefer to say, "punishment"). Or take pedophiles, a group that seems an even better candidate for suspect status. They have no doubt suffered a history of discrimination as well as a very strident social stigma. Like other kinds of sexual attraction, there is evidence that pedophilia is biological in nature.[43] If pedophiles meet the test of subordination, how can a principle of AS rule them out? How can theorists of a "politics of difference" not take them into account alongside

---

[42] See, e.g., Blair 2001, Raine et al. 1998.
[43] See, e.g., Hendricks 1988, Wright et al. 1990.

gays, women, and blacks? It will not do simply to assert that the history of discrimination is justified in the case of murderers or pedophiles, but unjustified in the case of blacks and women.[44] The assertion begs the question as to why. What makes some discrimination justifiable, and others not? After all, someone could just as easily say that racial discrimination is justifiable – and people no doubt have. AD and AS turn out over-inclusive.

Perhaps the distinction lies in the appeal to behavior. As Ely writes:

A law making burglary a crime is not suspicious – or, if you prefer, the suspicion is immediately allayed – because the goal of making life unpleasant for burglars is immediately translatable into the goal of discouraging people from breaking into our homes. It would not make sense, however, to defend a law disadvantaging blacks on the ground that we are trying to discourage people from being black.[45]

Thus, segregation does not regulate behavior but laws against murder and pedophilia do. Equal protection, under Ely's argument, is about making sure laws do not discriminate against status rather than behavior. Blackness is a status and is therefore not a legitimate ground for discrimination; whereas behaving in a certain way – killing or stealing – can be, or so Ely's argument suggests.

Yet, this alleged clarification of what AD and AS mean does not really help us out – bringing us to the way these principles are under-inclusive. They fail to repudiate laws that jeopardize liberty. After all, a law against sodomy is unapologetically a law that regulates behavior. As a general rule, case law does not regard mere disparate impact – the law happens to affect a certain group more than others – as sufficient to trigger presumptive discrimination.[46] Disparate impact may be evidence of a violation of AD or AS but it is not conclusive. How, then, can sodomy laws be seen as violating AD or AS? As it turns out the law in *Bowers* was facially neutral – presumably applying to homosexuals and heterosexuals. Nevertheless, the *Bowers* Court assumed that such laws, as applied, primarily discriminated against gays. But the Court did not afford gays suspect status. Had they done so – fully endorsing the principle of AD or AS – perhaps such laws could have been struck down under equal protection.

In *Watkins v. U.S. Army* (9th Cir. 1988) the Ninth Circuit did, in fact, conclude that gays constituted a suspect class invalidating the military's explicit ban on homosexuals (this was before the military's current Don't Ask Don't Tell policy). Reasoning that gays have suffered a history of discrimination on the basis of an immutable characteristic – sexual

---

[44] Cf. Goldman 2005.   [45] John Ely 1980: 154.
[46] *Washington v. Davis*, 426 U.S. 229 (1976).

orientation – the Ninth Circuit subjected the regulation to heightened scrutiny finding it unjustifiable.[47] Though that opinion (along with its recognition of gays as a suspect class) was ultimately vacated by the full Ninth Circuit,[48] perhaps this suggests that a thorough understanding of AD and AS can do the equality and freedom work.

Nevertheless, this is still not sufficient. Indeed, Ely's interpretation will actually justify state regulation of a litany of other behaviors. For instance, his interpretation will allow laws banning orgies and one-night stands. All these are behaviors, not statuses. So here's the rub. We do not deem the distinction between orgy participants and non-orgy participants or one-night stand enthusiasts and non-one-night stand enthusiasts as suspect. Under AD, such laws do not seem to invoke a morally irrelevant characteristic. This is because almost everyone can refrain from an orgy or a one-night stand. With nothing to define this assertion of "relevance," the AD approach is unable to prohibit such laws. It cannot ensure freedom.

The principle of AS also suffers the same fate. Only subordinated groups have standing under it. But laws banning orgies or one-night stands do not seem to discriminate against a particular *subordinated* minority. It's hard to see how participation in an orgy or a one-night stand is part of any identity formation. By its very terms, a one-night stand seems to be a random, single event unconnected to any long-term conception of identity. I doubt that those who speak of oppressed groups would include orgy or one-night-stand enthusiasts along with blacks, gays, or women. But it is precisely this argument that one could make in defense of the pedophile who considers her behavior at the core of her identity.

Then we see why the AS argument is both over- and under-inclusive. On one hand, if we accept that pedophilic behavior is at the core of a pedophile's identity, equality demands that we decriminalize such behavior. Existing laws outlawing pedophilia would turn out to be pretexts for outlawing a certain kind of status or identity. On the other hand, if the one-night stand or any other act in question has nothing to do with identity formation – it was done to fulfill a dare or to impress a friend, how can we claim that prohibiting it violates AS? The right to equality argument ends up simultaneously protecting too much and too little.

Equality obsesses about group status. In Nancy Fraser's language, our allegiance to the equality argument has led to an affirmation of group differentiation[49] which has in turn fueled the problematic nature/nurture debate.[50] This is because for equality to be in play, the group status must

---

[47] Ibid.: at 1448–1452.   [48] *Watkins v. U.S. Army*, 875 F.2d 699 (9th Cir. 1989) (en banc).
[49] Fraser 1997.
[50] Edward Stein (2001) discusses the ethical problems with this biological inquiry.

be biological – an immutable characteristic. If sexual orientation is to be considered along with race, it must be un-chosen. Gays and lesbians no doubt portray their desires as such when they adopt the locution of sexual orientation instead of sexual preference. That is, in order to invoke the right to equality, being gay must *not* be a choice. One must be born gay just as one is born black or white. But according to many biologists and anthropologists there is nothing biological about the category of race.[51] If anything, there may be more genetic diversity within alleged races than between them.[52] If race – the paradigmatic instance where the right to equality applies – may not be a biological characteristic but rather a social and legal construct, it seems perverse that sexual orientation must be portrayed as such to utilize the right to equality.

But my justificatory constraint provides a more robust, non-contingent solution. After all, what does it matter if sexual attraction is chosen, given, or a mixture of both? Indeed, why should the reason I decide to have sex with a man even matter? What if I don't even consider myself gay or bisexual – I do not fit into one of the suspect classes? What if the sex act is purely a physical thing, a night of experimentation, or even a favor for a friend? These may sound like silly rhetorical questions, but they quickly get to the core of my dissatisfaction with the conventional equality arguments. In these cases, it seems I'd have no standing to invoke the protection of equality. If we accept Ely's interpretation, the right to equality turns out to protect too little. Sexual freedom or any freedom for that matter should not have to hinge on why I decide to have sex, what I hope to gain from it, or what group, if any, I happen to belong to. If equality kicks in only under certain conditions – for example, I need to be gay – we cannot genuinely achieve it.

Moreover, this kind of thinking needlessly invites the objection that gays or other groups seek "special rights." After all, adding sexuality as another prohibited class – with its focus on the relevant group – no doubt suggests that the group is getting extra protection. If a law is illegitimate because it discriminates against a certain group, that group seems to benefit.

If we want to secure the options to engage in orgies or one-night stands, appeal to AD and AS is hardly the way to do it. In many ways, we revisit the arguments of Chapter 3. The problem is that we need the conceptual tools to permit laws against murder or pedophilia but reject laws that seek to institute a Puritan code, regulating other kinds of behavior. Appeal to AD and AS cannot do the necessary distinguishing work.

---

[51] See, e.g., Braman 1999, Livingstone 1962, Lewontin 1997.   [52] Lewontin 1997: 7.

Unsurprisingly, constitutional law looks to both fundamental rights and equal protection in ensuring equality and freedom. Conventional wisdom suggests that the right to privacy protects us from laws banning orgies or the one-night stand. This may explain why the constitutional division of labor is so ingrained. But if the equality arguments for sexual freedom require privacy, we revisit the problems above. Complementary arguments inherit the weaknesses of their component parts. Again, privacy only protects by tolerating, by invariably demeaning the sexual act as it hides it behind closed doors.

We should reject such a bifurcation. We need simply ask whether the law at issue seeks to minimize demonstrable harm. This is how we ensure equal protection. Rather than analyzing what group or class the law discriminates against or whether it violates a fundamental right, we need only ask the reason or rationale behind it. The minimization of harm explains the substantive criminal law. Behavior that leads to non-consensual demonstrable harm – such as murder and pedophilia – may certainly be prohibited. The polity has good reason to regulate it. Consensual orgies and sodomy, on the other hand, do not lead to such harm. The state has no good reason to pass laws regulating such behavior or a law mandating racial segregation or one that regulates the sexual activity of redheads and blonds. These laws fail regardless of the group I happen to belong to – if any at all. Thus, we nip the "special rights" objection in the bud. We need not speak in the slippery language of identity. We better secure equality by turning to reasons rather than rights. There is no "group" that benefits, because the law simply fails for not seeking to minimize demonstrable harm. If rational review is re-conceptualized in this way, we can ditch the Court's perverse equal protection analysis. Doing so better ensures equality. After all, the Court has largely already rejected the rights to property, religion, and privacy.

This shift to a simplified rational review is salient in the debate over same-sex marriage. Currently, much of the debate over the prohibition on same-sex marriage rests on the issue of class or classification. Though the decision was effectively undone by a state constitutional amendment, in *Baehr v. Lewin* (Hawaii 1993) the Hawaii Supreme Court, the first American court to do so, held that a ban on same-sex marriage triggers heightened scrutiny under the state's equal protection clause. It reasoned that such a ban is a kind of sex discrimination invoking a suspect classification. It recognized the fact that "[p]arties to a same-sex marriage could theoretically be either homosexuals or heterosexuals."[53] A gay man and a

---

[53] *Baehr* at 544.

lesbian would have no problem getting married. In this way, the prohibition is, at least formally, discriminatory on the basis of sex. The state looks to the sex and not to the person's sexual orientation in granting marriage licenses. But, and the Hawaii decision does not mention this, suppose a state asked individuals their sexual orientation before issuing the marriage license? If at least one party acknowledged being gay, the state would refuse the license. This would be a genuine case of sexual orientation discrimination. Under this kind of prohibition, a gay man and a lesbian woman could not get married.

This hypothetical case exemplifies *Baehr*'s problematic appeal to suspect class/classification. If we deem sexual orientation a suspect classification, this imaginary law would get heightened scrutiny. But suppose the Hawaii law only banned gays with red hair from getting married? Or banned gay black women from getting married? Or any other such combination?[54] Do we create more suspect classifications or classes? This highlights the theoretical problem with such doctrines. They, like their rights counterpart, seek to categorize whom the law discriminates against – gays or redheads – rather than focus on the *reason* behind such prohibitions. Simply put, such prohibitions are irrational. Just as the state has no good reason to segregate on the basis of race or to regulate certain consensual behavior, it also has no good reason to ban same-sex marriage or ban marriages between redheads and blonds. The pathology of suspect class/classification drives litigants to garner heightened or more exacting scrutiny from the Court. We need only see that such legislation is irrational, because it seeks to do something other than minimize demonstrable harm.

Use of rational review to invalidate such a prohibition is not a novel legal argument. In *Goodridge v. Dep't of Public Health* (Mass. 2003) the Supreme Judicial Court of Massachusetts, albeit under the state constitution, did just that, putting Justification into constitutional practice. This case stands as proof positive that Justification is workable. The Court begins its argument by noting that there may very well be due process and equal protection questions triggering heightened scrutiny. However, without reaching these constitutional questions, the state's highest court held that the ban fails on *rational review grounds alone*. It did *not* engage in a heightened scrutiny analysis. *Goodridge* simply turned its complete attention to the state's reason for enacting the prohibition. And in so doing, the Court rejected all the following rationales put forth by Massachusetts for the prohibition: "(1) providing a 'favorable setting for procreation', (2) ensuring the optimal

---

[54] Crenshaw 1989.

setting for child rearing, which the department defines as 'a two-parent family with one parent of each sex', and (3) preserving scarce State and private financial resources."[55]

The Court rightly reasoned these rationales fail in good faith to minimize demonstrable harm. First, the harm of a non-favorable setting for procreation – though a legitimate purpose – was limited irrationally only to same-sex marriages. The Supreme Judicial Court reasoned that in order to minimize this harm, the state would have to proscribe many more kinds of non-marital relationships where child rearing takes place.[56] Effectively, the Court adopts the "only" provision of my constraint, pointing to the fact that merely prohibiting same-sex marriage but not single parenting, for example, does something else in addition to minimizing harm. Second, the Supreme Judicial Court contends that the state offers no evidence that "forbidding marriage to people of the same sex will increase the number of couples choosing to enter into opposite sex marriages in order to have and raise children" or that a same-sex marriage is not an optimal setting for child rearing.[57] A mere claim that something is harmful is not enough. In line with my argument, the state of Massachusetts did not engage demonstrability in good faith. Third, once again implicitly accepting the "only" provision of my theory of Justification, the opinion reasons that the state does not truly care about preserving financial resources in the way it provides the marriage benefit to opposite sex couples.[58] Said differently, the ban on same-sex marriage is an illegitimate "one step at a time" measure to save on scarce resources. The Massachusetts decision makes clear that a genuine rational review inquiry is sufficient to smoke out such liberty-compromising legislation. The majority opinion did *not* ground its decision on the fact that a right to marry is fundamental or that the law violates a right to equality improperly discriminating on the basis of sex or sexual orientation. It did not engage arguments about the rights of groups or individuals by flagging the same-sex prohibition for higher scrutiny. A rational basis test was sufficient. For the Supreme Judicial Court, just reasons not rights did the work.

A democratic role for judicial review

In fact, abandoning conventional equal protection jurisprudence along with much fundamental rights analysis entails a more democratic role for judicial review. My theory of Justification and a corresponding single tier of rational review inform a more democracy-affirming role for the Court.

---

[55] *Goodridge* at 331.   [56] Ibid.: at 332–333.   [57] Ibid.: at 334–335.   [58] Ibid.: at 336–337.

In coming back to judicial review, we end where we began. In the Introduction, I laid out the essential motivation for my overall argument – finding how best to balance and realize the values of liberty and democracy. Such review stands at the center of this balancing act, at the center of a superior account of limited government.

Promoting freedom or equality can compromise democracy and vice versa. These values can conflict. The Court has the potential to be, as Alexander Bickel famously argued, "counter-majoritarian."[59] We need a theory of judicial review that best balances them. I suggest that a conception of judicial review where the Court should intervene only when the law seeks to do something other than minimize demonstrable harm is our best option.

Holding onto rights and their emphasis on substantive results (as outlined in Chapter 1) leads us to the counter-majoritarian extreme. Ronald Dworkin, for instance, argues that the Court should enforce such values.[60] He contends, in line with his commitment to rights:

My own view is that the Court should make decisions of principle rather than policy – decisions about what rights people have under our constitutional system rather than decisions about how the general welfare is best promoted – and that it should make these decisions by elaborating and applying the substantive theory of representation taken from the root principle that government must treat people as equals.[61]

The Court must make such substantive choices. For Dworkin the Court's counter-majoritarian character is no problem at all, because in enforcing equality it must constrain majoritarian decision-making.[62] Consequently, Dworkin's position values liberty but fails to incorporate genuine room for democracy. His conventional, static notion of rights as pre-political "trumps" suffers from the "democratic deficit" laid out in the beginning of the book. Focus on the conventional account of limited government leaves out the value of democracy.

But caring only about democracy leads us to the other extreme. John Ely argues that the Court should step in only when democracy breaks down, only when the democratic system malfunctions.[63] Only when groups are excluded from the democratic legitimation process should the Court intervene. Ely's commitment to the procedural requirements of democracy, then, has much in common with Habermas' presuppositions of equality and reciprocity. But like Habermas' discourse theory, Ely's procedural conception of judicial review is incapable of ensuring liberty. Again, though

---

[59] Bickel 1986.   [60] R. Dworkin 1985: Ch. 2, 23–28.   [61] Ibid.: 69.
[62] Whittington 1999: 27.   [63] John Ely 1980: 101–104.

a majority could not (under this mere procedural model of judicial review) prevent gays from voting or running for office, it could certainly curtail their sexual freedom. Such laws do not run afoul of democratic proceduralism. As long as gays have an equal say in the democratic decision to pass the sodomy law, under the Habermas–Ely approach the Court may not invalidate it. Such a limited role for judicial review no doubt fills the "democratic deficit" left by a strict rights-based approach. However, democracy is left unconstrained. There is no limit on it.

Now perhaps Habermas and Ely would retort that their theories are more than mere procedure. Habermas, as outlined in Chapter 3, does at times appeal to a right of equality as informing his discourse theory. Similarly, Ely endorses the "discrete and insular" argument of *Carolene Products* arguing that legislation that encroaches upon suspect classes should be deemed presumptively invalid.[64] In putting forth this theory of judicial review, Ely endorses the AS approach. But, as argued above, these exhortations to "equality" or "suspect class" turn out to prove too much and too little. They fail to do the necessary, normative distinguishing work in appropriately limiting democratic government.

We need something in between, something that, as Ian Shapiro argues, is "more than process, less than substance."[65] Robert Burt[66] presents such a middling position arguing that Courts should step in only when democratic decision-making leads to "domination."[67] Specifically, Burt argues that the Court should not forestall debate by declaring a clear winner as, for example, it did in *Roe*. By basing its decision on the right to privacy, it categorically decided the issue of whether women had a right to abort. The pro-life position was the clear loser leaving any democratic accommodation impossible. As Scalia similarly opines, the Court's abortion cases preempt "all participants, even the losers, the satisfaction of a fair hearing and an honest fight."[68] The *Roe* Court effectively fashioned a statute in laying out the trimester framework for the regulation of abortion. For Burt, the Court should intervene just enough to uphold what he terms an "equality principle" simultaneously allowing for a more balanced democratic debate.[69] For example, in *Brown*, the Court invalidated segregation but left the legislature to fashion an appropriate constitutional remedy.[70]

Shapiro likens Burt's approach to that of Justice Ginsburg.[71] Ginsburg also criticizes *Roe* as suggesting a theory of judicial review that preempts debate by hastily reaching a substantive outcome. *Roe* "invited no

---

[64] Ibid.: Ch. 6.   [65] Shapiro 2003a: 66.   [66] Burt 1992.   [67] Shapiro 2003a: 66.
[68] *Casey* at 10002, dissenting.   [69] Burt 1992: 358–359.   [70] Ibid.: 374–349.
[71] Shapiro 2003a: 67; see R. Ginsburg 1992.

dialogue with legislators. Instead it seemed entirely to remove the ball from the legislators' court."[72] She like Shapiro looks to *Casey* as a paradigmatic example of a more satisfactory middling approach.[73]

Shapiro contends that *Casey* "set some basic parameters within which legislatures must now fashion regulations that govern abortion."[74] By refraining from laying out exactly when the legislature may curtail abortion, the undue burden standard invites and requires democratic elaboration. It invites the democratic majority to decide the issue of demonstrability – whether a particular prohibition on abortion demonstrably harms women. In other words, the *Casey* decision rightly leaves it to the democratic decision-making process to decide the scope and terms of "undue." Echoing the concerns of the dissenters in *Casey*, Shapiro concedes that such an open-ended standard may invite more litigation. At least the rigid trimester framework of *Roe* was clear and easily implemented. Yet, for Shapiro such ambiguity and inefficiency are a price worth paying to promote and foster democracy, and I agree.[75] A good-faith commitment to demonstrability will no doubt invite democratic disagreement.

But the Shapiro–Burt–Ginsburg theory of judicial review, though somewhat instructive, fails to spell out the *actual* limits on democratic decision-making. Burt's emphasis on maintenance of an "equal principle" or a notion of anti-domination suffers from the same problems of meaning explored in the exhortations of equal liberty or equal protection. When do we know that domination has occurred, permitting the Court to step in? Burt is right that, in deciding cases, the Court should permit maximum democratic flexibility. But he, like Shapiro and Ginsburg, does not proffer a concrete regulatory principle to do so. (Interestingly, and it is worth mentioning again, Ginsburg's recent dissent in *Gonzales* does seem to endorse a turn away from rights and towards reasons.)

In any case, like the reflexive theorists of Chapter 2, they fail in connecting liberty with democracy. For instance, Shapiro fails to realize that fostering such democratic decision-making is best realizable by rejecting rights.[76] Adhering to rights effectively undercuts the creativity of the democratic process on both sides of the political spectrum. Again, there may be other ways, besides a right to abort, to remedy the burden of pregnancy. What if the state decided to compensate women for their pregnancy rather than freely allowing them the ability to abort? What if the state decided to pass a series of harsh Good Samaritan laws forcing others to carry a similar burden? The doctrine of fundamental rights preempts a range of

---

[72] R. Ginsburg 1992: 1205.   [73] Ibid.: 1199–1200.   [74] Shapiro 2003a: 69.
[75] Ibid.: 70–73.   [76] Ibid.: 69.

alternatives. *Lochner* with its emphasis on a right to property limits the polity from redistributing wealth or reconsidering the value of private property. The commitment to rights discourse invites the Court, as it did in *Bowers*, to interpret the scope of the constitutional right to privacy narrowly so as to exclude gay sex from its ambit. Similarly, the doctrines of suspect class and classification needlessly trigger heightened scrutiny when the polity passes affirmative action legislation to minimize harm.

We need not wrestle with the separate questions of "who governs me" and "how far ought government to interfere with me." By specifying the appropriate reason on which the polity may act – harm minimization – we necessitate democratic decision-making while ensuring equality and freedom. Rejecting rights including the focus on suspect class or classification, re-conceptualizing rational review to track this theory of Justification proffers a more appropriate theory of judicial review. It re-conceptualizes limited government balancing and realizing the values of liberty and democracy. It requires the Court to step in when the state fails this justificatory constraint, only when the polity proffers an illegitimate reason for its action – something other than harm minimization.

Conclusion

Occam's razor contends that all other things being equal the simplest theory is the correct one. All along my goal was to propose a sounder account of limited government, an account that better balances and realizes the values of liberty and democracy. Constraining the rationale on which the polity may act frees us from the problematic baggage of rights, channeling democratic debate in a more fruitful direction. In making this turn to legislative rationale or purpose convincing, I have proposed a concrete, and hopefully persuasive, theory of Justification, one that even resonates with American constitutional law. My primary aim was to convince you that we should re-conceptualize limited government by looking to the democratic polity's reason for acting. Reasons not rights ought to do the normative work.

The lack of robust democratic debate is not the problem with contemporary politics. Rather, contemporary politics seems beset by the problem of unnecessary, often fruitless debate on some matters and not enough on others. While the debate over same-sex marriage is so heated and the abortion controversy so exasperating, their Social Security or welfare counterpart is not. My theory of Justification stands as a corrective. If the polity may only seek to minimize demonstrable, non-consensual harm, there is no good reason to prohibit same-sex marriage just as there's no good reason to regulate the sexual activity of redheads or blonds. On the other hand, reasonable people can and should disagree over what welfare policy (if any) best minimizes harm. With abortion, it should be about how far we are willing to compel individuals to go to save others.

Simultaneously, my justificatory constraint makes liberty the normative presumption. By constraining democratic decision-making, *all* laws must be appropriately justified. Even conventional criminal legislation must pass this constraint. By shifting the normative attention away from individuals and groups and to the state itself, no law is presumptively valid. This may stand to enliven democratic discourse and even participation. We do better to limit democratic government not by carving out those areas, interests, or spheres off limits to state regulation but by limiting the reason or rationale on which it may act, a re-conceptualization that has already taken place in American constitutional law. Doing so ensures equality and freedom, permitting the democratic polity to pass a wide range of legislation it deems desirable.

Underlying my argument, then, is a commitment to democracy as well as liberty. Just as a judge offers jurors instructions before they deliberate, I ask you to keep both values in mind as you evaluate my argument. Simply caring about one or the other will not lead you to my theory of Justification. Only in seeking to balance these values do we see the appeal and purchase of Mill's "harm principle" understood as a justificatory constraint on state action. If I am correct, we ensure liberty – avoiding majority tyranny – while deferring to and permitting democratic decision-making. We should reject rights, turning to legislative purpose as the transformative account of limited government.

Bibliography

Abraham, Henry J. 1990. "Of Courts, Judicial Tools, and Equal Protections." In *The Constitutional Bases of Political and Social Change in the United States* (Shlomo Slonim, ed.) Westport, Conn.: Praeger Publishers.

Ackerman, Bruce. 1980. *Social Justice and the Liberal State*. New Haven, Conn.: Yale University Press.

    1983. "What is Neutral about Neutrality?" *Ethics* 93(2) (January): 372–390.

    1994. "Political Liberalisms." *The Journal of Philosophy* 91(7) (July): 364–386.

    1998. *We the People: Transformations*, Vol. 2. Cambridge, Mass.: Belknap Press.

Ackerman, Bruce and Anne Alstott. 1999. *The Stakeholder Society*. New Haven, Conn.: Yale University Press.

Alexander, Larry. 1998. "Affirmative Action and Legislative Purpose: correspondence to Jed Rubenfeld (1997) 'Affirmative Action'." 107 *Yale Law Journal* 2679.

Allen, Anita L. 1999. "Coercing Privacy." 40 *William and Mary Law Review* 723 (March).

American Heritage Dictionary. 2001. New York: Dell.

Anderson, Perry. 1974. *Lineages of the Absolutist State*. London: Verso.

Appiah, K. Anthony. 1994. "Identity, Authenticity, Survival: Multicultural Societies and Social Reproduction." In *Multiculturalism: Examining the Politics of Recognition* (Amy Gutmann, ed.) Princeton, N.J.: Princeton University Press.

    1996. "Against National Culture." In *Text and Nation: Cross-Disciplinary Essays on Cultural and National Identities* (Laura García-Moreno and Peter C. Pfeiffer, eds.) Columbia, S.C.: Camden, 1996.

Archard, David. 1990. "Freedom Not to be Free: The Case of the Slavery Contract in J.S. Mill's 'On Liberty'." *The Philosophical Quarterly* 40(161) (October): 453–465.

Arkes, Hadley. 1995. *The Return of George Sutherland: Restoring a Jurisprudence of Natural Rights*. Princeton, N.J.: Princeton University Press.

Arneson, Richard L. 1980. "Mill versus Paternalism." *Ethics* 90(4) (July): 470–489.

Bailyn, Bernard. 1967. *The Ideological Origins of the American Revolution*. New York: Belknap Press.

Balkin, Jack. 2001. *What Brown v. Board of Education Should have Said: The Nation's Top Legal Experts Rewrite America's Landmark Civil Rights Decision* (Jack M. Balkin, ed.) New York: New York University Press.

2005. *What Roe v. Wade Should have Said: The Nation's Top Legal Experts Rewrite America's Most Controversial Decision* (Jack M. Balkin, ed.) New York: New York University Press.

Balkin, Jack and Reva B. Siegel. 2003. "The American Civil Rights Tradition: Anticlassification or Antisubordination." 58 *University of Miami Law Review* 9.

Barber, Benjamin R. 1983. "Unconstrained Conversations: A Play on Words, Neutral and Otherwise." *Ethics* 93(2) (January): 330–347.

Barnett, Randy E. 2003. *Kennedy's Libertarian Revolution, National Review Online* (July 10, 2003), www.nationalreview.com/comment/comment-barnett071003. asap

Barry, Brian. 1995. *Justice as Impartiality*. New York: Oxford University Press.
    2001. *Culture and Equality*. Cambridge, Mass.: Harvard University Press.

Barry, Kathleen. 1995. *The Prostitution of Sexuality*. New York: New York University Press.

Beard, Charles. 1913. *An Economic Interpretation of the Constitution of the United States*. New York: Macmillan.

Beatty, David M. 1994. "Human Rights and the Rule of Law." In *Human Rights and Judicial Review: A Comparative Perspective* (David M. Beatty, ed.) Boston: Kluwer Press.

Becker, Gary S. 1985. "Human Capital, Effort, and the Sexual Division of Labor." *Journal of Labor Economics* 3(1) Part 2: Trends in Women's Work, Education, and Family Building: S33–S58.

Bedi, Sonu. 2007. "What is so Special About Religion? The Dilemma of the Religious Exemption." *Journal of Political Philosophy* 15(2) (June): 235–249.

Benhabib, Seyla. 1986. *Critique, Norm, and Utopia: A Study of the Foundations of Critical Theory*. New York: Columbia University Press.
    1992. *Situating the Self*. New York: Routledge.
    2002. *The Claims of Culture: Equality and Diversity in the Global Era*. Princeton, N.J.: Princeton University Press.
    2004. *The Rights of Others: Aliens, Residents, and Citizens*. Cambridge: Cambridge University Press.

Bentham, Jeremy. 1987 [1843]. "Anarchical Fallacies." In *Nonsense Upon Stilts: Bentham, Burke and Marx on the Rights of Man* (J. Waldron, ed.) London: Methuen.

Berlin, Isaiah. 1970 [1958]. "Two Concepts of Liberty." In *Four Essays on Liberty*. Oxford: Oxford University Press.

Bickel, Alexander M. 1986. *The Least Dangerous Branch: the Supreme Court at the Bar of Politics*. New Haven, Conn.: Yale University Press.

Blair, R. J. R. 2001. "Neurocognitive models of aggression, the antisocial personality disorders, and psychopathy." *Journal of Neurology, Neurosurgery and Psychiatry* 71: 727–731.

Boas, Franz. 1940. *Race, Language and Culture*. New York: Free Press.

Bork, Robert H. 1990. *The Tempting of America*. New York: Touchstone.

Braman, Donald. 1999. "Of Race and Immutability." 46 *University of California, Los Angeles Law Review* 1375.

Brest, Paul, Sanford Levinson, Jack M. Balkin, Akhil Reed Amar, and Reva B. Siegel. 2006. *Processes of Constitutional Decisionmaking: Cases and Materials*. 5th edn. New York: Aspen Publishers.

Brettschneider, Corey. 2007. *Democratic Rights: The Substance of Self-Government.* Princeton, N.J.: Princeton University Press.

Breyer, Stephen. 2005. *Active Liberty: Interpreting our Democratic Constitution.* New York: Knopf.

Burke, Edmund. 1973 [1790]. *Reflections on the Revolution in France.* New York: Anchor.

Burt, Robert A. 1992. *The Constitution in Conflict.* Cambridge, Mass.: Belknap Press.

Calabresi, Guido. 1990. The Supreme Court: 1990 Term. "Foreword: Antidiscrimination and Constitutional Accountability (What the Bork-Brennan Debate Ignores)." *Harvard Law Review* 105(80).

Calabresi, Guido and Douglas A. Melamed. 1972. "Property Rules, Liability Rules, and Inalienability: One View of the Cathedral." *Harvard Law Review* 85(6).

Carter, Stephen L. 1993. *The Culture of Disbelief: How American Law and Politics Trivialize Religious Devotion.* New York: Doubleday.

Chapman, Philip. 2004. Note, "Beyond Gay Rights: Lawrence v. Texas and the Promise of Liberty," 13 *William and Mary Bill of Rights Journal* 245.

Chemerinsky, Erwin. 2003. "Mock Brief for Petitioners in *Brown.*" 52 *American University Law Review* 1391.

    2005. *Constitutional Law.* 2nd edn. New York: Aspen Press.

Cohen, G. A. 1989. "On the Currency of Egalitarian Justice." *Ethics* 99(4): 906–944.

Cohen, Jean. 2002. *Regulating Intimacy: A New Legal Paradigm.* Princeton, N.J.: Princeton University Press.

Colker, Ruth. 1986. "Anti-Subordination Above All Else: Sex, Race, and Equal Protection." 61 *New York University Law Review* 1003.

Cover, Robert M. 1983. "The Supreme Court: 1982 Term. 'Foreword: Nomos and Narrative.' " 97 *Harvard Law Review* 4: 4–67.

Crenshaw, Kimberly. 1989. "Demarginalizing the Intersection of Race and Sex: A Black Feminist Critique of Antidiscrimination Doctrine, Feminist Theory, and Antiracist Politics." *University of Chicago Legal Forum* 139.

Dahl, Robert. 1971. *Polyarchy: Participation and Opposition.* New Haven, Conn.: Yale University Press.

    2001. *How Democratic is the American Constitution?* New Haven, Conn.: Yale University Press.

Davenport, Christian. 2007. *State Repression and the Domestic Democratic Peace.* New York: Cambridge University Press.

Davidson, Julia O'Connell. 1998. *Prostitution, Power and Freedom.* Cambridge: Polity Press.

Devigne, Robert. 2006. *Reforming Liberalism: J.S. Mill's Use of Ancient, Religious, Liberal, and Romantic Moralities.* New Haven, Conn.: Yale University Press.

Devlin, Lord Patrick. 1971 [1965]. "Morals and the Criminal Law; Hart." In *Morality and the Law* (Richard Wasserstrom, ed.) Belmont, Calif.: Wadsworth Publishing.

Dobzhansky, T. 1955. *Evolution, Genetics, and Man.* New York: Wiley & Sons.

Duncan, Richard F. 2005. "Free Exercise and Individualized Exemptions: Herein of Smith, Sherbert, Hogwarts, and Religious Liberty." 83 *Nebraska Law Review* 1178.

Dworkin, Andrea. 1981. *Pornography: Men Possessing Women.* New York: Pedigree.

Dworkin, Ronald. 1978. *Taking Rights Seriously.* Cambridge, Mass.: Harvard University Press.

1984. "Rights as Trumps." In *Theories of Rights* (Jeremy Waldron, ed.) Oxford: Oxford University Press.

1985. *A Matter of Principle.* Cambridge, Mass.: Harvard University Press.

1986. *Law's Empire.* Cambridge, Mass.: Harvard University Press.

1993. *Life's Dominion: An Argument about Abortion, Euthanasia, and Individual Freedom.* New York: Knopf.

Dyzenhaus, David. 1997. "John Stuart Mill and the Harm of Pornography." In *Mill's On Liberty: Critical Essays* (Gerald Dworkin, ed.) Lanham, Md.: Rowman & Littlefield.

Eisenberg, Melvin A. 2002. "Symposium: A Tribute to Professor Joseph M. Perillo, The Duty to Rescue in Contract Law." 71 *Fordham Law Review* 647.

Eisgruber, Christopher and Lawrence G. Sager. 2007. *Religious Freedom and the Constitution.* Cambridge, Mass.: Harvard University Press.

Ely, James W. 2005. "'Poor Relation' Once More: The Supreme Court and the Vanishing Rights of Property Owners." *Cato Supreme Court Review* (Mark K. Moller, ed.) Washington, D.C.: Cato Institute.

Ely, John. 1973. "The Wages of Crying Wolf: A Comment on Roe v. Wade." 82 *Yale Law Journal* 920.

1980. *Democracy and Distrust: A Theory of Judicial Review.* Cambridge, Mass.: Harvard University Press.

Employment Division, Dept. of Human Resources v. Smith, 494 U.S. 872 (1990).

Engels, Friedrich. 1942 [1884]. *Origin of the Family, Private Property, and the State.* New York: International Press.

Epstein, Richard A. 1988. "The Mistakes of 1937." 11 *George Mason University of Law Review* 5.

1995. *Cases and Materials on Torts.* 6th edn. New York: Aspen.

Ericcson, Lars O. 1980. "Charges against Prostitution: An Attempt at a Philosophical Assessment." *Ethics* (90): 335–366.

Farnsworth, E. Allan. 1999. *Contracts.* 3rd edn. New York: Aspen.

Farrell, Robert C. 1999. "Successful Rational Basis Claims in the Supreme Court from the 1971 Term Through Romer v. Evans." 32 *Indiana Law Review* 357.

Federalist Papers. 1961 [1788]. (Jacob E. Cooke, ed.) Hanover, N.H.: Wesleyan Press.

Feinberg, Joel. 1988. *The Moral Limits of the Criminal Law.* Vols. 1–4. Oxford: Oxford University Press.

Finnis, John. 1994. "Law, Morality, and 'Sexual Orientation'." 69 *Notre Dame Law Review* 1049.

Fishkin, James S. 1983. "Can There Be a Neutral Theory of Justice?" *Ethics* 93(2) (January): 348–356.

Flathman, Richard E. 1983. "Egalitarian Blood and Skeptical Turnips." *Ethics* 93 (2) (January): 357–366.

Franco, Paul. 1990a. "Michael Oakeshott as Liberal Theorist." *Political Theory* 18 (3): 411–436.

1990b. *The Political Philosophy of Michael Oakeshott*. New Haven, Conn.: Yale University Press.

Fraser, Nancy. 1997. *Justice Interruptus: Critical Reflections on the "Postsocialist" Condition*. New York: Routledge.

Galston, William. 1991. *Liberal Purposes*. Cambridge: Cambridge University Press, 1991.

Gaus, Gerald F. 1996. *Justificatory Liberalism*. Oxford: Oxford University Press.

Gaventa, John. 1980. *Power and Powerlessness*. Chicago: University of Illinois Press.

George, Robert P. 1993. *Making Men Moral: Civil Liberties and Public Morality*. New York: Oxford University Press.

Gerencser, Steven A. 1995. "Voices in Conversation: Philosophy and Politics in the Work of Michael Oakeshott." *The Journal of Politics* 57(3): 724–742.

Gilroy, Paul. 1993. *The Black Atlantic: Modernity and Double Consciousness*. Cambridge, Mass.: Harvard University Press.

Ginsburg, Douglas H. 1995. "Delegation Running Riot," *Regulation* No. 1 (reviewing David Schoenbrod, *Power Without Responsibility: How Congress Abuses the People Through Delegation* (1993)).

Ginsburg, Ruth Bader. 1992. "Speaking in a judicial voice." 67 *New York University Law Review* 1185–1209 (December).

Glasser, Charles J. Jr. (ed.). 2006. *International Libel & Privacy Handbook: A Global Reference for Journalists, Publishers, Webmasters and Lawyers*. New York: Bloomberg Press.

Glendon, Mary Ann. 1993. *Rights Talk: The Impoverishment of Political Discourse*. New York: Free Press.

Goldberg, Suzanne B. 2004a. "Equality Without Tiers." 77 *Southern California Law Review* 481.

2004b. "Morals-Based Justifications for Lawmaking Before and After Lawrence v. Texas." 88 *Minnesota Law Review* 1233.

Goldman, Jeffrey M. 2005. "Protecting Gays from the Government's Crosshairs: a Reevaluation of the Ninth Circuit's Treatment of Gays under the Federal Constitution's Equal Protection Clause following Lawrence v. Texas." 39 *University of San Francisco Law Review* 617.

Gould, Stephen. 1981. *The Mismeasure of Man*. New York: Norton.

Grant, Robert. 1990. *Oakeshott*. London: Claridge Press.

Gray, John. 1983. *Mill on Liberty: A Defense*. London: Routledge.

Gunther, Gerald. 1972. "Foreword: In Search of Evolving Doctrine on a Changing Court: A Model for A Newer Equal Protection." 86 *Harvard Law Review* 1.

Gutmann, Amy. 1985. "Communitarian Critics of Liberalism." *Philosophy and Public Affairs* 14(3): 308–322.

Gutmann, Amy and Dennis Thompson. 1996. *Democracy and Disagreement*. Cambridge, Mass.: Harvard University Press.

Habermas, Jürgen. 1990. *Moral Consciousness and Communicative Action* (Lenhardt and Nicholsen, trans.) Cambridge, Mass.: MIT Press.

1996. *Between Facts and Norms: Contributions to a Discourse Theory of Law and Democracy* (William Rehg, trans.) Cambridge: MIT Press.

2001. "Remarks on Legitimation through Human Rights." *The Postnational Constellation: Political Essays* (Max Pensky, trans. and ed.) Cambridge: Polity Press.

Hall, Stuart. 1992. "New ethnicities." In *'Race', Culture and Difference* (James Donald and Ali Rattansi, eds.) London: Sage.

Harcourt, Bernard. 1999. "The Collapse of the Harm Principle." *Journal of Criminal Law and Criminology*, Vol. 90.

Hart, H. L. A. 1994 [1961]. *The Concept of Law*. 2nd edn. Oxford: Oxford University Press.

Hartz, Louis. 1955. *The Liberal Tradition in America*. New York: Harcourt, Brace & World.

Hayward, Clarissa. 2000. *Defacing Power*. Cambridge: Cambridge University Press.

Hendricks, S. E., D. F. Fitzpatrick, K. Hartmann, M. A. Quaife, R. A. Stratbucker, and B. Graber. 1988. "Brain structure and function in sexual molesters of children and adolescents." *Journal of Clinical Psychiatry* (March) 49(3): 108–112.

Holmes, Stephen. 1997. *Passions and Constraints: On the Theory of Liberal Democracy*. Chicago: Chicago University Press.

Human Rights Campaign. Statewide Marriage Laws (2005): www.hrc. org/Template.cfm?Section=Center&CONTENTID=28225&TEMPLATE=/ ContentManagement/ContentDisplay.cfm

Hutchinson, Darren Lenard. 2003. "Unexplainable on Grounds Other Than Race, The Inversion of Privilege and Subordination in Equal Protection Jurisprudence." 2003 *University of Illinois Law Review* 615.

Jaggar, Alison. 1980. "Prostitution." In *The Philosophy of Sex* (Alan Soble, ed.) Totowa: Rowman & Littlefield, pp. 353–358.

Jeffreys, Sheila. 1990. *Anticlimax: A Feminist Perspective on the Sexual Revolution*. New York: NYU Press.

1997. *The Idea of Prostitution*. Melbourne, Australia: Spinifex.

Kalven Jr., Harry. 1960. "The Metaphysics of the Law of Obscenity." *1960 Supreme Court Review* 1: 1–45.

Koppelman, Andrew. 1990. "Forced Labor: A Thirteenth Amendment Defense of Abortion." 84 *Northwestern University Law Review* 480.

Kramer, Matthew H., N. E. Simmonds, and Hillel Steiner. 1998. *A Debate Over Rights: Philosophical Enquiries*. Oxford: Clarendon Press.

Kukathas, Chandran. 2003. *The Liberal Archipelago: A Theory of Diversity and Freedom*. Oxford: Oxford University Press.

Kymlicka, Will. 1995. *Multicultural Citizenship*. Oxford: Clarendon Press.

Larmore, Charles E. 1987. *Patterns of Moral Complexity*. Cambridge: Cambridge University Press.

1996. *The Morals of Modernity*. Cambridge: Cambridge University Press.

Lewontin, Richard. 1997. *Critical Race Theory: Essays on the Social Construction and Reproduction of Race* (E. Nathaniel Gates, ed.) Vol. 1. London: Routledge.

Livingstone, Frank. 1962. "On the Non-Existence of Human Races." 3 *Current Anthropology* 279.

Locke, John. 1988 [1690]. *Second Treatise of Government* (Peter Laslett, ed.) Cambridge: Cambridge University Press.

2003 [1689]. *Letter Concerning Toleration* in *Two Treatises of Government and A Letter Concerning Toleration* (Ian Shapiro, ed.) New Haven, Conn.: Yale University Press.

Lukes, Steven. 1982. "Of Gods and Demons: Habermas and Practical Reason." In *Habermas: Critical Debates* (John B. Thompson and David Held, eds.) Cambridge, Mass.: MIT Press.

Lyons, David. 1994. *Rights, Welfare, and Mill's Moral Theory*. Oxford: Oxford University Press.

MacDonald, Margaret. 1984. "Natural Rights." In *Theories of Rights* (Jeremy Waldron, ed.) Oxford: Oxford University Press.

Macedo, Stephen. 1995. "Homosexuality and the Conservative Mind." 84 *Georgetown Law Journal* 261.

MacIntyre, Alasdair. 1984. *After Virtue: A Study in Moral Theory*. 2nd edn. Notre Dame, Ind.: Notre Dame University Press.

Mackie, J. L. 1977. *Ethics: Inventing Right and Wrong*. New York: Penguin.
1988. *Whose Justice? Which Rationality?* Notre Dame: Notre Dame Press.

MacKinnon, Catharine A. 1987. *Feminism Unmodified: Discourses on Life and Law*. Cambridge, Mass.: Harvard University Press.
1989. *Toward a Feminist Theory of the State*. Cambridge, Mass.: Harvard University Press.

Mapel, David R. 1990. "Civil Association and the Idea of Contingency." *Political Theory* 18(3): 392–410.

Marx, Karl. 1994 [1891]. *Selected Writings*. Indianapolis: Hackett.

McClain, Linda C. 1995. "Inviolability and Privacy: the Castle, the Sanctuary, and the Body." 7 *Yale Journal of Law and the Humanities*. Winter.

McConnell, Michael W. 1997. "The Importance of Humility in Judicial Review: A Comment on Ronald Dworkin's 'Moral Reading' of the Constitution." 65 *Fordham Law Review* 1269.

McGuigan, Patrick B. and Dawn M. Weyrich. 1990. *Ninth Justice: The Fight for Bork*. Washington, D.C.: Free Congress Research and Education Foundation (University Press of America).

McLeod, W. H. 1989. *Who is a Sikh? The Problem of Sikh Identity*. Oxford: Clarendon Press.

McMahon, Christopher. 2000. "Discourse and Morality." *Ethics* 110 (April): 514–536.

Meiklejohn, Alexander. 1948. *Free Speech and its Relation to Self-Government*. New York: Harper.

Merriam-Webster Online. www.merriam-webster.com

Michelman, Frank. 1988. "Law's Republic." *Yale Law Journal* 97(8): 1493–1537.

Mill, J. S. 1979 [1861]. *Utilitarianism* (George Sher, ed.) Indianapolis: Hackett.
1989 [1859]. *On Liberty* (Stefan Collini, ed.) Cambridge: Cambridge University Press.
1989 [1869]. *The Subjection of Women* (Stefan Collini, ed.) Cambridge: Cambridge University Press.

Minnesota Statutes Annotated (M.S.A.) 2001. §.604A.01: Good Samaritan Law.

Montagu, A. 1997. *Man's Most Dangerous Myth*. 6th edn. Walnut Creek, Calif.: Altamira Press.

Munoz, Vincent Phillip. 2003. "James Madison's Principle of Religious Liberty." *American Political Science Review* 97(1).

Murray, John Courtney. 1993. *Religious Liberty: Catholic Struggles with Pluralism.* Louisville, Ky.: Knox Press.

Nemko, Amy H. 1998. "Single-Sex Public Education After VMI: The Case for Women's Schools." 21 *Harvard Women's Law Journal* 19.

Nozick, Robert. 1974. *Anarchy, State, and Utopia.* New York: Basic Books.

Oakeshott, Michael. 1962. "Rationalism in Politics." In *Rationalism in Politics.* Indianapolis: Liberty Press.

  1975. *On Human Conduct.* Oxford: Oxford University Press.

Okin, Susan Moller. 1989. *Justice, Gender, and the Family.* New York: Basic Books.

  1999. "Is Multiculturalism Bad for Women?" In *Is Multiculturalism Bad for Women?* (with respondents), (Joshua Cohen, Matthew Howard, and Martha C. Nussbaum, eds.) Princeton, N.J.: Princeton University Press.

Oxford English Dictionary Online. www.oed.com

Parekh, Bhikhu C. 2000. *Rethinking Multiculturalism: Cultural Diversity and Political Theory.* Basingstoke: Macmillan.

Parijs, Philippe van. 1995. *Real Freedom for All.* Oxford: Oxford University Press.

Partial Birth Abortion Act of 2003, 18 U.S.C. § 1531.

Pascoe, Peggy. 1996. "Miscegenation Law, Court Cases, and Ideologies of 'Race' in Twentieth Century America." *The Journal of American History*, 83(1): 44–69.

Pateman, Carole. 1988. *The Sexual Contract.* Oxford: Polity Press.

Pettit, Philip. 1997. *Republicanism: A Theory of Freedom and Government.* Oxford: Oxford University Press.

Plant, Raymond. 1972. "Social Thought." In *The Twentieth-Century Mind 1918–1945* (C. B. Cox and A. E. Dyson, eds.) Oxford: Oxford University Press.

Poe, S. and C. N. Tate. 1994. "Repression of Human-Rights to Personal Integrity in the 1980s – A Global Analysis." *American Political Science Review* 88(4): 853–872.

Posner, Richard. 1992. *Sex and Reason.* Cambridge, Mass.: Harvard University Press.

Quinton, Anthony. 1978. *The Politics of Imperfection.* London: Faber & Faber.

Radin, Margaret Jane. 1987. "Market-Inalienability." 100 *Harvard Law Review* 1849.

Raine, Adrian, J. Reid Meloy, Susan Bihrle, Jackie Stoddard, Lori LaCasse, and Monte Buchsbaum. 1998. "Reduced Prefrontal and Increased Subcortical Brain Functioning Assessed Using Positron Emission Tomography, Predatory and Affective Murderers." *Behavioral Sciences and the Law* 16: 319–322.

Rawls, John. 1971. *A Theory of Justice.* Revised edn. Cambridge, Mass.: Harvard University Press.

  1996. *Political Liberalism.* New York: Columbia University Press.

Rees, J. C. 1966. "A Re-Reading of Mill on Liberty." In *Limits of Liberty: Studies of Mill's On Liberty* (Peter Radcliff, ed.) Belmont, Calif.: Wadsworth Publishing.

Regan, Donald H. 1979. "Rewriting Roe v. Wade." 77 *Michigan Law Review* 1569.

Rehg, William. 1991. "Discourse and the Moral Point of View: Deriving a Dialogical Principle of Universalization." *Inquiry* 34: 27–48.

Religious Freedom, Restoration of Act (RFRA) of 1993, H.R. 1308.

The Restatement of Contracts (Second). 1981: §§ 346, 359–369.

The Restatement (Second) of Torts. 1965: § 314.

The Restatement (Second) of Torts. 1979: § 895F.

Rockefeller, Steven. C. 1994. "Comment" on Taylor's *The Politics of Recognition*. In *Multiculturalism* (Amy Gutmann, ed.) Princeton, N.J.: Princeton University Press.

Roper v. Simmons. 543 U.S. 551 (2005).

Rubenfeld, Jed. 1989. "The Right to Privacy." 102 *Harvard Law Review* 737.

1997. "Affirmative Action." 107 *Yale Law Journal* 427.

2005. *Revolution by Judiciary: The Structure of American Constitutional Law.* Cambridge, Mass.: Harvard University Press.

Sandel, Michael. 1982. *Liberalism and the Limits of Justice*. Cambridge: Cambridge University Press.

1984. "The Procedural Republic and the Unencumbered Self." *Political Theory* 12(1): 81–96.

1996. *Democracy's Discontent: America in Search of a Public Philosophy.* Cambridge, Mass.: Harvard University Press.

Saks, Michael J. 1998. "Merlin and Solomon: Lessons from the Law's Formative Encounters with Forensic Identification Evidence." 49 *Hastings Law Journal* 1069.

Scalia, Antonin. 1997. *A Matter of Interpretation: Federal Courts and the Law.* Princeton, N.J.: Princeton University Press.

Scanlon, T. M. 1998. *What We Owe to Each Other.* Cambridge, Mass.: Belknap Press.

Schauer, Frederick. 1979. "Speech and 'Speech' – Obscenity and 'Obscenity': An Exercise in the Interpretation of Constitutional Language." 67 *Georgetown Law Journal* 899.

2003. *Profiles, Probabilities, and Stereotypes.* Cambridge, Mass.: Harvard University Press.

Scheffler, Samuel (ed.). 1998. *Consequentialism and its Critics.* Introduction. Oxford: Oxford University Press.

Schneiders, Sandra M. 2004. *Beyond Patching: Faith and Feminism in the Catholic Church.* Revised edn. New York: Paulist Press.

Shachar, Ayelet. 2001. *Multicultural Jurisdictions: Cultural Difference and Women's Rights.* Cambridge: Cambridge University Press.

Shapiro, Ian. 1986. *The Evolution of Rights in Liberal Theory.* Cambridge: Cambridge University Press.

1999. *Democratic Justice.* New Haven, Conn.: Yale University Press.

2001. *Abortion: The Supreme Court Decisions 1965–2000* (ed.) Introduction. Indianapolis: Hackett.

2003a. *The State of Democratic Theory.* Princeton, N.J.: Princeton University Press.

2003b. "John Locke's Democratic Theory." In *Two Treatises of Government and A Letter Concerning Toleration* (Ian Shapiro, ed.) New Haven, Conn.: Yale University Press.

2003c. *The Moral Foundations of Politics*. New Haven, Conn.: Yale University Press.

Siegel, Reva B. 2005. *What Roe v. Wade Should have Said: The Nation's Top Legal Experts Rewrite America's Most Controversial Decision* (Jack M. Balkin, ed.) New York: New York University Press.

Siegan, Bernard H. 1980. *Economic Liberties and the Constitution*. Chicago: Chicago University Press.

Skinner, Quentin. 1997. *Liberty before Liberalism*. Cambridge: Cambridge University Press.

Skipper, Robert. 1997. "Mill and Pornography." In *Mill's On Liberty: Critical Essays* (Gerald Dworkin, ed.) Lanham, Md.: Rowman & Littlefield.

Stein, Edward. 2001. *The Mismeasure of Desire: The Science, Theory, and Ethics of Sexual Orientation*. Oxford: Oxford University Press.

Steinberger, Peter J. 2000. "The Impossibility of a 'Political' Conception." *The Journal of Politics* 62(1) (February): 147–165.

Stoney, David. 2005 "Fingerprint Identifications." In *Modern Scientific Evidence: The Law and Science of Expert Testimony*, Vol. 4 § 34 (David L. Faigman *et al.*, eds.) St. Paul, Minn.: West Group.

Sullivan, Kathleen M. and Gerald Gunter (eds.) 2001. *Constitutional Law*. 14th edn. New York: Foundation Press.

Sunstein, Cass R. 1999. "Should Sex Equality Law Apply to Religious Institutions?" In *Is Multiculturalism Bad for Women?* (with respondents), (Joshua Cohen, Matthew Howard, and Martha C. Nussbaum, eds.) Princeton, N.J.: Princeton University Press.

Taylor, Charles. 1992 [1979]. "Atomism." In *Communitarianism and Individualism* (Shlomo Aviner and Avner De-Shalit, eds.) Oxford: Oxford University Press.

1994. "The Politics of Recognition." In *Multiculturalism* (Amy Gutmann, ed.) Princeton, N.J.: Princeton University Press.

Ten, C. L. 1980. *Mill on Liberty*. Oxford: Clarendon Press.

Thompson, Judith Jarvis. 1971. "A Defense of Abortion." *Philosophy and Public Affairs* 1(1): 47–66.

1975. "The Right to Privacy." *Philosophy and Public Affairs* 4: 295–314.

1976. "Killing, Letting Die, and the Trolley Problem." 59 *The Monist*: 204–217.

Title VII, 42 U.S.C. 2000e-1(a).

Tocqueville, Alexis de. 2000 [1835, 1840]. *Democracy in America* (Vols. 1 and 2) (Harvey C. Mansfield and Delba Winthrop, eds. and trans.) Chicago: University of Chicago Press.

Tribe, Laurence. 1988. *American Constitutional Law*. 2nd edn. New York: Foundation Press.

Tribe, Laurence and Michael C. Dorf. 1990. "Levels of Generality in the Definition of Rights." *University of Chicago Law Review* 57(4) (Fall): 1057–1108.

Turkington, Richard C. and Anita L. Allen. 2002. *Privacy Law: Cases and Materials*. 2nd edn. St. Paul, Minn.: West Group.

Tushnet, Mark. 2001. "The Redundant Free Exercise Clause." 33 *Loyola University Chicago Law Journal* 71.

Unger, Roberto Mangabeira. 1996. *What Should Legal Analysis Become?* London: Verso.

UNESCO. *Statement on the Nature of Race and Race Differences* by Physical Anthropologists and Geneticists – June 1951.

Urbinati, Nadia. 2002. *Mill on Democracy: From the Athenian Polis to Representative Government.* Chicago: Chicago University Press.

Vermont Statutes Annotated (V.S.A). 1968. 12 § 519: Emergency Medical Care.

Waldron, Jeremy. 1985. "What is Private Property?" *Oxford Journal of Legal Studies* 5(3). 313–349.

    1987. "Mill and the Value of Moral Distress." *Political Studies* XXXV, 410–423.

    1999. *Law and Disagreement.* Oxford: Clarendon Press.

    2007. "Mill on Liberty and on the Contagious Diseases Acts." In *J. S. Mill's Political Thought: A Bicentennial Reassessment* (Nadia Urbinati and Alex Zakaras, eds.) Cambridge: Cambridge University Press.

Walston, Roderick E. 2001. "The Constitution and Property: Due Process, Regulatory Takings, and Judicial Takings." 2001 *Utah Law Review* 379.

Walzer, Michael. 1983. *Spheres of Justice.* New York: Basic Books.

Warren, Samuel D. and Louis D. Brandeis. 1890. "The Right to Privacy." 4 *Harvard Law Review* 193.

West, Robin. 1992. "Reconstructing Liberty." 59 *Tennessee Law Review* 441.

    2005. *What Roe v. Wade Should have Said: The Nation's Top Legal Experts Rewrite America's Most Controversial Decision* (Jack M. Balkin, ed.) New York: New York Press.

Whittington, Keith E. 1999. *Constitutional Interpretations: Textual Meaning, Original Intent, and Judicial Review.* Lawrence: University of Kansas Press.

Williams, Bernard. 1983. "Space Talk: The Conversation Continued." *Ethics* 93 (2) (January): 367–371.

Winkler, Adam. 2006. "Fatal in Theory and Strict in Fact: An Empirical Analysis of Strict Scrutiny in the Federal Courts." 59 *Vanderbilt Law Review* 793.

Wolgast, Elizabeth H. 1994. "The Demands of Public Reason." *Columbia Law Review* 94(6) (October).

Wollheim, Richard. 1973. "John Stuart Mill and the Limits of State Action." *Social Research* 7: 1–30.

    1975. (ed.) Introduction, *John Stuart Mill: Three Essays.* Oxford: Oxford University Press.

Wood, Gordon. 1969. *The Creation of the American Republic, 1776–1787.* Chapel Hill: University of North Carolina Press.

Wright, Percy, Jose Nobrega, Ron Langevin, and George Wortzman. 1990. "Brain Density and Symmetry in Pedophilic and Sexually Aggressive Offenders." *Annals of Sex Research* 3: 319–328.

Y. al-Hibri, Azizah. 1999. "Is Western Patriarchal Feminism Good for Third World/Minority Women?" In *Is Multiculturalism Bad for Women?* (with respondents), (Joshua Cohen, Matthew Howard, and Martha C. Nussbaum, eds.) Princeton, N.J.: Princeton University Press.

Young, Iris Marion. 1990. *Justice and the Politics of Difference.* Princeton, N.J.: Princeton University Press.

Index